CH01176786

The Metropolitan-Vickers
Type 2 Co-Bo Diesel-Electric Locomotives

D5701, Carlisle, 8 July 1966. View from Currock Road bridge looking west towards Rome Street Junction, with Bog Junction immediately behind the photographer. (Colour-Rail)

LOCOMOTIVE
· PORTFOLIOS ·

The Metropolitan-Vickers

Type 2 Co-Bo Diesel-Electric Locomotives

From Design to Destruction

ANTHONY P. SAYER

Pen & Sword TRANSPORT
AN IMPRINT OF PEN & SWORD BOOKS LTD.
YORKSHIRE – PHILADELPHIA

First published in Great Britain in 2020 and reprinted in 2022 by
Pen & Sword Transport
An imprint of Pen & Sword Books Ltd
Yorkshire - Philadelphia

Copyright © Anthony P. Sayer, 2020, 2022

ISBN 978 1 52674 281 0

The right of Anthony P. Sayer to be identified as Author of this work has been asserted by him in accordance with the Copyright, Designs and Patents Act 1988.

A CIP catalogue record for this book is available from the British Library.

All rights reserved. No part of this book may be reproduced or transmitted in any form or by any means, electronic or mechanical including photocopying, recording or by any information storage and retrieval system, without permission from the Publisher in writing.

Typeset in Palatino by Aura Technology and Software Services, India.
Printed and bound in India by Replika Press Pvt. Ltd.

Pen & Sword Books Ltd incorporates the Imprints of Pen & Sword Books Archaeology, Atlas, Aviation, Battleground, Discovery, Family History, History, Maritime, Military, Naval, Politics, Railways, Select, Transport, True Crime, Fiction, Frontline Books, Leo Cooper, Praetorian Press, Seaforth Publishing, Wharncliffe and White Owl.

For a complete list of Pen & Sword titles please contact:

PEN & SWORD BOOKS LTD
47 Church Street, Barnsley, South Yorkshire, S70 2AS, England
E-mail: enquiries@pen-and-sword.co.uk
Website: www.pen-and-sword.co.uk

Or

PEN AND SWORD BOOKS
1950 Lawrence Rd, Havertown, PA 19083, USA
E-mail: Uspen-and-sword@casematepublishers.com
Website: www.penandswordbooks.com

Front cover:
D5716, Crewe Works (Erecting Shop Yard), 1 November 1964.
(Arnold W. Batson (Transport Treasury))

Back cover:
D5702, Grange-over-Sands, 3 August 1968. (Michael Atkinson)

CONTENTS

Preface 7
Acknowledgements 8
Abbreviations 9

Chapter 1	Class Introduction 10
Chapter 2	Some Technical Aspects 19
Chapter 3	Locomotive Design 27
Chapter 4	Delivery and Acceptance Testing 43
Chapter 5	Allocations 45
Chapter 6	Overhaul History 48
Chapter 7	Individual Locomotive Histories 57
Chapter 8	Early Performance 125
Chapter 9	Pre-Dukinfield Storage 138
Chapter 10	Pre-Dukinfield Storage Locations 142
Chapter 11	Dukinfield Rehabilitation 145
Chapter 12	Post-Dukinfield Performance 152
Chapter 13	The Re-Engining Proposal and Other Developments 161
Chapter 14	Accident and Fire Damage 171
Chapter 15	Operations: A High-Level Summary 175
Chapter 16	Detail Differences 201

Chapter 17	Liveries	204
Chapter 18	Unique Identifiers	216
Chapter 19	Storage 1965-68	234
Chapter 20	Storage Locations 1965-68	236
Chapter 21	Withdrawal	253
Chapter 22	Disposal	256
Chapter 23	Post Withdrawal	259
Chapter 24	Conclusions	264
	Bibliography	270

PREFACE

Like my previous book in the modern traction *Locomotive Portfolios* series, this one also devotes itself completely to a single class of locomotives for the first time, the Metropolitan-Vickers diesel-electric Co-Bo Type 2s. The nearest the class previously got to such exclusivity was in a part-work magazine published in 2017 in which the 'Metrovicks' shared space with the ten English Electric 'Baby Deltics'.

Whilst performing the obligatory scan of past material published on the subject, it became very noticeable that there was no generally accepted family name for this fleet of twenty locomotives. The term 'Co-Bos' is frequently used, reflecting their unique wheel arrangement, and, more recently, the nondescript 'Class 28' title following the introduction of the TOPS system. However, it is the various abbreviations of the manufacturer's company name, Metropolitan-Vickers, which represents the most commonly used collective noun for the class; there are numerous versions (Met-Vicks, Met-Vickers, Metro-Vicks, etc) but the name used throughout this book (except where described otherwise in quotations) is 'Metrovicks'.

For a class of only twenty locomotives, the Metrovicks have attracted a disproportionately high quantity of column-inches in books, magazines, websites, etc, and, as frequently seems to be the case these days, much of it seems to be repetitions of previously published material, unfortunately including many factual errors. With this book, I have again gone back to absolute basics in an attempt to get at the truth, firstly by utilising British Railways archive material to shed much new light on the history of the class (ordering, design, re-engining, withdrawal, etc), and, secondly, by building-up individual locomotive histories from primary source material (people's personal observations, visit reports, etc) to establish the works histories for each locomotive of the class, together with their respective detail difference and liveries.

My only sightings of the Metrovicks was a fleeting glimpse of the condemned line-up at Carlisle New Yard whilst travelling the West Coast Main Line on a Motorail train on 4 September 1969, dumped alongside a fair few Claytons! A few sightings of S15705, TDB968006 and preserved D5705 (the same locomotive, of course!) resulted in my seeing twelve of the fleet of twenty.

Numerous references are made to No.1 and No.2 ends of locomotives. For clarity, No.1 end is defined as the end containing the radiator compartment. Mention is also made to '1-2' or '2-1' sides of the locomotives; the '1-2' side is the side of the locomotive where the No.1 end is to the left and No.2 end to the right.

Anthony Sayer
May 2020

ACKNOWLEDGEMENTS

Official sources have provided a major input in developing the class and individual locomotive histories and I would like to personally thank the teams of people at the National Archive (Kew), the National Railway Museum (York), the Barrow Archive and Local Studies Centre and the Derby Industrial Museum for their kind assistance. My thanks also go to Chris Hawkins of Irwell Press for pointing me in the direction of other key archive records not held by the above institutions.

A considerable number of quotes have been taken from the *Railway Observer*, the magazine of the Railway Correspondence and Travel Society (RCTS); these have been reproduced with the very kind permission of W. Gordon Davies of the RCTS.

My 'back to basics' approach has, by necessity, relied heavily on a massive amount of personal observation information in various forms. I have made every attempt to credit everyone concerned in the Bibliography. My thanks go to you all, and if I have failed to include anyone in the reference list, I sincerely apologise, but my thanks are there nonetheless.

This book has used over 180 photographs to support the text. The aforementioned plethora of repeated book and magazine column inches of text on the class, applies equally to the availability of photographs, with many images reproduced time and time again. Whilst it has been possible to find a significant amount of previously unpublished written material to include here, the same cannot generally be said about the photographic side of things. As a consequence, I have tried to select the least frequently previously reproduced images, and for the more commonly used pictures, to strategically position them within the various chapters to provide as much context as possible.

My thanks go to the following organisations and individuals for the photographs used herein: Paul Chancellor (Colour-Rail), Robin & Sarah-Jane Fell (Transport Treasury), John Chalcraft (Rail-Photoprints), Rail-Online, W. Gordon Davies and John Broughton (RCTS Archive), Martin High (Transport Topics), Mick Mercer (Rail Image Collections), Peter Waller (Online Transport Photography) and Mike Claxton ('Rail Pictorial: The Paul Claxton Collection'). Also Michael Atkinson, Stewart Blencowe, Tom Bowman, David Dippie, Ernie's Railway Archives, Stephen Fisher, Bill Hamilton, Mark Hoofe, Mike Jackson, Andrew Lance, Dave Lennon, Keith Long, R. Lush, Noel A. Machell, Stuart Martin, Mick Mobley, Peter Sedge, Clinton P.R. Shaw, N. Skinner, John Grey Turner, Mark Walker collection, Ray Winthrop, George Woods, Bill Wright, together with 'Regional Bus Photos', '70023venus2009' and the Modern Traction Photo Group.

There are images from a very small number of photographers where it has proved impossible to obtain the appropriate permission to use their photographs despite every endeavour being made to track down the individuals concerned. In addition, there are one or two images where the identity of the photographer is totally unknown. Lack of accreditation on slides or prints has prevented any possibility of determining their provenance. In both cases, anyone who feels that they have not been adequately credited should please contact me via the publisher to ensure that the situation is corrected in future editions.

And finally, thanks to Rob Mason (Chairman of the Class 15 Preservation Society) for permission to reference the engineering drawing covering the little-known investigation to re-engine the Metrovick fleet with Sulzer engines.

ABBREVIATIONS

AEI	Associated Electrical Industries.
BLS	British Locomotive Society.
BR	British Railways/British Rail.
BRB	British Railways Board.
BRB W&EC	BRB Works & Equipment Committee.
BRCW	Birmingham Railway Carriage & Wagon Co. Ltd.
BTC	British Transport Commission.
CIE	Córas Iompair Éireann (Irish Transport System).
CM&EE	Chief Mechanical & Electrical Engineer.
EHC	Engine History Card
FDTL	BRB *'Fires on Diesel Train Locomotives'* Reports.
GEC	General Electric Company.
LCGB	Locomotive Club of Great Britain.
LMR	London Midland Region, British Railways.
LMS	London Midland & Scottish.
MV	Metropolitan-Vickers
NBL	North British Locomotive Co. Ltd.
NTP	National Traction Plan.
RCTS	Railway Correspondence and Travel Society.
SLS	Stephenson Locomotive Society.
s.p. or sp	Stabling point.
SR	Southern Region, British Railways.
S(u)	Stored unserviceable.
TOPS	Total Operations Processing System
T&RS	Traction & Rolling Stock.
WAGR	Western Australian Government Railways.
WCML	West Coast Main Line

Chapter 1
CLASS INTRODUCTION

1.1 Background.

During the 1950s, Metropolitan-Vickers was a well-established company involved in the building of electric locomotives and British Thomson-Houston (BTH) and the General Electric Company (GEC) were well-known suppliers of railway electrical equipment.

Both BTH and Metropolitan-Vickers had been bought in 1928 by Associated Electrical Industries (AEI), but they continued to function as separate entities.

GEC took over AEI (and, therefore, BTH and Metropolitan-Vickers) in 1967, with English Electric following a year later, thus producing a significantly enlarged GEC and the largest UK electrical manufacturing group.

1.2 Metrovick Precursors.

In 1953, the Western Australian Government Railways (WAGR) placed an order with Metropolitan-Vickers for forty-eight 1,045hp 3ft 6in gauge mixed-traffic locomotives specifically with low axle-loading. These X-class locomotives were delivered between 1954 and 1956 and utilised a Crossley two-stroke HST V8 diesel engine. Although Crossley Brothers had been building reliable engines for many years, particularly for marine applications, it had never built an engine for railway traction applications prior to the WAGR contract; at the time the contract was awarded, the HST Vee engine was still very much on the drawing board.

In May 1954, Metropolitan-Vickers received an order from Córas Iompair Éireann, the Irish Transport System (CIE) for ninety-four locomotives with Crossley engines, sixty rated at 1,200hp and thirty-four at 550hp. The A-class batch of sixty locomotives had an uprated version of the engine used in the WAGR fleet. Introduction into traffic commenced in September 1955.

It was this 1,200hp version of the engine that was installed in the twenty Co-Bo Metrovick locomotives ordered by British Railways in November 1955.

1.3 Order Placement.

The BTC Works & Equipment Committee (W&EC) Meeting Minute 293 (dated 17 November 1954) recorded approval in principle for 160 diesel-electric locomotives at a total estimated cost of £9.28m, 130 for construction by contractors and 30 in BR Workshops.

The breakdown of the locomotives to be built by contactors was forty in the 600-800hp range (Type A), eighty in the 1000-1250hp range (Type B) and ten in the 2000-and-over hp range (Type C); locomotives to be built by BR Workshops were split twenty in the 1000-1250hp range and ten in the 2000-and-over hp range. The remaining fourteen locomotives of the so-called 'Pilot Scheme' fleet of 174 locomotives were constructed with hydraulic transmissions.

The twenty diesel-electric locomotives in the 2000-and-over hp range were approved by the W&EC on 9 February 1955 (Minute 357/40) and authorised by the BTC on 17 February 1955 (Minute 8/74[o]) at a cost of £1.68m and were included in the 1956 Building Programme.

The W&EC Meeting Minute 388/26 (dated 23 March 1955) approved the construction of the remaining 140 diesel-electric locomotives provisionally as part of the 1957 and 1958 Locomotive Building Programmes, at a total estimated cost of £7.60m. Advance authority was given by the BTC on 24 March 1955 (Minute 8/142[i]).

Tenders for the 130 complete locomotives and power equipment for the 30 locomotives to be built in BR Workshops were invited from 16 contractors, including five overseas companies. Notwithstanding gauge considerations, the tenders received from firms abroad were higher than for comparable British types of locomotives and, therefore, only tenders submitted by the selected British companies were accepted.

The recommended tenders (i.e. those which were considered to best meet requirements) for the 130 complete diesel-electric locomotives to be built by contractors amounted to £8,513,450 and for the 30 power equipment sets for the locomotives to be built in British Workshops, £1,478,600 i.e. a total of £9,992,050 against the originally authorised expenditure of £9,280,000, an increase of £712,050 (7.6 per cent).

With respect to the locomotives in the 1000-1250hp category, five contractors were nominated for the supply of the required eighty locomotives, as follows:

Main Contractor	No. of Locos	Total Price	Delivery of First Units
English Electric	10	£714,000	30 months
Metropolitan-Vickers	20	£1,428,000	24 months
Birmingham Railway Carriage & Wagon	20	£1,260,750	20-23 months
Brush Electrical Engineering	20	£1,413,000	21 months
North British Locomotive Co.	10	£624,000	21 months
		£5,439,750	

It will be noted that a strict least-cost selection process was not applied, '. . .the aspect of lowest cost being conditioned by the wish to gain experience with a wide variety of makers and designs'. However, the combination of engine builders and electrical contractors recommended was '. . . mainly governed by the selection of the lowest combined tender' where alternatives were available.

A memorandum dated 29 September 1955 submitted by Chief Electrical Engineer, Chief Mechanical Engineer, Chief Financial Officer, Chief Operating and Motive Power Officer, Chief Commercial Officer and Chief Stores Officer to the W&EC recommended acceptance of the tenders for the 160 locomotives at a total cost of £9.92m and the proposed distribution of orders between manufacturers. The W&EC approved the memorandum on 12 October 1955 (Minute 517/16) subject to '. . . no actual orders being placed with Metropolitan-Vickers Co. Ltd. until a satisfactory guarantee had been received from the firm in respect of the performance of the Crossley engines to be fitted to the locomotives (this proviso is made because of the unsatisfactory performance of the Crossley engines now in service in diesel shunting locomotives on the London Midland Region)'.

Orders for the twenty Type B Co-Bo's were placed with Metropolitan-Vickers on 16 November 1955. The 1957 Locomotive Building and Condemnation Programmes were presented to the W&EC, via a Memorandum dated 2 December 1955, ready for their meeting on 7 December 1955; W&EC Minute 567 (Supplementary Item No.30) recorded the inclusion of the twenty Metrovicks without any form of qualification, and the Building Programme was accepted and submitted to the BTC for authorisation which was duly completed on 15 December 1955 (Minute 8/590).

The excess tender prices for the Type A and B 'Pilot Scheme' locomotives over the original March 1955 estimates were authorised as part of the 1957 Building and Condemnation Plans, hidden away amongst other orders for diesel shunters and steam locomotives and residual scrap values for redundant steam locomotives.

1.4 Why Twenty?

It is well documented that Roland C. Bond (BTC Chief Mechanical Engineer) wanted to gain some experience with 2-stroke engines but quite why twenty of the Metrovick locomotives were ordered (as opposed to a more conservative batch of ten) is unknown, particularly given (i) the relatively high unit cost of these locomotives compared with the other Type B alternatives, (ii) the quite explicit reservations recorded regarding the performance of the Crossley power units (see below), and, (iii) known problems with Crossley-engined shunting locomotives already in service with BR (D3117-D3126).

On 1 January 1957, Bond submitted a memorandum to the Technical Development and Research Committee entitled *Main Line Diesel Locomotives - Experience in Eire*, reproduced here in full:

'Close contact is maintained with the Irish Railways on their experience with dieselisation and a report has recently been received from two Motive Power Department Officers who visited Eire. This report draws attention to two matters which may be considered as teething troubles with the Crossley engines. There have been several piston failures due to unsatisfactory temperature distribution under traction conditions. The firm is aware of this and has redesigned the pistons, so that replacement pistons to Eire and all which will be supplied in the BR engines will be to the new design. Secondly the fuel injectors have been found unsatisfactory which agrees with our initial experience with Crossley engines on the diesel shunting locomotives. We have now replaced them with C.A.V. injectors with satisfactory results and the same will be arranged on all further Crossley engines to be delivered to us.

'The report also refers to the dirty condition of the engine compartments due to oil leakage from the engine itself. This is a very undesirable condition and Messrs. Crossley are being contacted as to the measures they will have to take to avoid this trouble on the BR engines. The type test of 100 hours under fluctuating load which is called for in the specification will give an opportunity for our inspectors to examine the performance of the engines as regards oil leakage before they are mounted on to the locomotive chassis.'

1.5 Introduction to Traffic.

Construction of the first Co-Bo, D5700, commenced at Bowesfield Works, Stockton-on-Tees, in late 1956 under Lot No.255. The first complete locomotive emerged from the works in July 1958. The actual cost of the locomotives as recorded on the Engine History Cards was £78,436 for D5700-7, £78,437 for D5708-18, and £78,534 for D5719, giving a total cost of £1,568,829 (average £78441.45 per locomotive). This compares adversely to the original price of £1,428,000, a mark-up of nearly 10 per cent which would appear to be in excess of the price variation clause included within the contract.

D5716, Bedford. 18 May 1959. Straight out of the box! (*Colour-Rail*)

D5711, 14E Bedford, 10 January 1960.
(*Colour-Rail*)

1.6 Drawing the Line at Twenty.

The 'Pilot Scheme' provided six Type B (later Type 2) designs for testing purposes over a three-year period (five from contractors and one from BR Workshops); the quite deliberate objective was to ultimately determine a limited number of types for volume production commencing 1961/62 based on operational experience gained.

However, facing deteriorating financial results, the BTC abandoned the three year trial period, and extended and accelerated the introduction of diesel locomotives as fast as British production capacity would allow, believing that dieselisation and the consequent elimination of steam would dramatically improve the position. Minute 9/384 of the BTC Meeting of 26 July 1956 records that:

The Commission . . . discussed the purchase of additional main line locomotives and agreed that they would be prepared to consider requests for a number of these without further trials, provided that:

1. There is sufficient technical evidence to show that the type of locomotive desired is fully and without doubt able to meet requirements which are comparable to those in the service for which it is intended.
2. The substitution of the diesel locomotives for steam locomotives is economically justified by the manner in which they will be operated.'

The dangers of giving up the trial period were made clear by R.C. Bond but Chairman Sir Brian Robertson insisted that the Board's decision was adhered to with the specific condition that good reliable locomotives were introduced.

The Commission also insisted that the number of different designs of locomotives should be reduced to an absolute minimum. This, as already mentioned, was one of the key objectives of the 'Pilot Scheme' process but it had now become necessary to recommend the smallest possible number of types without any operating experience having been obtained with the locomotives then on order. The only way of achieving this was to base recommendations on engineering judgement, knowledge of various firms' products, and the operating experience of other railways.

A Memorandum to the Works and Equipment Committee dated 20 September 1956 proposed, under the requirements of BTC Min. 9/384, that fifty-six Type B (1000-1250hp) locomotives should be included in the 1958 Locomotive Building Programme i.e. ten to be built in BR Workshops at an estimated cost of £760,000 and forty-six by contractors at an estimated cost of £3,496,000. This proposal was approved by the W&EC on 26 September 1956 (Minute 750 [Item 26]) and passed up to the Commission for authorisation. Minute 9/477 of the BTC meeting of 27 September 1956 recorded the necessary authorisation.

A Memorandum to W&EC dated 15 November 1956 proposed that five contractors should be invited to tender for the fifty-six locomotives, these being Brush, English Electric, Metropolitan-Vickers, North British Locomotive (NBL), and Birmingham Railway Carriage & Wagon (BRCW). This list reflected the desire not to proliferate types beyond those already part of the 'Pilot Scheme' types. The W&EC approved the shortlist at their meeting on 21 November 1956 (Minute 782 [Item 4]).

Following receipt and analysis of the tenders, a further Memorandum to the W&EC dated 4 April 1957 recommended the placing of orders for forty-six locomotives with NBL (twenty-eight [D6110-37]) and BRCW (eighteen [D5320-D5337]), at a total cost of £3,162,080. Minute 876 (Item No.15) of the W&EC meeting of 10 April 1957 recorded approval for the placing of these contracts. Clearly Metropolitan-Vickers were unsuccessful with their bid, but it is unknown if this was based purely on price or whether product quality issues were also taken into account. The remaining ten locomotives of the 1958 Building Programme (D5020-D5029) were allocated to be constructed in BR workshops; these deployed Sulzer engines and were allocated to the Eastern Region.

A Memorandum to the BTC dated 16 May 1957 acted as a cover note for a Report entitled *Modernisation of British Railways: Report on Diesel and Electric Traction and the Passenger Services of the Future*. This report was described as 'the definitive modernisation plan for traction and passenger traffic' and effectively updated significant parts of the 1955 Modernisation Plan. It highlighted 'the very much more rapid introduction of diesel locomotive traction than had first been intended', stating that the Plan for diesel locomotive manufacture up to 1962 'sets a production task of magnitude' envisaging the ordering of a further 1,889 main-line diesel locomotives during the period 1957-62.

The BTC at their meeting on 23 May 1957 (Minute 10/212) approved the general concept of the extension and acceleration of introduction of diesel traction as contained in the report, without commitment to the exact pace of extension, stating that:

'The Commission would be prepared to go further than they have already gone in regard to ordering diesel main line locomotives, in spite of the risk of unsatisfactory performance in the early stages, if the Regions presented them with a limited number of firm plans for their use in specific areas, containing as clear a justification as possible.'

The Commission estimated that:

'The maximum number of diesel main line locomotives likely to be procurable was about 500 in one year, and the Commission would be prepared to include up to this number in their locomotive orders for 1959 to meet the requirements of such schemes.'

The Commission asked that the question of limiting the number of types of main-line diesel locomotives types be specifically addressed, and to advise on what was practicable. The Report *Main Line Diesel Locomotives: Limitation of Variety* (R.C. Bond & S. Warder, 26 July 1957) was produced in response to this request.

At the time of this report, 444 locomotives had been authorised, of which orders had been placed for 230 locomotives or equipment sets, i.e. the original 174 Pilot Scheme Locomotives authorised in the 1956 and 1957 Building Programmes and 56 Type 2 locomotives authorised for the 1958 Programme. The remaining 214 authorised locomotives included 116 diesel-hydraulic locomotives for the Western Region and 98 diesel-electrics for the Southern Region.

The principles used in the *Limitation of Variety* report governing the selection of locomotive types for ordering beyond those already ordered were reliability and as much standardisation as British production capacity would allow. On the basis of these key considerations, the recommendation was that any diesel-electric locomotive orders placed in the 1959 Building Programme should be limited to the following types, subject to the phasing of the Regions' specific requirements and manufacturing capacity:

		Engine	Transmission	Mechanical parts
Type 1	1,000hp	English Electric	English Electric	English Electric
Type 2	1,160hp	Sulzer	BTH	BR
Type 3	1,750hp	English Electric	English Electric	English Electric
Type 4	2,500hp	Sulzer	Crompton	BR

English Electric and Sulzer engines featured strongly. It was considered that English Electric had the largest experience and productive capacity of any British manufacturer and had the resources to ensure the delivery of a reliable product, whilst the Sulzer engine was the best known and widely used outside of the USA, and was recognised for excellent design and workmanship. Paxman engines were proposed as a reserve type, whilst Crossley and Mirrlees engines were not included in the recommendations list on the basis that both companies were deemed to have less experience of traction requirements than either EE or Sulzer.

Subsequent discussions with industry soon showed, however, that it was not possible to adhere strictly to the recommendations and, to meet BR's demands for Type 2 locomotives and to capitalise on available production capacity, Brush, BRCW and NBL were subsequently awarded orders for more of their Type 2 diesel-electric locomotives (see later).

In reaction to the BTC decision recorded in Meeting Minute 10/212 (23 May 1957), the Regions submitted a range of Area Schemes requiring a total of 782 diesel locomotives, significantly in excess of the suggested five hundred. In a Memorandum to the BTC dated 11 September 1957, the W&EC suggested that the Commission approve in principle a 1959 Building Programme of around 782 diesel locomotives. At the BTC Meeting on 19 September 1957 (Minute 10/400), the Commission approved, in principle, a 1959 Building Programme of the order of 750 to 800 locomotives composed of the types recommended in the *Limitation of Variety* report. It was recognised that this was a large requirement and production capacities may dictate some deferral into 1960. However, a subsequent capital investment restriction in late 1957 severely limited the purchase of locomotives for delivery in 1959 and it was, therefore, impossible to take full advantage of building capacity for main-line diesel locomotives in that year.

The revised 1959 Building Programme included eighty-four Type 2 diesel-electric locomotives (plus shunting and electric locomotives); all of these Type 2s were to be built in BR Workshops employing Sulzer engines (subsequently D5030-D5113). The W&EC approved the building of the eighty-four locomotives at their meeting on 22 January 1958 (Minute 1110, Item No.20) and authorised by the BTC on

13 February 1958 (Minute 11/53). The remaining diesel locomotive requirements were deferred into 1960 and 1961. Contactors were invited to tender in advance of these later Building Programmes but exactly which contractors were involved is unknown.

The financial situation eased during 1958 and as a consequence there were two Supplements to the 1959 Building Programme, with locomotive types selected on the basis of tenders already received, as follows:

First Supplement (ninety locomotives), including sixty Type 2s:
    40 Brush (D5520-D5559) Authorised 26 June 1958.
    20 NBL (D6138-D6157) Authorised 10 July 1958.
Second Supplement (forty-nine locomotives), including twenty-nine Type 2s:
    20 Brush (D5560-D5579) Authorised 20 November 1958.
    9 BRCW (D5338-D5346) Authorised 20 November 1958.

None of the locomotives in the First and Second Supplements featured in the *Limitation of Variety* recommendations but were repeat orders for locomotives of types already in service. The key question is; were Metropolitan-Vickers invited to tender for the 1960/61 requirements? And, with competitive quotes, could they have been awarded orders?

In late 1958, a memorandum was produced for discussion at the Chairman's Conference on Modernisation; this was produced by R.C. Bond (by now BTC Technical Advisor) and entitled *Main Line Diesel Locomotives: The Approach to Standardisation* (dated 10 November 1958).

The recommendations concerning the preferred diesel-electric manufacturers for each of the Types 1-4, as detailed in the *Limitation of Variety* report, were reiterated. However, this memorandum went a stage further by explicitly listing the designs which it was proposed should be *excluded* from any future orders, as below:

		No. Series	Engine	Electrical Equipment
Type 1.	North British Locomotive	D8400	Paxman	General Electric Company.
Type 2.	Metropolitan-Vickers	D5700	Crossley	Metropolitan-Vickers.
	English Electric	D5900	Small Napier 'Deltic'	English Electric.
	North British Locomotive	D6100	M.A.N.	General Electric Company.

Notes of the Chairman's Conference, which took place on 13 November 1958, record that 'The Chairman . . . fully agreed with the proposals set out in the Technical Advisor's paper for the elimination of a number of locomotive types'.

Bond's memorandum also supported repeat orders for types of locomotives not included in the *Limitation of Variety* recommendations, i.e. BTH Type 1, Brush and BRCW Type 2s and English Electric Type 4, to enable financial capital allocations to be used to the full during 1959/60.

A further report covering limitation of variety was produced in 1959 entitled *Standardisation of Main Line Diesel Locomotives* (BR General Staff, 8 June 1959). By this date, approximately 150 diesel-electric main line locomotives were in service; however, there was still insufficient experience with the new traction to statistically challenge the logic of the *Limitation of Variety* report recommendations. This report, once again, explicitly listed the 'excluded' types of diesel-electric locomotives. Following on from this report and in a Memorandum to the BTC from the General Staff dated 22 June 1959, the Commission were recommended to:

(a) endorse the principles embodied in the Report on *Limitation of Variety* of main line diesel locomotives (nearly two years after it was published in 26 July, 1957!)

(b) note the further progress currently attained towards standardization (*as described in the report*), and

(c) approve the proposal to specifically exclude the four specified types from the forthcoming 1960 and 1961 programmes.

The BTC Minutes of the Meeting on 25 June 1959 (Minute 12/253) recorded that the Commission accepted these recommendations with only a few minor caveats. Quite why it took nearly two years to formally ratify the *Limitation of Variety* report is unclear, although it has to be said that the 1957 report, whilst clear about what was included in the list of recommended types, was not explicit about which types should NOT be included.

This lack of clarity, against the backdrop of expanded and accelerated production pressures and combined with individual manufacturing company constraints across the UK, allowed the NBL and Brush Type 2 diesel-electric fleets to be expanded from ten to fifty-eight, and, from twenty to eighty respectively (and ultimately 263 in the latter case).

Theoretically, these pressures could also have allowed the Metrovick fleet to expand had their tender for at least some of the fifty-six Type 2 locomotives included in the 1958 Locomotive Building Programme been financially more attractive.

Experience in Australia and Ireland may well have been the key influencing factor in this particular decision regardless of price, but the 1959 *Standardisation of Main Line Diesel Locomotives* report formally and finally precluded any further orders being placed with Metropolitan-Vickers.

1.7 Timeline.

Key Milestones	Date	Comments
WAGR (Australia) X/XA-class introduction:	05/54>	48 locos (8-cyl HST-V8, 1045hp).
BR Crossley-engined Shunter (D3116-27) introduction:	06/55>	10 locos (6-cyl ESNT6, 350hp).
CIE (Ireland) A-class introduction to traffic:	09/55-01/57	60 locos (8-cyl HST-V8, 1200hp).
W&EC approval for 100 Type 2 'Pilot' diesel locos:	23/03/55	
BTC advance authority for 'Pilot' locos:	24/03/55	
Memorandum to W&EC re. composition of 'Pilot' fleet:	29/09/55	
W&EC Approval for 'Pilot' fleet including 20 locos from Metropolitan-Vickers):	12/10/55	
Order placed for 20 locos from Metropolitan Vickers:	16/11/55	
BTC approval of final prices of 'Pilot' fleet:	15/12/55	
BTC extension/acceleration of diesel orders (1) (Min.9/384):	26/07/56	
1958 Locomotive Building Programme authorised:	27/09/56	
Placement of orders against 1958 Building Programme:	10/04/57	Inc 56 Type 2s; no Metrovicks.
BTC extension/acceleration of diesel orders (2) (Min.10/212):	23/05/57	
R.C. Bond/S. Warder *Limitation of Variety* Report:	26/07/57	Metropolitan-Vickers, NBL and Brush not included in Type 2 recommended list.
1959 Locomotive Building Programme authorised:	13/02/58	84 Type 2s (to be built in BR Workshops).
1959 Supplementary Locomotive Building Programmes authorised (to capitalise on available production capacity):	26/06/58+ 20/11/58	Inc 89 Type 2s (60 Brush, 20 NBL, 9 BRCW)

18 • THE METROPOLITAN-VICKERS TYPE 2 CO-BO DIESEL-ELECTRIC LOCOMOTIVES

Key Milestones	Date	Comments
D5700 into traffic:	07/58	
R.C. Bond Report: *Main Line Diesel Locomotives: The Approach to Standardisation*:	10/11/58	Metrovick <u>explicitly excluded</u> from future orders
Central Staff Report *Standardisation of Main Line Diesel Locomotives*:	08/06/59	
BTC acceptance of *Limitation of Variety* Report:	25/06/59	

Observations:
a) The Crossley-engined BR shunters had only been in traffic for four months at the time of the W&EC meeting of 12 October 1955. The WAGR operator in Australia had had seventeen months of experience by this time but the extent to which the British Railways were cognisant of events there is unknown.
b) In September 1956 fifty-six additional Type 2 diesel-electrics were authorised for the 1958 Locomotive Building Programme; orders were subsequently placed with BR/Sulzer (10), BRC&W/Sulzer (18) and NBL/MAN (28). Certainly by December 1956, and maybe earlier, R.C. Bond was in contact with the CIE and was aware of the difficulties being experiencing with the A-class fleet. This may well have influenced the decision not to proliferate the Metrovick fleet.
c) At the time when the 1959 Locomotive Building Programme was authorised (February 1958), the *Limitation of Variety* recommendations of July 1957 had been published although to what extent these ultimately precluded any further orders being placed with Metropolitan-Vickers is unclear.

Metrovick, Bowesfield Works, Stockton. Advanced state of construction, with the locomotive being propelled around the Bowesfield site by a mobile crane. Note the bodyshell of a South African Railways Class 5E1 (Series 1) Bo-Bo 3kV electric locomotive in the background. 135 of these locomotives were built by Metropolitan-Vickers, here at Bowesfield Works, between 1959 and 1961. The rail track looks to be dual gauge, presumably 4ft 8½in for the British Railways locomotives and 3ft 6in for the South African electrics. (*Tom Bowman*)

Chapter 2
SOME TECHNICAL ASPECTS

2.1 General

The order for the twenty locomotives was awarded to Metropolitan Vickers Electrical Co Ltd of Trafford Park, Manchester as the main contractor. Metropolitan-Vickers provided the electrical equipment and entered into a partnership with Crossley Brothers (Openshaw) to supply their two-stroke HST V8 engine. Some mechanical parts and internal components were subcontracted to affiliate Beyer Peacock Ltd of Gorton, Manchester. Body construction and equipment assembly was undertaken at the Metropolitan-Vickers' Bowesfield Works at Stockton-on-Tees.

2.2 Leading Particulars.

Former class codes: D12/1 (1955 classification), later 12/5 (1962 classification).
TOPS Code: Class 28.
Number Series: D5700-19.
Engine:
Crossley HST V8-cylinder two-stroke. Maximum continuous rated output: 1,200hp at 625rpm.
Firing Order: 1A, 1B, 4A, 4B, 2A, 2B, 3A, 3B.
Cylinder bore: 10½in, piston stroke: 13½in.
Cooling water capacity: 90gal.
Lubricating oil capacity: 30gal.
Dry weight: 30,500lb (13,800kg).
Main generator:
Metropolitan-Vickers TG.4204.
Continuous ratings: 1070A/750V and 1650A/475V both at 625rpm.
Auxiliary generator:
Metropolitan-Vickers AG.103AZ.
Continuous rating: 110V, 62kW at 625/400rpm.
Traction motors:
5 Metropolitan-Vickers MV.137BZ nose-suspended, single-reduction gear drive.
Gear ratio: 15:67.
Continuous rating: 475V, 330A, 180hp, 510rpm.

Performance:
Maximum tractive effort: 50,000lb at 23% adhesion at 2,900A main generator.
Continuous tractive effort: 25,000lb at 13.5mph at 1,650A main generator.
Rail hp: 942hp.
Full engine output: available between 4.3 and 61mph.
Continuous rating: available between 13.5 and 75mph.
Braking:
Metcalfe/Oerlikon.
Air for loco, vacuum for train giving a brake force of 76% of loco weight in working order.
Brake force: 35 tons
Sanding equipment: Pneumatic.
Maximum Permitted Speed: 75mph
Train Heating equipment: Spanner 'Swirlyflo' boiler (steaming capacity 1,500lb/hr).
Tank capacities: Engine and boiler fuel: 510gal. Boiler water: 600gal.
Wheel arrangement: Co-Bo.
Weight (operational): 97tons 3cwt
N.B. The 'Engine History Cards' show 91tons 5cwt 'Working Weight' i.e. including liquids.
Overall length: 56ft 7½in

20 • THE METROPOLITAN-VICKERS TYPE 2 CO-BO DIESEL-ELECTRIC LOCOMOTIVES

Height: 12ft 8½in
Width: 9ft 2½in
Wheel diameter: 3ft 3½in
Bogie wheelbase: Bo-bogie: 8ft 6in, Co-bogie: 12ft 1½in
Bogie pivot centres: 32ft 4in
Total wheelbase: 42ft 7in
Minimum curve negotiable: 3½ chains without gauge widening at dead slow speed.
Route availability: 8.
Multiple-working operation: Red circle.
Purpose: Mixed-traffic locomotives.

See Diagram below for additional details.

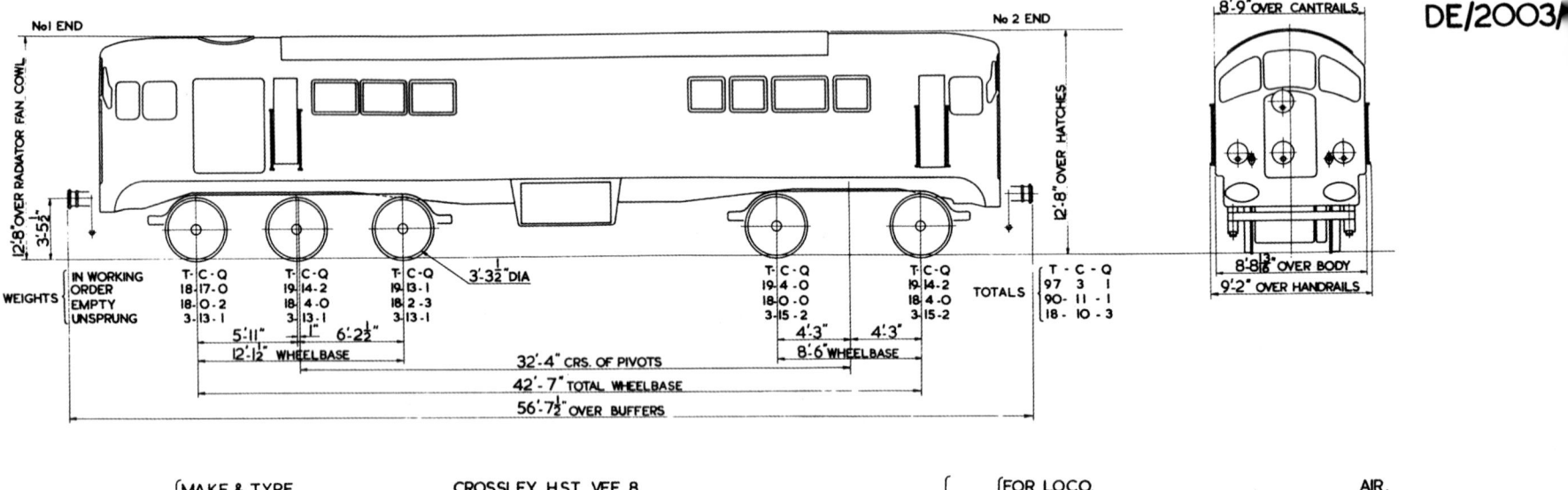

ENGINE	MAKE & TYPE	CROSSLEY H.S.T. VEE 8.
	No. OF CYLS. & CYCLE	8 CYL. 2 STROKE.
	MAX. CONT. RATED OUTPUT	1200 H.P. AT 750 R.P.M.
MAIN GENERATOR	MAKE & TYPE	METROPOLITAN-VICKERS T.G. 4204.
TRACTION MOTORS	MAKE & TYPE	METROPOLITAN-VICKERS M.V. 137 BZ.
	No.	FIVE.
	TYPE OF SUSPENSION	NOSE.
	TYPE OF GEAR DRIVE	SINGLE REDUCTION.
PERFORMANCE	MAX. TRACTIVE EFFORT	50,000 LBS. AT 23% ADHESION. AT 2900 AMPS. MAIN GENERATOR.
	CONT. TRACTIVE EFFORT	25,000 LBS. AT 13·5 M.P.H. AT 1650 AMPS. MAIN GENERATOR.
	RAIL H.P. AT CONT. RATING	900 H.P.
	FULL ENGINE OUTPUT	AVAILABLE BETWEEN 4·3 & 61 M.P.H.
BRAKING	TYPE FOR LOCO	AIR.
	TYPE FOR TRAIN	VACUUM.
	BRAKE FORCE % OF LOCO. WEIGHT IN WORKING ORDER	76%
SPEED	MAX. PERMITTED SERVICE SPEED	75 M.P.H.
CURVE	MIN. RAD. CURVE WITHOUT GAUGE WIDENING. AT DEAD SLOW SPEED.	3½ CHAINS.
TRAIN HEATING EQUIPMENT	BOILER MAKE & TYPE	SPANNER 'SWIRLYFLO'.
	STEAMING CAPACITY	1500 LBS/HOUR.
TANK CAPACITIES	ENGINE FUEL BOILER FUEL	510 GALLS.
	BOILER WATER	600 GALLS.

1200 H.P. M·V. TYPE 2 C-B DIESEL ELECTRIC LOCOMOTIVE.

Line Drawing DE/2003/1 of Metropolitan-Vickers Type 2 1,200hp diesel-electric. (*BR Main-Line Diesel Locomotive Diagrams, September 1961*)

2.3 Equipment Layout and Superstructure.

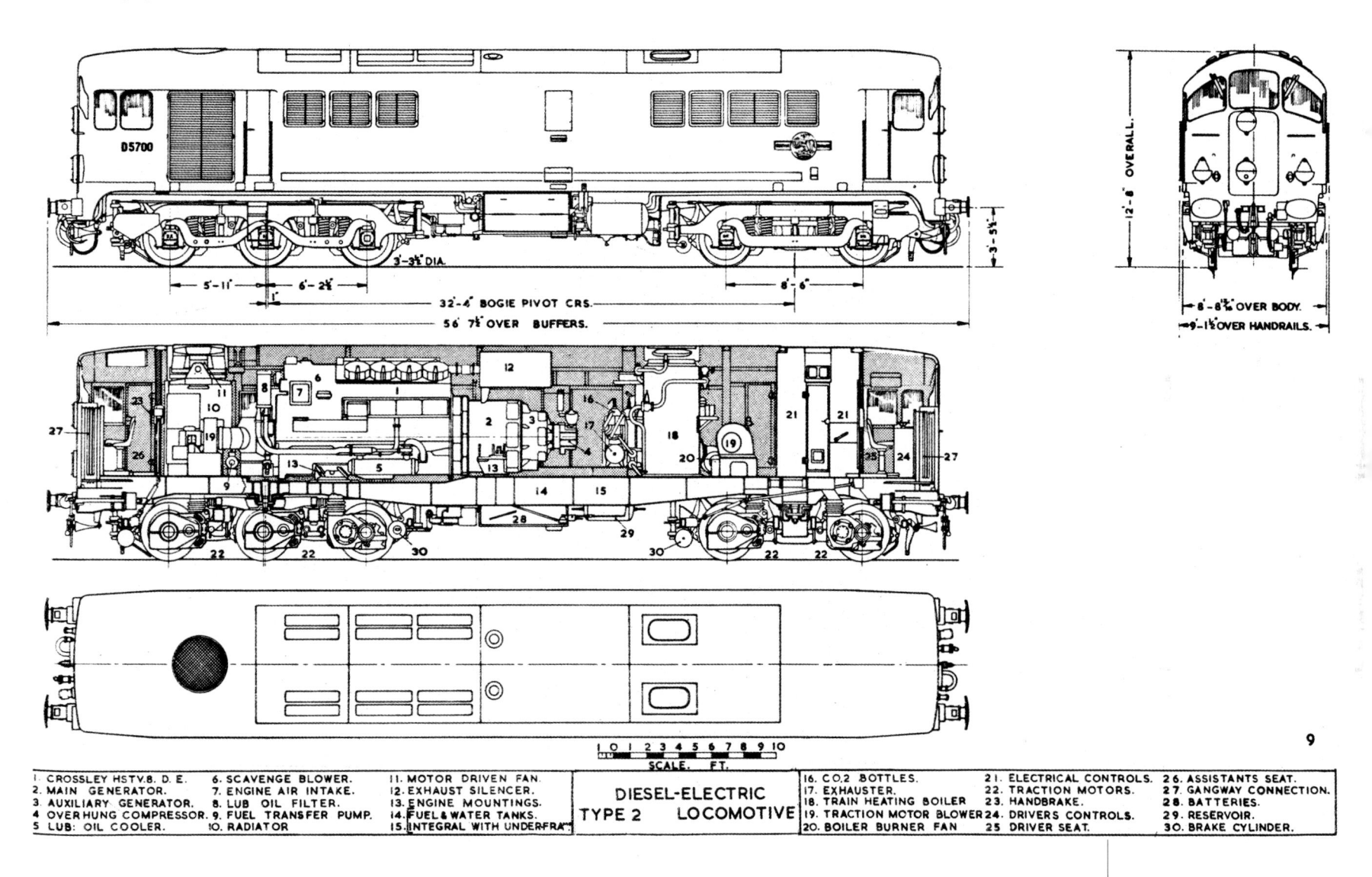

1. CROSSLEY HSTV.8. D.E.	6. SCAVENGE BLOWER.	11. MOTOR DRIVEN FAN.	16. CO₂ BOTTLES.	21. ELECTRICAL CONTROLS.	26. ASSISTANTS SEAT.
2. MAIN GENERATOR.	7. ENGINE AIR INTAKE.	12. EXHAUST SILENCER.	17. EXHAUSTER.	22. TRACTION MOTORS.	27. GANGWAY CONNECTION.
3. AUXILIARY GENERATOR.	8. LUB OIL FILTER.	13. ENGINE MOUNTINGS.	18. TRAIN HEATING BOILER	23. HANDBRAKE.	28. BATTERIES.
4. OVERHUNG COMPRESSOR.	9. FUEL TRANSFER PUMP.	14. FUEL & WATER TANKS.	19. TRACTION MOTOR BLOWER	24. DRIVERS CONTROLS.	29. RESERVOIR.
5. LUB: OIL COOLER.	10. RADIATOR	15. INTEGRAL WITH UNDERFRA	20. BOILER BURNER FAN	25. DRIVER SEAT	30. BRAKE CYLINDER.

DIESEL-ELECTRIC TYPE 2 LOCOMOTIVE

The Metrovick locomotive body was an all-steel fabrication, with a heavy underframe onto which side and end skeletal members were fitted. These were plated in medium-gauge steel. Access to internal equipment was provided by removable roof hatches and side inspection doors.

The internal layout was fairly conventional with a full-width cab at each end each with a left-hand driving position. Entrance into the cab, however, was distinctly unusual with the cab-door entrance on the driving side being located some 12ft inward (with cab access through part of the equipment room). The secondman's door was located conventionally immediately ahead of the cab bulkhead

At the No.1 end, a cooler group was located with side radiator elements and a roof-mounted fan. To the rear of this was the Crossley HST V8 engine. Coupled to the inner end of the engine was the Metropolitan-Vickers main and auxiliary generator group, providing power for both traction and auxiliary equipment. Towards No.2 end was the control equipment, brake frame and

Line Drawing of Metropolitan-Vickers Type 2 D5700.
(BR Main-Line Locomotive Layout Diagrams)

Spanner Mk1 steam train-heating boiler. An internal cab-to-cab walkway was provided. The water and fuel tanks were located within the underframe.

The locomotives used the Metcalfe-Oerlikon vacuum-controlled direct air brake system, manufactured by Davies & Metcalfe. The locomotive itself had air brakes, which were controlled either by a driver's direct air brake valve, used when shunting or running light, or by a driver's vacuum brake valve when the unit was hauling vacuum-fitted vehicles.

The cab layout also incorporated some unusual features. The power controller, located on the driver's right-hand side, was a wheel (with knob) instead of the more common push/pull lever. The power controller had ten notches, which progressively increased the engine speed and traction output. In front of the driver was the usual instrumentation including various gauges, ammeters and speedometer. On the driver's left were two brake controllers, a straight air brake valve for the locomotive and a proportional valve for the train, which progressively applied both the locomotive brakes and the train's vacuum brakes. A floor-mounted Driver's Safety Device (DSD) 'dead man's' pedal was fitted. The secondman's side of the cab included a horn valve and a DSD hold-over button. Electrical heating was provided in the driving cabs with foot warmers at the driving positions. The cab windows had demisters.

In the middle front of the cab fronts was a communicating gangway door which provided access between pairs of locomotives.

Front-end equipment on the Metrovicks consisted of standard drawgear, plus vacuum brake, steam heat and air control pipes. Air-operated warning horns were fitted just below the buffer beams.

Horizontally-hinged front-end train identification discs were installed; when open these could show a white light. In addition, two red electric tail lights were positioned on either side of the front gangway doors.

D5700, Derby Works (Open Day), 30 August 1958. The finished article in pristine condition. Note the position of the fire alarm window cutting into the bodyside stripe which caused Jack Howe so much consternation (see Section 3.9).
(Rail-Online)

Some Technical Aspects • 23

D5718, 10A Carnforth, 22 April 1968. (*Mark Walker collection*)
Front end detail:
'Pantograph' windscreen wipers.
Indicator discs on protruding sub-frames (to allow the discs to span the protruding lights behind) (x4).
Rear lights (x2).
Lamp irons (x3)
Electrification warning signs (x2)
Buffer beam equipment, from left to right:
- Left buffer
- Air control pipe (below right of buffer)
- Red circle multiple-working jumper cable
- Vacuum brake pipe.
- Drawgear (hook and screw coupling)
- Steam heating pipe.
- Red-circle multiple working jumper receptacle.
- Air control pipe (below left of buffer)
- Right buffer

Two warning horns below the buffer beam, the left one pointing forwards, the right directed sideways.

2.4 Crossley Engine.

2.4.1 General.

The Crossley HST V8 engine was unusual with respect to British Railways traction on two counts, the two-stroke arrangement and the Exhaust Pulse Pressure-Charging system developed by Crossley. R.C. Bond, the BTC Chief Mechanical Engineer was keen to try out a diesel running on the two-stroke cycle as a comparison with the alternative four-stroke engine type, hence the order with Crossley. It has been argued that the Crossley engine would probably not have been accepted by the BTC but for the joint-venture with Metropolitan Vickers which the BTC held in high regard.

2.4.2 Two-Stroke Engines.

The following extract from *Trains Illustrated* (February 1958, pp86-89, 'The A.B.C. of the diesel engine – Part One', R. Tourret) provides an excellent and succinct insight into two-stroke engines and their pros and cons:

'A diesel engine is an internal combustion engine. In other words, its fuel is burnt in the cylinders, in contrast to the steam engine, in which the hot gases are produced in a boiler separate from the cylinders.

'An internal combustion engine can be of either reciprocating or rotating type (the latter is the gas turbine engine . . .). This is the sequence of events in a reciprocating engine: a charge is drawn into the cylinder, this air is compressed, fuel is injected and the mixture is ignited; combustion then occurs at an extremely rapid rate, almost equivalent to an explosion, driving the piston down the cylinder and providing the power; finally, the exhaust products are expelled and the cylinder is ready to receive a fresh charge of air.

'In practice, this induction-compression-power-exhaust sequence can conveniently be accomplished in two revolutions of the crankshaft, i.e. with the piston moving up and down the cylinder twice. Firstly the piston moves down the cylinder and sucks in air; secondly, the piston moves up to compress the air; thirdly, fuel is injected and the following combustion pushes the piston down the cylinder; finally, the piston moves up the cylinder to expel the exhaust gases . . . the cylinder is fitted with inlet and exhaust valves. The inlet valve opens for the induction stroke and the exhaust valve for the exhaust stroke; otherwise the valves remain closed.

'In this sequence, called a four-stroke cycle, only one stroke in four is a power-stroke. To give a more regular torque, it is therefore usual to have a number of cylinders in one engine – four, six, eight or more – so that at a given time there is always at least once cylinder firing and giving power.

'As another means of obtaining power pulses more frequently, a two-stroke cycle is sometimes used. This gives one power stroke in two. There is the same induction-compression-power-exhaust sequence, but a separate stroke is no longer allowed for each phase. As the piston moves up, first the inlet valve is open and the fresh charge drives the exhaust gases out; then, as the piston moves up, the air is compressed. It is to be noted here that the air is not sucked in but has to be blown in . . . At the top of the stroke, fuel is injected and the resultant explosion drives the piston down. At the end of the stroke the exhaust valve opens and the exhaust gases are expelled by the incoming fresh charge of air. With engines operating on the two-stroke cycle, it is possible to dispense with valves in favour of inlet and/or outlet ports in the cylinder walls, which are opened or uncovered by the piston as it moves.

'Although a two-stroke engine has the advantage over a four-stroke (there are twice as many power strokes) twice as much power is not obtained as might at first be thought. To start with, the exhaust process is not so efficient as in a four-stroke type and some spent gases may remain in the cylinder; conversely, some fresh charge can be blown right through the cylinder and out through the exhaust. In addition, because the fresh air must be blown in, some power has to be taken from the engine to induce its entry and this power is wasted so far as useful work is concerned. All in all, therefore, two-stroke engines tend to give about the same power as four-stroke engines of the same size.

'When the charge of air has been compressed, the fuel has to be ignited ... With a diesel engine, the fresh air is compressed to a greater extent (than a petrol engine), i.e. the compression ratio is higher and may be 15 or 20-1, instead of 6 or 10-1 as in a petrol engine. Since the temperature of the air rises as it is compressed, the temperature at the end of the compression stroke in a diesel engine is quite high. It is, in fact, high enough to ignite the fuel immediately it is injected into the cylinder.'

2.4.3 The Crossley HST V8 engine and Exhaust Pulse Pressure Charging.
An article in the January 1959 edition of *Trains Illustrated* (pp12-3, 'Type "2" 1,200 hp diesel-electric Co-Bo units for BR') describes the Crossley HST V8 engine in some detail:

'The Crossley engine employed is the only conventional two-stroke cycle type featured in current BR locomotive orders. As its designation suggests, the HST Vee 8 has its eight cylinders arranged in 'V' formation; its continuous rating is 1,200 hp at 625 r.p.m. and the one-hour rating is 1,320 hp at the same r.p.m. Its makers advance particular claims for the engine's mechanical simplicity, which achieves a high power per cylinder without the complication of exhaust turbo-charging. A port-controlled loop scavenge system eliminates the necessity for cylinder head valves or operating gear, and a feature known as Exhaust Pulse Pressure-Charging, which has been highly developed by Crossley, is also incorporated. By this means some of the scavenge air that has passed through the cylinder into the exhaust manifold is forced back into the cylinder by the exhaust pressure pulse from an adjacent cylinder; this occurs at the instant of port closure, thus creating a positive pressure of about 10 lb./sq. in. at the commencement of compression.'

The Exhaust Pulse Pressure-Charging offered cheap pressure-charging and did away with the expensive and potentially troublesome turbo-charging arrangement used in most other designs.

As R.M. Tufnell describes (*The Diesel Impact on British Rail*, Mechanical Engineering Publications, 1979.).'Their 'HST' range had several appealing features, such as its low speed of 625 rev/min and its absence of valves and valve gear ... '; however, the engine 'had a poor power/weight ratio. The two-stroke principle had been proved in traction by the success of the General Motors EMD 567 range. ... Two-stroke engines had to be provided with some form of forced induction for their air supply and whereas the EMD engine used two compact high-speed rotary "Roots" type compressors, Crossley used a single chain-driven blower mounted at the free end of the crankshaft, which considerably increased the bulk and weight of the engine.'. Furthermore, 'Crossley Bros., unfortunately, did not have the time or the money to get their HST engine to the same output or degree of reliability as that achieved by General Motors.'

2.5 Electrical Equipment.
2.5.1 Main and Auxiliary Generators.
The main and auxiliary generators were of integral construction. The frame was flange mounted on the end of the engine and the armatures were mounted on a common hollow shaft, which was solid coupled to the engine crankshaft at one end and carried on a single roller bearing on the other.

The main generator supplied power to the five traction motors, the excitation being automatically controlled on eight of the ten master-controller notches by the load regulator. The auxiliary generator supplied power for all motor-driven auxiliaries, battery charging, control equipment, lighting, cab heating, main generator excitation, and train heating boiler controls.

2.5.2 Auxiliaries.
There were three motor blowers, two for traction motor cooling and one to pressurise the generator compartment for forced cooling of the generator.

The main Worthington-Simpson compressor was flange-mounted to the auxiliary generator and driven from it. This supplied compressed air for the locomotive brakes, electro-pneumatic control gear, horns, windscreen wipers and sanding gear.

Two Westinghouse exhausters were provided to operate the brakes on vacuum-fitted rolling stock.

2.5.3 Traction Motors.
The Metrovicks were fitted with five Metropolitan-Vickers MV.137BZ axle-hung traction motors: these motors were four-pole series-wound machines of the nose-suspended type.

2.5.4 Power Control.
The master controller provided the driver with the means of selecting the direction of travel and the power level provided by the engine. The selector handle had four positions i.e. forward, off, engine-only and reverse, the handle being in the engine-only position when starting the Crossley engine. The power wheel had ten notches to provide increments of power up to the maximum of 1,200hp on notch 10. The use of the notched or stepped system of control eliminated the need for additional flexible air connections between locomotives when operating in multiple, and also ensured correct load sharing at all times.

In notches 1 and 2, the engine ran at its idling speed, and the main generator was excited by the two stages of primary field strength. From notch 3 (which corresponded to about 25 per cent of traction hp) to notch 10 (full load) the engine speed was automatically set, by the engine speed regulator, to give increments of power, thus ensuring that the engine operated at optimal conditions. Thereafter, adjustment of the electrical load was controlled by the automatic load regulator. Field-weakening was controlled direct by the load regulator, without separate contactors. There were two weak-field running steps, but each was approached through intermediate steps to avoid an abrupt change of field strength.

On notch 10, full power was available between 4.3 and 61mph, this range being controlled by control of generator excitation up to about 25mph and by traction motor field weakening thereafter.

The so-called 'Red Circle' electro-magnetic multiple control equipment permitted up to three like-fitted locos to be driven in multiple by one driver. In reality the only other 'Red Circle' fitted locomotives were D5500-19, D6100-37 and D8400-9; given the sphere of operation of these classes it is highly unlikely that the Metrovicks were operated in multiple with any locomotive other than another Metrovick!

2.6 Bogies.
The key distinguishing feature of the Metrovicks was the Co-Bo wheel arrangement and resulted from the positioning of the engine/generator towards No.1 end necessitating a six-wheel bogie at that end. The all-up weight of 97 tons and a maximum axle-loading in excess of 19 tons 14cwt resulted in a route availability of a somewhat restrictive 'RA8'.

Whether the Co-Bo wheel arrangement was in direct response to British Railways invitation to tender specification or whether Metropolitan-Vickers deliberating designed for a 50,000lb maximum tractive effort is unknown. However, by deploying five driven axles, Metropolitan-Vickers achieved the highest maximum tractive effort of all of the Pilot-Scheme Type 2 designs.

The cast-steel Commonwealth-style bogies were produced by English Steel Castings Corporation and supplied ready manufactured to Metropolitan-Vickers at Bowesfield Works. Traction motors, as already mentioned, were supplied by Metropolitan-Vickers, with brake equipment by Davies & Metcalfe.

Springing was by the semi-equalising method, with beams spanning the distance between the axles; the bogie frame was supported on helical springs resting on these beams. A number of refinements in the suspension were deployed, including the addition of Metalastik bonded rubber 'sandwiches' interposed between the axlebox top and the equalising beams; the introduction of Ferobestos pads into the spring seats; and the use of Woodhead-Monroe shock absorbers.

Chapter 3
LOCOMOTIVE DESIGN

3.1 General.
The National Archive carries quite a considerable amount of written correspondence between the BTC, Metropolitan-Vickers and the external Design Consultant employed on the Metrovick contract. This correspondence, however, provides only a partial insight into the design of the Metrovick diesels but the information to be gleaned makes for very interesting reading nonetheless. Unfortunately however, the archive material itself is incomplete, with several letters between the interested parties clearly missing; however, worse than this, the Metropolitan-Vickers and Design Consultant design drawings frequently referred to in the documentation are almost non-existent with only two drawings apparently being preserved for posterity. In addition, all verbal interactions between the key players are inevitably unavailable (i.e. face-to-face dialogue, telephone conversations and minutes of meetings held between the interested parties).

Recognising these limitations, it is still worth reviewing the available paperwork as it does illustrate many of the challenges experienced with the design of the Metrovicks and at least in part explains some of the apparent oddities in the final design. The documents also clearly highlight significant friction between the BTC Design Managers (and the Design Consultant) and the Metropolitan-Vickers engineers.

The key protagonists in the available archives are as follows:

R.C. Bond	BTC, Chief Mechanical Engineer, London.
E.S. Cox	BTC, Assistant Chief Mechanical Engineer, London.
C. Barman	BTC, Executive, Design Panel, London.
G. Williams	BTC, Design Officer (from July 1957), Design Panel, London.
J.F. Harrison	BTC, CM&EE, LMR, Derby.
C.S. Cocks	BTC, LMR, Derby.
H. West	MV (General Manager?).
F. Whyman	MV Chief Engineer, Traction Projects Department.
N. Thorneley	MV Deputy Chief Engineer, Traction Projects Department.
R.M. Kay	MV Appearance Design Engineer.
?.Bowers	MV Drawing Office.
J. Howe	Consultant, Chartered Architect & Industrial Designer; assisted MV with appearance design and subsequently employed by the BTC as design consultant.

External design work on the Metrovicks appears to have started in earnest during early 1956. Metropolitan-Vickers employed Appearance Design Engineers and had also recruited the services of Jack Howe as the Design Consultant by this time.

Messrs. Cox and Barman from the BTC first visited Metropolitan-Vickers in Manchester on 28 February 1956 to discuss the 'appearance design' of the Metrovicks. Mr Howe and one of the MV Design Engineers were also in attendance. Unfortunately, the various points discussed at this meeting go unrecorded. However, Cox and Barman subsequently recognised that there would be 'a very great advantage to us [BTC] if Mr Howe could be employed by the Commission so that he might act for them as design consultant in this matter [design of the Metrovicks] . . .'. In a letter to H. West of Metropolitan-Vickers dated 9 March 1956, Barman stated: 'I myself feel sure that such an arrangement would help to make the consultations between your firm and ourselves more effective and indeed I think it might well be found to save valuable time'.

Metropolitan-Vickers agreed and from mid-March 1956 Howe effectively operated with two bosses, an arrangement which inevitably caused some difficulties as the work progressed.

3.2 Front-End Design (cab windows and gangway doors).

During March 1956, Barman received a 'new' drawing (No. A2109429) from Metropolitan-Vickers, the reference to 'new' presumably referring to an update subsequent to the 28 February meeting between MV and the BTC. Barman passed this drawing onto Howe on 16 March 1956 with a cover letter stating that MV '. . . have carried the design for their locomotive a little further . . .' and that '. . . The drawing also shows two alternative treatments for the front'. Barman put his cards on the table very early on by stating, 'The one we want, of course, is the flush fronted one.'

On 27 March 1956, Howe forwarded a copy of Drawing No.125/1 to Barman together with a perspective drawing which he had produced showing 'a possible solution to this problem, which, with your agreement, I will pass to Metropolitan-Vickers for them to consider in the light of the practical requirements'. Quite what the 'problem' was that Howe was referring to is unclear but presumably relates to the two alternative front-end 'treatments'. On 28 March 1956, the drawing was sent to Metropolitan-Vickers.

On 3 April 1956, F. Whyman, Metropolitan-Vickers' Chief Engineer, responded to Howe with respect to Drawing No.125/1, as follows:

'We have gone rather carefully into you drawing and photograph but feel that the locomotive will look very stark and severe.

'We are worried about the appearance of the cab end or front which, to us, is very reminiscent of an old-fashioned vestibule Colonial coach with its appearance of an overhanging roof and the very ugly flat portions outside the windows where flat glass instead of curved have been used. I think you are going to find it very difficult to get any reasonable appearance without using curved windows with such a large expanse of glass and as the toughened glass used for these windows cannot be cut, we cannot see the slightest reason why curved special sections could not be stored as spares instead of rectangular or other shaped flat sections, and I think you would be well advised to have another go at the British Railways on this subject to at least remove the ugly flat window sills outside the windows.

'The somewhat overhanging roof only slightly radiused at the end again looks to us extremely old-fashioned and the whole arrangement of windows and overhanging roof will give very high wind resistance to motion which is to be avoided.'

Howe responded to Whyman on 5 April 1956:

'I entirely agree with you regarding the use of flat glass for the cab windows. This, as you know, was discussed at our meeting at Trafford Park and again when I met Mr Cox and the other designers in London. He was most insistent that flat glass should be used and I therefore accepted the ruling although I would very much prefer it to be curved. If this were so it would overcome one or two difficulties which you are worried about, namely, the slight overhang of the roof and the wide sills externally.'

On 23 April 1956, Howe sent a letter to N. Thorneley (Whyman's deputy at Metropolitan-Vickers):

'This is to confirm the discussion we had with

Mr Whyman on Friday last when the following points were agreed:

1. British Railways have agreed that curved glass can be used in the cab windows and the arrangement will not be as indicated in my drawing 125/1A, a copy of which I left with you.
2. I wish to avoid a definite break between the cladding on the front of the cab and the buffer beam, but as this appears to present difficulties in maintaining access to the buffer bolts, the buffer beam itself may be curved and in the same plane as the face above.
3. Owing to the difficulty of forming the doors to the corridor link if curved in two planes, I agree that these shall be vertical up to the top of the cab windows.'

It was probably at this point that the final configuration of the Metrovicks was conceived, although, as will be seen, the subject of the cab front-end design rumbled on for another twenty-two months!

The dimensions of the front-end gangways doors became a significant topic over the ensuing few months, to the extent that Howe saw the possibility of a substantial front-end re-design. The following letter from Howe to Barman dated 15 June 1956 illustrates the point:

'While I was there [at Derby the previous week reviewing the 'Peak' locomotive design work] I discovered that the head of the corridor link doors is some 6" lower than the Metrovick design and there appears to be no reason why these should differ. I understand it was thought at one time that the MV job need not link with theirs, but it seems obvious to me that it would be very desirable to do so. I have written to Whyman suggesting that this should be dropped as it will enable a continuous horizontal window to be accommodated above with good sight lines and ample space for controls. Enclosed is a very rough sketch showing this arrangement [drawing No.125/2]. I have not received Whyman's reaction but I plan to go to Manchester at the end of next week when the whole thing can be discussed. I have asked him to re-consider the sloping window and although I am sure he will not like it, it will be a great improvement.'

Fortunately, Drawing No.125/2 (dated 12 June 1956) is one of only two drawings to be found in the National Archive and shows a locomotive with substantially different looks relative to that which became the final product. Unfortunately, no comments from Whyman have been found.

J. Howe Drawing No.125/2 dated 12 June 1956. The front end design, although not used on the British Metrovicks, bears a remarkable similarity with the 135 Class 5E1 (Series 1) electric locomotives (numbered E364-E498) built by Metropolitan-Vickers at Bowesfield for the South African Railways, albeit with the corridor/gangway connection extended to roof height. (*Courtesy National Archive, Kew*)

The gangway door issue raised its head again in another letter (dated 25 June 1956) from Howe to Barman:

'It appears that the lowering of the corridor link doors may not be possible due to a policy question on multiple working which has not yet been resolved. Consequently, they [MV] are not prepared to make this amendment yet upon which depends my latest revision to the cab windows. In any case they are very much opposed to the sloping window which I had hoped could be incorporated.'

Clarification on the so-called 'multi-unit operation scheme' was provided by J.F. Harrison in a letter to Howe dated 27 June 1956:

'With reference to your [separate] letter of 26th instant, as you state in your letter the height of the gangway door on the Metro-Vickers locomotives depends on a decision as to whether they are, or are not, coming into the multiple operation scheme along with the other contractors. This decision rests entirely between Metro-Vickers and the B.T.C.

'If they decide to come into the multi-unit operation scheme then the height of the gangway doors on the Metro-Vickers locomotives will have to conform with the dimension shown on the attached copy of drawing DD.4536. If, however, they decide not to come into the scheme then they are, within reason, free to choose the height of the gangway door to suit the layout of the locomotive, the only requirement being that the M.V.E. locomotives will couple together satisfactorily and work in multiple with each other.'

A letter from J. Howe to F. Whyman dated 28 June 1956 reads:

'When I was in Manchester last week I was most interested to see the full size cab model of the new British Railways locomotive. I have been, and still am, somewhat worried about the arrangement of the windows and I sent to Mr Thornley [sic] a rough sketch showing an alternative. This was based on a reduced height of linked gangway which has been, I understand, adopted as standard for all locomotives being made by other manufacturers. I understand that the adoption of this standard by MetroVick depends upon a policy decision in regard to multiple unit operation between yourselves and the British Transport Commission.

'If this door could be lowered as suggested, it would, I think, just enable a continuous horizontal front window to be employed [as per Howe's Drawing No.125/2]. Not only would this, in my opinion, give a more attractive appearance, but would provide a more ample observation area for the driver.'

At this point the trail seems to go cold in terms of correspondence held within the National Archives. Drawing No.125/1B was produced during early August 1956 although it is not clear from the archives which front-end style was portrayed.

There is no indication, one way or the other, whether Metropolitan-Vickers accepted being part of the 'multiple operation scheme'. However, the following letter from R.C. Bond to J.F. Harrison dated 2 October 1956 makes interesting reading, bringing driver visibility issues into the equation:

'Mr Barman has let me see some drawings prepared for the styling of the above locomotive, including the firm's latest layout Drawing No.G.O.61078.

'There is one . . . feature on this drawing which I do not like very much and that is the arrangement of the front cab windows, the bottom edge of which continues in a straight line across the cab front at the level of the top of the gangway doors. This means that the men sitting in the driving position will have a very restricted view forward unless he is seated so high that he cannot conveniently lean out of the cab side window. Here again the firm has taken a different line from all of the other constructors who have found means of dropping the level of the cab front windows in the vicinity of the driver's face.'

On the basis of this letter, it could be construed that MV did accept being part of the 'multiple operation scheme' and Howe's front-end design proposal as illustrated in his Drawing No.125/2, only for it to be criticised by Bond on the basis of inadequate driver's visibility.

Bond's comments effectively refer to the front-end window arrangement deployed on the BR/Sulzer, BRCW and Brush Type 2 diesels as being a preferable arrangement.

The next relevant letter which surfaces is one from Howe to C.S. Cocks (Derby(as distinct from E.S. Cox, London)) dated 2 November 1956:

'I was with Mr Whyman and Mr Thorneley of Metropolitan Vickers last week and learnt of the modifications that had been made in regard to the cab windows. I was not able to comment very much at the time because they are related to other external features [notably the positioning of the cab doors - see below] . . .

'This is most disappointing because I completed a drawing three months ago [maybe Drawing No.125/2, although this was actually produced in June 1956] based on agreed information, which, subject to detail modifications, was thought to represent the approved design. This opinion was certainly shared by Mr Christian Barman, Mr Bond and Mr Cox in London.'

By December 1956, matters had moved on. At this time much debate was being focussed on cab door positioning and bodyside grille arrangements; in fact on 13 December 1956, Howe forwarded Drawing No.125/3 (also dated 13 December) and the only other drawing available in the National Archives covering the Metrovicks) to M. Thorneley showing alternative bodyside grille options. However, a crucial feature of this drawing was that the front cab windows had moved on (or migrated back) to the curved 'wrap-around' design which the Metrovicks were finally delivered.

Drawing No.125/1C was forwarded from Howe to Barman together with a covering letter on 22 February 1957, which was passed on to Bond for final approval four days later. Bond notified his approval to Barman on 1 March 1957. Drawing No.125/1C was presumably the same as Drawing No.125/3 with respect to the front windows.

The archive information then goes very quiet for thirteen months. It will have been noted above that Howe was not pleased with the front-window design which manifested itself in Drawing No.125/3. It appears that maybe Howe saw an opportunity in January 1958 to finally get his way in deploying his design as proposed in Drawing 125/2, thereby dispensing with the 'wrap-around' window arrangement. The following sequence of letters illustrates Howe's attempts at rejuvenating his design and why, in the end, his efforts were thwarted.

Letter: J. Howe to F. Whyman, 23 January 1958:

'I must apologise for the delay in dealing with the question of the cab windows but unfortunately none of the people in the Transport Commission who I wanted to contact have been available until two days ago. I saw Mr Christian Barman and Mr E.S. Cox and they agreed that it would improve the design of this locomotive enormously if the window could be cut back as I suggested when we last met. Mr Cox has written to Mr Harrison at Derby and it is possible that by now he has been in touch with you.

'I am sorry that this should have cropped up at the present stage and fully appreciate your point of view from the manufacturing angle but if you could see your way to make this amendment it would, I know, remove one bad design feature in an otherwise excellent job, and I think it might also, in the long run, prove to be a manufacturing advantage because of the difficulty which Stockton has experienced in fitting the first windows.'

Letter: F. Whyman to J. Howe to, 27 January 1958:

'Thanks for your letter of the 23rd January which came as a surprise to me when I saw it this morning. I thought at our last meeting I made it quite clear that any change to the window or similar changes at this stage of the job were quite unthinkable, so you will appreciate how surprised I am to find you have furthered this with British Railways in an endeavour to have a change made.

'The position as I see it is, the drawings were in your possession before the windows were made and no objections were raised and whilst I agree that a change would marginally improve the appearance . . .

in order to ensure reasonable delivery at reasonable cost these points will have to be noted for the benefit of future designs, but physical changes at this stage will not be possible.

'Quite apart from the actual delay that would arise from a change such as you suggest which would be of the order of 3 to 4 months, the psychological effect on the Works of seeing such changes done when so much urgency is attached to the completion of the job would be extremely discouraging and take away all future sense of urgency.

'. . . so far as we are concerned here everything possible will be done to avoid changes of this nature.'

Letter: J. Howe to F. Whyman, 29 January 1958:

'Thank you for your letter dated 27th January which I have received this morning.

'When I was last with you we discussed this matter and both expressed our respective views and when I left you it was agreed that I should go to the Drawing Office with Mr Bowers and look into the position in regard to these windows. This I did and as a result the action which I have taken was agreed. I did tell Mr Bowers that I would deal with the matter immediately but unfortunately there was a slight delay because I was unable to contact people concerned at the Transport Commission. In the circumstances I feel that the remarks in your first paragraph are a little out of perspective.

'You will appreciate that I am acting as Consultant to the British Transport Commission in connection with this project and I felt bound to raise this point in order to obtain their views on the matter.

'I note from your letter you will resist any proposed change . . .'

Behind the scenes, Howe had clearly escalated the matter within the BTC given the following correspondence:

Letter: R.C. Bond to C. Barman, 11 February 1958:

'With reference to your recent meeting with Mr Cox and the letter to Mr Harrison . . . which was dictated in your presence; the proposal contained therein has now been discussed with the firm and I am now informed that the whole of the cab window frames and glasses are completed to the original design and considerable difficulty and a five months delay would be experienced in the replacement at this stage of the window and frame sets.

'Mr Harrison has therefore recommended, and I have agreed, that no change should be made in the design of the front end of this particular group of locomotives.

'In connection with this matter Mr Harrison reports that no fitting or bedding problems are anticipated in the present design and the arrangement of the corner pillar and swept window as it stands appears to be exceptionally good for side visibility.'

The foregoing provides some insight into the front-end design of the Metrovicks. The impression is that Metropolitan-Vickers created something approaching the original front-end design way back in early-1956 and it was broadly this which ultimately saw the light of day in 1958, despite Howe's best efforts.

Driver visibility was critical and appears to have prevented the design illustrated in Drawing No.125/2. On the basis of various BR drawings, it appears that Metropolitan-Vickers did adopt the 'multiple operation scheme'; the top and bottom heights of the gangway doors for the Metrovicks are shown to be identical with other Type 2 classes, suggesting that the height level was indeed dropped to conform. However, to achieve the required window depth on the outer two windows a very curved bottom profile was used (with wrap-around), instead of the arrangement used on BR/Sulzer, BRCW and Brush locomotives.

The May 1961 edition of *Trains Illustrated* (pp299-304) carried part 3 of an article entitled 'Design on the Railway'. With regards to cab windows the commentary is succinct:

'The side windows of the cab must be placed low enough to enable the driver to look back along the train, whilst those in the front must be high enough to clear the communicating doors and the driver's control desk. To combine these two groups of windows into a neat single unit of design is no simple matter; it has been achieved very successfully on the D5300, D5500 . . . locomotives, less well on the D5000 and D5700 designs.'

3.3 Bodyside design (doors)

The positioning of the cab doors on the Metrovicks has always been a topic of debate and the following correspondence indicates fairly extensive debate during the design phase itself.

The topic first surfaced in the Archive information available with a letter from J. Howe to F. Whyman dated 2 August 1956:

'Thank you for your letter of the 31st July enclosing a copy of your drawing number A2109397 . . . I would like to mention the following: You had hopes, I believe, of convincing British Railways that a door on the driver's side of the cab was not essential but I notice that two doors have now been included. Have you agreed with them that this shall be so?'

Nearly two months later, the subject attracts further attention, including a letter from C. Barman to E.S. Cox dated 28 September 1956:

'I understand Metropolitan-Vickers claim that progress on this locomotive is now held up for lack of a decision on the cab access doors, and I think Mr Bond told us the other day that this question is being discussed at a meeting at Derby next week.

'It occurs to me that you may be interested to see the three drawings I send you herewith. Drawing (a) shows our original design with two normal cab doors one on either side of the cab. Drawing (b) shows the new layout proposed by Metropolitan-Vickers and our drawing (c) shows how this arrangement will look as far as the exterior is concerned.

'Apart from appearance, a grave difficulty of this new proposal is that the driver cannot reach the nearside access door without making a circuit round the boiler. Mr Howe, our designer, who has made a careful study of the internal arrangements, is convinced that there should be no serious difficulty in pushing back the boiler and the cab partition to make room for two cab doors as in the original design.'

Cox replied to Barman on 2 October 1956:

'I have very much the same feelings as you regarding this locomotive and I attach a copy of a letter which Mr Bond has today sent to Mr Harrison with a view to having the matter looked at again at the meeting which is to be held with the firm on 11th instant.

'I am only too afraid, however, that the design has proceeded too far for any real alteration to be made, but will advise you of the outcome on my return from the meeting next week.'

The letter from Bond to J.F. Harrison is given below:

'Mr Barman has let me see some drawings prepared for the styling of the above locomotive, including the firm's latest layout Drawing No. G.O.61078.

'Unlike all other main line diesels, which are under design, it is proposed that there should be no door in the cab on the driver's side on this particular locomotive. Access from the driver's side of the locomotive at each end is from a door further along the body of the locomotive, and the driver, in order to reach his seat from this side, has to pass around the control cabinet at one end and through a tortuous passage round the circumference of the boiler at the other end. Since this locomotive is amongst the longest which has been offered, I cannot understand why with an engine of only 1200hp it is necessary to restrict the length of the cab to this extreme extent. Other things being equal it would be preferable that this locomotive, like all the others, should have cab access doors on each side immediately behind the driver's seat.

'Inspection of the above mentioned firm's drawing does seem to indicate an unusual waste of space within the locomotive body at the generator end and before finally approving this layout I think the matter should be discussed further with the firm.

'If the firm's design has proceeded so far that any material alteration will involve serious delays, then we may have to accept the position, but the arrangement at the driving ends does seem much inferior to what has been offered by other firms and this firm's product will be thrown up in an unfavourable light if no improvement can be made.'

D5705, 66A Polmadie, May 1960. The open driver's door illustrates well the unusual positioning; the driver entering the No.2 cab here will need to circumnavigate the electrical control cubicles before gaining access to the cab. *(Rail-Online)*

The result of the meeting held on 11 October 1956 eventually comes to light in a memo from Howe to Barman dated 22 February 1957:

'I am enclosing two copies of [Drawing No.] 125/1C which has been redrawn according to the latest information available from Metrovick and I will be glad if you would pass them to Mr Bond for his approval.

'I am sorry about the positions of the cab doors. As you are aware, they have become rather detached and have tended to break up the design, but as you know, this was the subject of a long discussion between myself, Metrovick and Derby and resulting in Derby agreeing to the omission of the driver's door.'

Quite why the boiler and the control cubicle had to be positioned where they were is never explained, despite the strong suggestion of their being sufficient space within the bodyshell for these components to be moved to allow more conventional cab door positioning. Once again we see evidence of the Metropolitan-Vickers engineers getting their way despite pressure being brought to bear by the customer; and again we see British Railways giving-in presumably to avoid jeopardising agreed delivery deadlines. It may be unfair, but there does seem to be an impression of Metropolitan-Vickers deliberately procrastinating long enough for design decisions to become a fâit d'accompli, subservient to engineering 'necessity'.

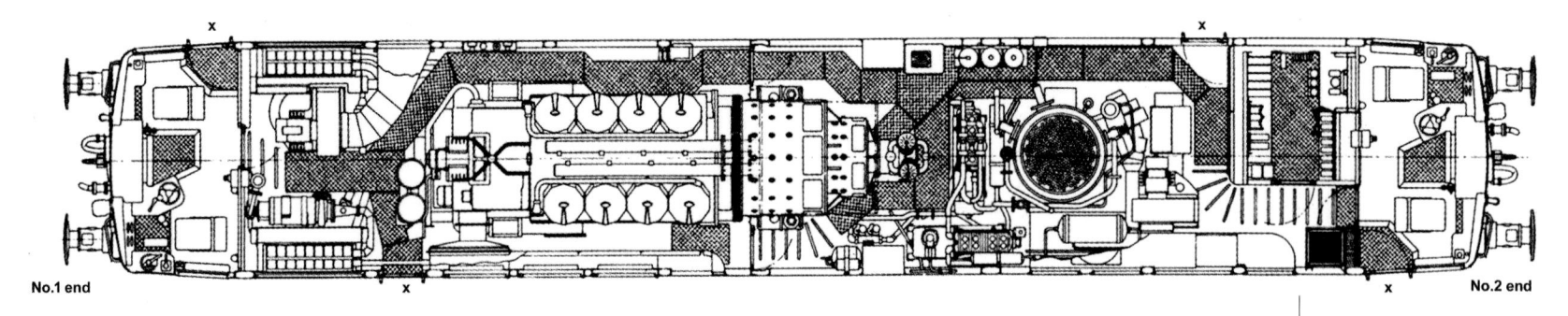

Metrovick Top Elevation. Note the position of the internal walkways and the 'cab' door positions (marked x). (*The Locomotive*)

3.4 Bodyside design (radiator grilles, air filter grilles, etc).

In a letter to C. Barman dated 27 March 1956, J. Howe commented, 'I do not know how their [Metropolitan-Vickers] drawing number A2109429 was produced because when I asked for an engine layout, I was told that it did not yet exist.' When Howe produced his own drawing (No.125/1) it was, as a consequence, with very limited supporting technical information, but designed to be a catalyst for debate. The bodyside grilles on Drawing No.125/1 were, therefore, positioned high up on the bodyside purely from an aesthetic perspective in an effort to avoid very large 'black holes' in the side of the locomotive.

On 3 April 1956, F. Whyman responded to Howe's drawing as follows:

'With reference to the various grilles, I see that you have arranged these at a high level no doubt to bring the lower edges in line with the driver's cab windows which in itself is, I think, a pleasing feature. Unfortunately since our last meeting we have more thoroughly explored the subject of roof radiators and have had to abandon any hope of utilising them. We are therefore back to the old type of radiator which requires an opening almost the full height of the locomotive side.

'I attach hereto a preliminary print of drawing A.2109384 which shows the internal layout that we have now crystallised and which should be of some assistance to you in seeing the limitations around which we have to work. I had hoped that it might be possible to have the conventional radiators with your small openings high up in the locomotive side supplemented by openings not seen in the floor which would allow the air that would normally come in through the bottom tier of louvres come unseen through the underneath. This however, appears impracticable for two reasons - (a) it would push the radiators too far into the locomotive in view of the fact that there is a motor blower inside them, (b) it would make it not possible readily to get at the radiator elements for installation or removal without having the whole of the wall sections removable. The objection to (b) I think could be partially overcome but the congested layout referred to under (a) would appear rather final.

'Again the rather shallow louvres you have indicated at a high level do make it difficult, if not impossible, to get in satisfactory filters and other requirements which would normally require double tiering, particularly for the engine combustion air as indicated on drawing also attached.'

Howe's responded to Whyman on 5 April 1956:

'I am naturally disappointed over the radiator openings and I hope it may be possible to modify the shape and perhaps the grille treatment so that they appear less like black holes in the side of the loco. In regard to the other grilles, it does seem to me that there is a certain amount of flexibility as regards position and shape.'

Two further letters from Howe to Metropolitan-Vickers confirm further meeting discussions on the subject. Letter: J. Howe to N. Thorneley, 23 April 1956:

'This is to confirm the discussion we had with Mr Whyman on Friday last.

'It is agreed that the radiator openings shall be accommodated in the sides of the locomotive approximately the area and shape shown in your drawing A2109429, but that these will be moved away from the cab doors approximately 1'. In order that these openings shall not appear too dominant it was agreed that you would endeavour to include a louvred grille instead of the weldmesh as shown at present.

'I would like the various intake and extract openings to be in the form and proportion shown on my drawing 125/1A, and it was agreed that you would endeavour to meet this requirement if possible. If it is necessary to form openings at a lower level than I have shown I would still like the same unit opening to be used below the upper one, separated by approximately 6".

Letter: J. Howe to N. Thorneley, 22 May 1956:

'This is to confirm the points discussed at our meeting on Friday last:
'The various air inlet and extract grilles will form a continuous line at high level broadly as indicated on my drawing number 125/1A and as I would prefer to keep the horizontal form, the intermediate vertical bars should be omitted on the face, but strengthening members can be incorporated on the back of the louvres.'

After this point, documentation on the grille subject in the Archives becomes very sporadic; all are reproduced here, although it is evident that there is some correspondence missing; the gist is, however, clear with ongoing mismatches between design preference and engineering reality.

Letter: J. Howe to F. Whyman, 2 August 1956:

'Thank you for your letter of the 31st July enclosing a copy of your drawing number A2109397.
'I would like to mention the following:
'I notice that the radiator grille has now moved away from the cab rather more than as shown on your perspective drawing and the relative position between it and the adjoining filter is very cramped. Again your perspective showed a better relationship which I would prefer to keep if possible. Also I believe that it will not be necessary to remove the grille from outside, and the heavy frame would appear to be unnecessary. I do not think it desirable that this should be made to match the filters and I would prefer to see here a simple trimmed opening with the louvres running behind and no projecting moulding at all.'

Letter: J. Howe to N. Thorneley, 13 December 1956:

'I am enclosing as promised, some sketches of the locomotive end where I was unhappy about the grille arrangement adjoining the radiator. These are lettered A B and C and my preference is in that order.
The rough sketch which I brought away showed the opening approximately 10 sq. ft. in area and I have worked on that assumption. Unfortunately, I have no details of the present position of vertical structural members and cannot say whether the suggestion will encroach upon them or not. I would, of course, very much prefer sketch A but you did mention the difficulty of providing sufficient space between the engine and the ducting. I would, however, like you to consider this very carefully as you may be able to overcome this problem.
'I am also assuming that these grilles will not be hinged on the outside but they will have a projecting frame as is the case of those on the opposite side of the locomotive.
'I would also like to restate my views about the radiator openings which I mentioned in my letter to Mr Whyman dated 6th November. I said that I would like the louvres to be immediately behind the simple opening in the cladding without any projecting frame. The external effect of this is illustrated on the photograph of the colour drawing I sent you. I am mentioning this because it was not clear from your details how you proposed to arrange this.'

Letter: J. Howe to C. Barman, 14 December 1956:

'I went to Trafford Park on Tuesday and found that

Metrovick had managed to overcome the filter problem quite satisfactorily on one side of the locomotive but had got themselves in a muddle on the other. I hope soon to be able to produce an up-to-date drawing so that we know where we are; but there are still a few details to sort out.

'I thought you would like to have the copy letter confirming the various points together with drawing number 125/3 showing possible filter re-arrangement.'

Letter: J. Howe to G. Williams, 3 September 1957:

'With reference to your letter dated the 10th July I found it necessary to produce a new coloured drawing of the above locomotive as there have been a number of changes since the last drawing was produced and this is enclosed . . . which, if it meets with Mr Bond's approval, can be sent to Metropolitan Vickers with his instructions.

'I would like to explain that originally I aimed at a regular pattern of filter grilles which would be the main horizontal feature of the exterior and it was intended that these should be coloured grey as against the green general background. Also the radiators were then intended to be removed when necessary from the inside and I have specified a simple opening in the body side with the grille immediately behind. MV have now found that it is impossible to remove the radiators internally and the treatment of the grille must be the same as for the filters. Formally I had aimed at 'losing' the radiator grille by painting it in body colour but now that the treatment is similar to the filters it seems reasonable to paint them the same and this I have done.'

Confidential letter: J. Howe to C. Barman, 28 July 1958:

'I went to Stockton last week and saw the first of the Metrovick diesel electric locomotives due for delivery.

I was asked to do this by C.H. Flurscheim, a director of M.V., and I have sent him a report, a copy of which is attached.

'The large louvres mounted outside the radiators were not pitched at the same angle as the filter louvres adjacent to them, thus there was little obscuration of the radiator behind which was the main object of providing the grille. The frames around the radiator and filter louvres were dissimilar although they had been originally detailed to match. It was not possible to judge the final effect and interrelationship of the louvres as painting was not complete but the smaller filter grilles appeared to be satisfactory.'

3.5 Bodyside Design (Cab/buffer beam)

The Archives include two pieces of correspondence on this topic.

Firstly, a letter: J. Howe to F. Whyman, 2 August 1956:

'Thank you for your letter of the 31st July enclosing a copy of your drawing number A2109397 . . . I would like to mention the following:

'We did agree some time ago, and this was incorporated in your perspective drawing, that the side cladding should carry down to the underside of the main beam. I notice on your elevation that this now finishes short. I think this is unfortunate, because it tends to lift the body above the structure and to divorce it from the bogies.'

Letter: J. Howe to N. Thorneley, 13 December 1956:

'The other point which was also mentioned in the letter and shown in red on a copy of your drawing A2109576 was the detail of the buffer beam where it joins the body at the side. This is also shown on the enclosed sketch and when I saw you in November I understood that this detail could be adopted without difficulty, but on Tuesday your draughtsman still appeared to be working to the previous line.'

This was never addressed and the locomotives were delivered with cabside cladding finishing short of the baseframe below the cabside windows, producing a rather awkward appearance. In this example, there appears to be absolutely no engineering reason given as to why this simple design modification could not have been accommodated.

D5703, 66A Polmadie, 19 August 1959. Note how the cabside panelling finishes short of the locomotive baseframe. The Metropolitan-Vickers works plate ('METROPOLITAN-VICKERS 1958') is clearly evident below the secondman's cabside window at solebar level.. *(David Dippie)*

3.6 Indicator Panels.

The Metrovicks were delivered with train identification discs; however, correspondence within the Archives indicate some debate surrounding the deployment of route indicator panels instead.

This topic first showed up in a letter from Howe to Barman dated 18 April 1957:

'I was with the Traction Department of Metropolitan-Vickers yesterday and there are one or two points which they would like settled as soon as possible. These are:

'A decision regarding the number of marker discs and lamps to be included or whether these are to be replaced by a route indicator. If the latter is definitely required must it be the standard Southern Region design or can it be modified as an integral part of the locomotive? If the latter is possible they will require to know the minimum sizes of letters and the number of digits to be accommodated.'

Subsequent correspondence involved Howe and Williams, as follows:

Letter: J. Howe to G. Williams, 10 July 1957:

'As regards the route indicator panel there are two possible solutions. One is to house the indicator to one side of the centre as I am doing on the Pullman job and the other to follow the same arrangement as the Derby design, but before coming to any decision on this I must find out from Metropolitan-Vickers whether the box can be accommodated in the cab as I know there is a lot of gear below the control desk which may get in the way.'

Letter: G. Williams to J. Howe, 10 July 1957:

'. . . with regard to the route indicator panel . . . The position of this box should now be indicated on the Metro-Vic locomotive, and the marker discs removed. There will be two digits, or one letter and one digit.'

Letter: G. Williams to J. Howe, 2 August 1957:

' . . . as you know we have not yet full information about the indicator box for the diesel-electric locomotives.'

Letter: J. Howe to G. Williams, 6 August 1957:

'Thanks for your letter of the 2nd August in connection with the above. You will remember that I said I was holding up the exterior decoration of the locomotive in the hope that something would have been settled about the train identification box but during my visit to Trafford Park last week MV Engineers informed me that they were going ahead with markers and that any modification would have to be dealt with later. I will therefore go ahead and produce the drawing you require irrespective of the possible change regarding train identification.'

3.7 Final Design Acceptance.

Acceptance of the final Metrovick design was achieved in March 1957, although certain elements were debated long after this:

Memo: C. Barman to R.C. Bond, 26 February 1957:

'At last I am able to submit a drawing of the above locomotive showing as nearly as possible what it will finally look like.'

Memo: R.C. Bond to C. Barman, 1 March 1957.

'Your memo of 26th February; I approve the final external design which has been proposed for this locomotive and presume that it is now agreed that this design shall be followed as closely as possible, subject to any over-riding requirements of siting of power equipment which Metro-Vickers may still have to decide.'

Memo: C. Barman to J. Howe, 5 March 1957.

'Just a line to confirm that Mr Bond has written Mr Harrison at Derby formally approving the design of the Metropolitan-Vickers B Type locomotive as recorded in your Drawing No.125/1.'

3.8 Working Relationships.

With incomplete evidence, it is difficult to fully understand the working relationship between British Railways, Metropolitan Vickers and the 'external' Design Consultant. However, there is enough information in the Archives to get a very strong flavour of many of the issues in play, and an insight how these relationships influenced the final locomotive design.

3.8.1 Metropolitan-Vickers and the Design Consultant.

Letters from Howe at various times describe a difficult working relationship with the Metropolitan-Vickers engineers. Howe's understanding of some of the design necessities of railway operations do seem to have been somewhat naive (e.g. driver visibility) and may have contributed to the situation, but it is clear that he did have to contend with some strong-minded characters at Metropolitan-Vickers. Howe certainly had strong views himself, particularly with respect to the front cab window debate; his insistence on trying to re-open old debates and overturn previous decisions must have annoyed the Metropolitan-Vickers engineers. It is very clear that the engineering-centric Metropolitan-Vickers team presented something of a challenge for Howe.

The Metropolitan-Vickers engineers seem to be constantly changing the engineering design arrangements, leading to a constant state of flux with respect to appearance design considerations, a situation which clearly frustrated Howe.

There is evidence in the archive material that Metropolitan-Vickers appeared at times to move ahead rapidly to a point where any aesthetic design intervention became impossible e.g. the cab window debate, indicator panels, etc. Equally, there were times when Metropolitan-Vickers appeared to deliberately procrastinate, which was maybe a strategy to ultimately create a fait accompli situation.

Without doubt, the 'twin-hatting' situation which Howe found himself must have been difficult for him personally and the distancing effect between Metropolitan-Vickers, the engineering manufacturer, and the BTC, the customer, must have impacted on the efficacy and timeliness of the decision-making process.

3.8.2 BR Involvement.

In many cases, British Railways seem to get involved only when 'encouraged' by Howe; this was probably deliberate and explains why Howe was employed by the BTC in the first place. This being the case, then it is arguable that Howe did not escalate issues quickly enough. It is arguable, however, that BR should have been considerably more pro-active as an organisation.

3.9 Howe's Final Verdict.

On 28 July 1958, J. Howe sent a letter to C. Barman together with a report of his visit to Stockton to see the complete locomotive prior to delivery:

'I went to Stockton last week and saw the first of the Metrovick diesel electric locomotives due for delivery.

'I was asked to do this by C.H. Flurscheim a director of M.V. and I have sent him a report, a copy of which is attached.

'I was pretty disgusted with what I saw and the report – which is very restrained – gives a fair idea of the job.

'As you know I have to assume a split personality on this project because, in a sense, I am working for two masters so perhaps at this stage you would use the report for your private information only and that any action necessary will be taken after we have had a chance of discussing it together.'

Here is Howe's report virtually in its entirety:

'On Friday 18th July 1958 a visit was paid to Stockton Works by Mr Ferguson, Assistant Chief Engineer, Traction Control Department, Mr Jack Howe, Design Consultant to the British Traction Commission and Metropolitan-Vickers Electrical Company Ltd., and Mr R.M. Kay, Industrial Design Engineer.

'The first of the diesel electric locomotives for British Railways was inspected and the driving cab of the second locomotive was inspected in detail with Mr Cowin, Works Manager.

'The general impression was that workmanship and finish were poor and not appropriate to a modern . . . locomotive. In many cases this was a matter of detail but the cumulative effect detracted from the desired impression.

'One particularly untidy mass of pipes, conduit and small equipment was seen under the centre of the locomotive. Mr Howe had on several occasions suggested to Traction Projects Department that this part of the locomotive be enclosed in common with the batteries, etc., and had indicated this on his drawing number 125/1E which was approved by the British Transport Commission. Further development of the exact form of this enclosure was dependent upon more detailed information regarding the equipment to be housed but such information was not forthcoming.

'The large louvres mounted outside the radiators were not pitched at the same angle as the filter louvres adjacent to them, thus there was little obscuration of the radiator behind which was the main object of providing the grille. The frames around the radiator and filter louvres were dissimilar although they had been originally detailed to match. It was not possible to judge the final effect and interrelationship of the louvres as painting was not complete but the smaller filter grilles appeared to be satisfactory.

'It was agreed that the layout of the cab should be improved both from the point of view of good appearance and convenience to the driver. Among details discussed were the screening of pipes, conduit, etc., boxing in or otherwise reducing the apparent bulk of vacuum brakes, and positioning instruments so that the most important were given the greatest prominence. It was thought that the shape of the main controller handle could be improved and that if the handle wheel type was, after careful consideration, considered to be the most appropriate form, the additional knob could be dispensed with.

'Mr Ferguson stated that he was prepared to give serious thought to the miniaturising of the main controller and of the handle required to operate it.

'Outside the cab it was noticed that the top marker light projected above the top line of the communicating door. This contributed to the general untidy appearance and Mr Howe stated that if this was the result of complying with British Railways precise dimensional requirements it was his experience that concessions could be made where difficulties of this kind occurred. The detailing of the marker lights and discs appeared to be unnecessarily complicated.

'It was noted that the main cab windows were glazed with an aluminium frame secured to the bodyside with a <u>large number</u> of countersunk screws. This necessitated considerable drilling, filling, rubbing down, etc., a most laborious and costly procedure. Mr Howe had previously discussed this problem with Traction Projects Department and strongly recommended the use of Claytonrite rubber strip glazing but this was rejected as being unreliable against wind pressure. It would have made this part of the work very much cheaper and easier, and a better finish would have been obtained. Furthermore by this method the whole of the painting can be completed before the glazing is carried out thus ensuring that all edges of openings are fully protected.

'The general impression regarding detailed design was that components had been added as the job progressed and had not become integrated as part of a unified whole. It appeared that there were many afterthoughts. An example of this is the position of the fire alarm window which, it was thought, would cut about half way through the grey band which BR require to be painted on the side of the locomotive. It was thought that within limits this window could have been located elsewhere. Similarly inside the cab a heater has been fixed on the wall over the manufacturer's name plate obscuring part of it.

'A cleaner and neater design of windscreen wiper would have been an advantage. The one selected appeared to be particularly antiquated and it was suggested that an electrically driven wiper would be appropriate.

'It was strongly recommended that in the event of further orders being placed for this design of locomotive full consideration will be given to the above observations and recommendations with a view to achieving greater apparent unity and interrelationship between component parts.'

A letter from Howe to G. Williams dated 4 December 1958 provide a couple of extra insights:

'You asked me to let you have my further views on the above locomotive as a result of seeing the finished product recently at Marylebone station.

'My remarks contained in the Report which I sent to Metropolitan-Vickers, of which you had a copy, are still valid in all respects and the following are therefore additional to those.

'Two of the cab windows at the No.2 end of the train were about 1½' out of alignment with the result that the gutter had to curve upwards from the straight to avoid the higher window. Errors of this kind seem to me to be quite inexcusable.

'As you know, one of the most unfortunate errors in this design is the lack of relationship between the front and the side cab windows. I will not go into the reasons for this because you know them already but if orders for more of these locomotives are to be placed (and I have heard unofficially that they are) then I feel very strongly that further consideration should be given to this detail. It is not easy to achieve without a major modification but the position would be very much eased if the Commission would agree to a lower headroom in the corridor link. This, I understand, is used very infrequently when the locomotives are running coupled and then only for the assistant driver to attend to the steam boiler.'

G. Williams replied to J. Howe on 5 December 1958:

'This is simply to acknowledge your letter of 4th December

which we discussed this morning.

'As you know, we are going to write to the Chief Mechanical Engineer, basing our remarks on your letter and report, in an attempt to stop the mistake being continued on any possible future batch.'

G. Williams subsequently sent a further letter to Howe on 8 January 1959:

'I had a word with Mr E.S. Cox the other day to prepare him for a report which I was beginning to draft on this locomotive, giving the Panel's criticisms of the design which would be very largely based on your confidential report of the 28th July, and later correspondence and discussions.

'Cox tells me, however, that there is no likelihood of further orders being placed for this locomotive.'

In Section 1.6, reference was made to R.C. Bond's memorandum entitled 'Main Line Diesel Locomotives: The Approach to Standardisation' (dated 10 November 1958). This memorandum listed the designs which it was proposed should be deleted from any future orders and included the Metrovicks; this listing was endorsed by the BTC Chairman on 13 November 1958.

3.10 Final Comments.

The Metrovick design attracted few, if any, accolades; ultimately comments like 'distinctly odd', 'strange' and 'bizarre' became the order of the day, with criticism being focussed particularly on the Co-Bo wheel arrangement, the wrap-around cab windows, the 'clumsy-looking' headcode discs and the location of the driver's cabside doors.

Metropolitan-Vickers Works Plate.

Chapter 4
DELIVERY AND ACCEPTANCE TESTING

4.1 Delivery Dates.
See Section 5.

4.2 Delivery – Promise v. Actual.
A BR document entitled 'Main-Line Diesel Position (Position at 1st June 1960)' (BR1712/377), highlighted the late delivery of the Metrovick fleet:

Original Delivery Promise	01/58
First Loco. Delivered	25/07/58

4.3 Acceptance Testing.
There were several references in the contemporary society magazines regarding testing of the Metrovicks, mainly via *The Railway Observer* and *Trains Illustrated*:

- 'The long-awaited trial runs of . . . locomotives ex-Metropolitan-Vickers Stockton works commenced on 7th July [1958]. A tight schedule with a fourteen-coach load had been arranged to Leeds, but trouble was experienced and several unscheduled stops had to be made, resulting in the return journey being about ninety minutes late. The engine noted on 14th July was . . . D5700.' (*RO*, August 1958)
- 'D5700 visited Tyneside on 15th July [1958]. It came down via the Team Valley line and returned via Sunderland, hauling a train of thirteen bogie coaches and carrying reporting number 78. It passed Pelaw at 4-10p.m. for Sunderland. (*RO*, August 1958)

D5719, Ripon (on a test train from Stockton), October 1959.
(Rail-Photoprints)

- 'New Metrovick diesels ex-Stockton have continued to make trial runs to Leeds, outward via Wetherby, returning via Harrogate, and D5703 was noted on 7th October [1958], with 13 bogies.' (*RO*, November 1958)
- 'In mid-October Nos. D5703/4 were running trials from the makers . . .' (*TI*, December 1958),
- 'Making the normal trial run on 13th November [1958], new diesel ex-Metropolitan Vickers Stockton works, D5705, with a load of 12 bogies, failed just before reaching Wormald Green on the outward journey with a blocked main injection pump. The Ripon pilot, J39 64857 was sent out and brought the complete train back to Ripon almost exactly an hour after it had first passed through . . . A new part was obtained from the works, and D5705 returned with its train under its own power during the afternoon, the run to Leeds being cancelled.' (*RO*, December 1958)
- 'D5705 made a second trial run through here [Harrogate] on 20th November [1958] . . . Dates of similar test runs are: D5706 27th November; D5707 11th December; D5708 18th and 31st December; D5709 1st January [1959].' (*RO*, February 1959)
- 'On 10th February [1959], two new Co-Bo's ex-Metro-Vick Bowesfield works [presumably D5710/1] passed through York station heading south, presumably en route for Derby . . .' (*RO*, March 1959)

4.4 Trials and Driver Training.

D5700 commenced trials and driver training from 28 July *1958* on the Churnet Valley line, later joined by D5701.

Chapter 5
ALLOCATIONS

Loco.	Introduction, Re-allocations and Withdrawal
D5700	1w/e 26/07/58 (25/07/58) 17A, 1w/e 03/02/62 12E/12C, 4w/e 06/11/65 12B, Withdrawn 1w/e 30/12/67
D5701	1w/e 06/09/58 (01/09/58) 17A, 1w/e 03/02/62 12E/12C, 4w/e 06/11/65 12B, 1w/e 17/02/68 12A*, 17/06/68 D10, Withdrawn 1w/e 07/09/68.
D5702	1w/e 04/10/58 (29/09/58) 17A, 1w/e 03/02/62 12E/12C, 4w/e 06/11/65 12B, 1w/e 17/02/68 12A*, 17/06/68 D10, Withdrawn 1w/e 07/09/68.
D5703	1w/e 25/10/58 (20/10/58) 17A, 1w/e 03/02/62 12E/12C, 4w/e 06/11/65 12B, Withdrawn 1w/e 30/12/67.
D5704	1w/e 08/11/58 (05/11/58) 17A, 1w/e 03/02/62 12E/12C, 2w/e 17/12/66 12B, Withdrawn 1w/e 30/12/67.
D5705	1w/e 06/12/58 (05/12/58) 17A, 1w/e 03/02/62 12E/12C, 2w/e 17/12/66 12B, 1w/e 17/02/68 12A*, 17/06/68 D10, Withdrawn 1w/e 07/09/68.
D5706	1w/e 06/12/58 (05/12/58) 17A, 1w/e 03/02/62 12E/12C, 2w/e 17/12/66 12B, 1w/e 17/02/68 12A*, 17/06/68 D10, Withdrawn - 1w/e 07/09/68.
D5707	1w/e 20/12/58 (19/12/58) 17A, 1w/e 03/02/62 12E/12C, 2w/e 17/12/66 12B, 1w/e 17/02/68 12A*, 17/06/68 D10, Withdrawn - 1w/e 07/09/68.
D5708	1w/e 10/01/59 (07/01/59) 17A, 1w/e 03/02/62 12E/12C, 2w/e 17/12/66 12B, 1w/e 17/02/68 12A*, 17/06/68 D10, Withdrawn 1w/e 07/09/68.
D5709	1w/e 10/01/59 (07/01/59) 17A, 1w/e 03/02/62 12E/12C, 2w/e 17/12/66 12B, Withdrawn 1w/e 30/12/67.
D5710	1w/e 14/02/59 (10/02/59) 17A, 1w/e 03/02/62 12E/12C, 2w/e 17/12/66 12B, Withdrawn 1w/e 30/12/67.
D5711	1w/e 14/02/59 (10/02/59) 17A, 1w/e 03/02/62 12E/12C, 2w/e 17/12/66 12B, 1w/e 17/02/68 12A*, 17/06/68 D10, Withdrawn 1w/e 07/09/68.
D5712	1w/e 07/03/59 (04/03/59) 17A, 1w/e 30/01/60 14A, 1w/e 02/07/60 17A, 1w/e 03/02/62 12E/12C, 2w/e 17/12/66 12B, 1w/e 17/02/68 12A*, 17/06/68 D10, Withdrawn 1w/e 07/09/68.
D5713	1w/e 07/03/59 (04/03/59) 17A, 1w/e 30/01/60 14A, 1w/e 16/07/60 17A, 1w/e 03/02/62 12E/12C, 2w/e 17/12/66 12B, Withdrawn 1w/e 30/12/67.
D5714	1w/e 14/03/59 (11/03/59) 17A, 1w/e 30/01/60 14A, 1w/e 22/10/60 17A, 1w/e 03/02/62 12E/12C, 4w/e 06/11/65 12B, 1w/e 17/02/68 12A*, 17/06/68 D10, Withdrawn 1w/e 07/09/68.

Loco.	Introduction, Re-allocations and Withdrawal
D5715	1w/e 11/04/59 (08/04/59) 17A, 1w/e 30/01/60 14A, 1w/e 22/10/60 17A, 1w/e 03/02/62 12E/12C, 4w/e 06/11/65 12B, 1w/e 17/02/68 12A*, Withdrawn 1w/e 04/05/68.
D5716	1w/e 16/05/59 (13/05/59) 17A, 1w/e 30/01/60 14A, 1w/e 13/08/60 17A, 1w/e 03/02/62 12E/12C, 4w/e 06/11/65 12B, 1w/e 17/02/68 12A*, 17/06/68 D10, Withdrawn 1w/e 07/09/68.
D5717	1w/e 13/06/59 (08/06/59) 17A, 1w/e 30/01/60 14A, 1w/e 06/08/60 17A, 1w/e 03/02/62 12E/12C, 2w/e 17/12/66 12B, 1w/e 17/02/68 12A*, 17/06/68 D10, Withdrawn 1w/e 07/09/68.
D5718	1w/e 11/07/59 (07/07/59) 17A, 1w/e 30/01/60 14A, 1w/e 06/08/60 17A, 1w/e 03/02/62 12E/12C, 2w/e 17/12/66 12B, 1w/e 17/02/68 12A*, Withdrawn 1w/e 04/05/68.
D5719	1w/e 17/10/59 (13/10/59) 17A, 1w/e 30/01/60 14A, 1w/e 06/08/60 17A, 1w/e 30/12/61 12E/12C, 2w/e 17/12/66 12B, 1w/e 17/02/68 12A*, 17/06/68 D10, Withdrawn 1w/e 07/09/68.

Sources: Engine History Card and SLS *Journal*.

Notes:
1. Depot codes: 12A Carlisle Kingmoor (diesel depot), 12B Carlisle Upperby,
    12C Barrow (from 09/09/63), 12E Barrow (up to 08/09/63).
    14A Cricklewood (London).
    17A Derby.
    D10 Preston Division.
2. The Engine History Card for D5719 shows the initial allocation date to 12E Barrow as both w/e 30/12/61 *and* w/e 03/02/62.
3. *D5701/2/5-8/11/2/4-9 were officially transferred to 12A Carlisle Kingmoor (New Diesel Depot) during 1w/e 17/02/68, a delayed re-allocation given that 12B Carlisle Upperby closed on 01/01/68.
4. New LMR divisional allocation codes were introduced in place of depot codes with effect from 0001hrs 17/06/68; the twelve remaining Metrovicks at that time (D5701/2/5-8/ 11/2/4/6/7/9) were transferred to D10 Preston Division.

D5716, 12C Barrow, 1965. Plenty of oil spillage indicating engine difficulties. Prior to the depot fire in July 1966.
(*Rail-Online*)

Allocations • 47

D5716, 12B Carlisle Upperby, 8 October 1967. *(Rail-Online)*

Chapter 6
OVERHAUL HISTORY

6.1 Works Responsibilities.
Maintenance Works for the Metrovicks:

Derby	From New
Horwich	From 24/03/62
Crewe	From 24/03/63

6.2 1958-64 Works Visits - *Engine History Card* (BR 5694) Information.
Engine History Card (EHC) information, which records much of the Works locomotive repair history, has been obtained for all twenty locomotives. Information within the EHCs is very useful, but does need to be deployed with care. As Ian Sixsmith in various of the Irwell Press *The Book of . . .* publications warns:

'Engine [History] Cards, whilst containing much useful and even fascinating information, should be regarded as a guide to what happened to the engine, not an unimpeachable document to be afforded the status of gospel. It seems to be stating the obvious that the Cards only show what was written on them at the time, and the temptation to read and interpret too much should be resisted. Nevertheless, the Cards are a marvellous, fascinating, invaluable record of what happened, yet there are often infuriatingly silent on events that we enthusiasts half a century or more later consider of vital interest and importance. They were filled in, by hand, by clerks and naturally enough contain errors.'

Overhaul categories:
Up to end-1963:

HC/HCas	Heavy Casual
LC/LCas	Light Casual
NC	Non Classified

From 1964 the following repair categories applied:

G/GEN	General
I/INT	Intermediate
L/LGT	Light
C	Classified (level unspecified)
Rect	Rectification i.e. re-call to works to correct faults.
U	Unscheduled (sometimes U/C and U/P, assumed to be Unclassified/ Unplanned).

Works repair information for each locomotive is presented in Section 7. However, it should be noted that entries on the History Cards ceased from mid-1964.

6.3 1964-68 Works Visits - Society and Personal Reports.
The latest Works visit recorded on the EHCs was for D5719 (Crewe 07/03/64-04/09/64). As a consequence, it has been necessary to derive subsequent works visits from various society reports and personal sightings. During the period February 1964 to July 1968, numerous reports have been perused, covering 134 different weekends (predominantly based on Sunday visits but with occasional Saturday reports). Additional midweek reports were reviewed, where available, but these were relatively few in number. The 134 discrete weekend reports over 54 months equates to 2.48 visits per month which represents a very extensive coverage particularly bearing in mind that four or five weekends per year were unavailable for enthusiast visits due to Easter, Summer, Christmas and New Year holiday closures.

Summaries of locomotive works visits are listed in Section 6.4 below, combining both EHC and sighting information. Full details of the Works visit sightings are included in Section 7 for each locomotive.

6.4 Metrovick Works History.

Loco. No.	Works	Pre Date	Period in Works	Post Date	Repair Class	Cumulative Mileage on Arrival	Source
D5700	Derby		07/08/59-18/09/59		LC	33446	EHC
	Derby		24/03/60-10/06/60		LC	61380	EHC
	Dukinfield		19/10/61-30/08/62		HC	99251	EHC
	Crewe	18/10/64	01/11/64-08/02/65	20/02/65	?	?	Sightings
	Crewe	28/02/66	06/03/66-20/03/66*	27/03/66	?	?	Sightings
D5701	Derby		19/09/58-22/09/58		NC	244	EHC
	Derby		22/08/60-12/11/60		LC	69800	EHC
	Derby		15/11/60-29/11/60		NC (Rect)	Not recorded	EHC
	Dukinfield		19/10/61-17/08/62		HC	86299	EHC
	Horwich		25/03/63-31/05/63		HC	117675	EHC
	Crewe	29/09/67	30/09/67-26/11/67	09/12/67	?	?	Sightings
	Crewe	31/03/68	07/04/68-21/04/68	28/04/68	?	?	Sightings
D5702	Derby		27/04/59-21/05/59		HC	16782	EHC
	Derby		20/08/60-25/10/60		LC	74832	EHC
	Dukinfield		16/10/61-19/12/62		HC	86214*	EHC
	Crewe	20/12/64	03/01/65	07/01/65	?	?	Sightings
	Crewe	24/01/65	07/02/65-23/05/65	30/05/65	?	?	Sightings
	Crewe	27/02/66	06/03/66-12/06/66	19/06/66	?	?	Sightings
	Crewe	06/08/67	20/08/67-01/10/67	17/10/67	?	?	Sightings
D5703	Derby		03/04/59-04/05/59		LC	7984	EHC
	St Rollox		12/09/59-26/09/59		LC	21059	EHC
	Dukinfield		18/09/61-23/05/62		HC	42914	EHC
	Crewe	20/12/64	03/01/65-23/05/65	06/06/65	?	?	Sightings
	Crewe	11/06/65	20/06/65	27/06/65	? (Rect?)	?	Sightings
	Crewe	19/03/67	09/04/67-10/09/67*	24/09/67	?	?	Sightings
D5704	Derby		08/07/60-21/09/60		LC	71460	EHC
	Dukinfield		18/09/61-08/06/62		HC	83737	EHC
	Dukinfield		06/08/62-14/08/62		NC (Rect)	88442	EHC
	Crewe	28/02/66	06/03/66-19/02/67*	05/03/67	?	?	Sightings

Loco. No.	Works	Pre Date	Period in Works	Post Date	Repair Class	Cumulative Mileage on Arrival	Source
D5705	Derby		04/12/59-13/01/60		NC	44051	EHC
	Derby		10/11/60-24/01/61		LC	96558	EHC
	Dukinfield		16/10/61-27/06/62		HC	107484	EHC
	Crewe	10/07/65	25/07/65-14/11/65	05/12/65	?	?	Sightings
	Crewe	11/09/66	18/09/66	02/10/66	?	?	Sightings
	Crewe	29/03/67	09/04/67-12/11/67	19/11/67	?	?	Sightings
D5706	Dukinfield		19/10/61-30/07/62		HC	81209	EHC
	Crewe	27/07/64	12/08/64-08/11/64	15/11/64	?	?	Sightings
	Crewe	05/12/65	xx/12/65-20/03/66	27/03/66	?	?	Sightings
	Crewe	02/09/67	10/09/67-01/10/67	29/10/67	?	?	Sightings
D5707	Dukinfield		19/06/61-29/03/62		HC	42887/42956*	EHC
	Crewe	29/03/67	09/04/67-11/06/67	16/06/67	?	?	Sightings
D5708	Dukinfield		10/07/61-19/04/62		HC	62508/62557*	EHC
	Crewe	29/09/67	01/10/67-26/11/67	28/01/68	?	?	Sightings
D5709	Dukinfield		05/06/61-23/02/62		HC	63171	EHC
	Crewe	06/06/65	20/06/65-19/02/67*	05/03/67	?	?	Sightings
D5710	Derby		26/01/60-28/03/60		NC	57606	EHC
	Derby		26/07/60-15/08/60		NC	77303	EHC
	Derby		18/10/60-02/01/61		LC	86984	EHC
	Dukinfield		18/09/61-08/06/62		HC	88561	EHC
	Crewe	13/12/64	20/12/64-28/02/65	14/03/65	?	?	Sightings
	Crewe	19/09/65	26/09/65-14/11/65	05/12/65	?	?	Sightings
	Crewe	03/04/66	24/04/66-19/02/67*	05/03/67	?	?	Sightings
D5711	Derby		11/04/59-28/04/59		LC	6988	EHC
	Derby		22/06/60-16/09/60		NC	56251	EHC
	Derby		11/11/60-03/02/61		LC	66081	EHC
	Dukinfield		23/10/61-07/12/62		HC	68141*	EHC
	Crewe	20/07/66	31/07/66-15/01/67	22/01/67	?	?	Sightings

Overhaul History • 51

Loco. No.	Works	Pre Date	Period in Works	Post Date	Repair Class	Cumulative Mileage on Arrival	Source
D5712	Derby		08/12/59-15/12/59		NC	34891	EHC
	Dukinfield		10/07/61-18/05/62		HC	38347/38364*	EHC
	Horwich		03/08/63-20/08/63		LC	101567	EHC
	Crewe	02/06/68	09/06/68	15/06/68	?	?	Sightings
D5713	Derby		29/12/59-01/01/60		NC	34739	EHC
	Derby		11/03/60-10/06/60		NC	38363	EHC
	Dukinfield		19/06/61-15/03/62		HC	41005	EHC
	Crewe	18/12/66	08/01/67-19/02/67*	05/03/67	?	?	Sightings
D5714	Derby		25/03/59-20/04/59		LC	3783	EHC
	Derby		18/12/59-29/12/59		NC	37761	EHC
	Dukinfield		22/10/61-08/11/62		HC	88852	EHC
	Crewe	04/10/64	10/10/64-20/12/64	03/01/65	?	?	Sightings
	Crewe	03/01/65	07/01/65-24/01/65	07/02/65	? (Rect?)	?	Sightings
	Crewe	10/10/65	16/10/65-14/11/65	05/12/65	?	?	Sightings
	Crewe	10/07/66	24/07/66-18/09/66	02/10/66	?	?	Sightings
D5715	Derby		15/04/59-01/05/59		LC	651	EHC
	Derby		23/12/59-26/12/59		NC	34758	EHC
	Dukinfield*		16/10/61-28/03/63		HC	73259	EHC
	Crewe	25/04/65	09/05/65-12/09/65	19/09/65	?	?	Sightings
	Crewe	02/01/66	16/01/66-29/05/66	05/06/66	?	?	Sightings
	Crewe	20/11/66	11/12/66-12/02/67	19/02/67	?	?	Sightings
	Crewe	01/08/67	02/08/67-06/08/67	19/08/67	?	?	Sightings
	Crewe	31/03/68	07/04/68-28/04/68*	04/05/68	?	?	Sightings
	Crewe	19/05/68	09/06/68*	23/06/68	?	?	Sightings
D5716	Derby		10/12/59-18/12/59		NC	30149	EHC
	Dukinfield*		18/10/61-05/10/62		HC	63647	EHC
	Crewe	01/03/64	25/03/64	31/03/64	?	?	Sightings
	Crewe	26/07/64	12/08/64-29/11/64	06/12/64	?	?	Sightings
	Crewe	25/10/65	31/10/65-13/02/66	19/02/66	?	?	Sightings

Loco. No.	Works	Pre Date	Period in Works	Post Date	Repair Class	Cumulative Mileage on Arrival	Source
D5717	Derby		18/12/59-29/12/59		NC	22532	EHC
	Derby		20/06/60-01/07/60		NC	40341	EHC
	Derby		17/07/60-20/10/60		LC	40924	EHC
	Dukinfield		16/10/61-23/01/63		HC	56719	EHC
	Crewe		27/01/64-02/05/64		Unscheduled	Not recorded	EHC
	Crewe	30/05/65	06/06/65	20/06/65	?	?	Sightings
	Crewe	29/05/66	05/06/66-02/10/66	09/10/66	?	?	Sightings
	Crewe	20/11/66	11/12/66-18/12/66	09/01/67	?	?	Sightings
	Crewe	18/06/67	02/08/67-27/08/67	10/09/67	?	?	Sightings
D5718	Derby		17/12/59-18/12/59		NC	19351	EHC
	Derby		16/02/60-28/04/60		LC	23281	EHC
	Derby		17/07/60-17/10/60		LC	33161	EHC
	Dukinfield		22/10/61-27/11/62		HC	36590	EHC
	Crewe	01/04/64	06/04/64	07/04/64	?	?	Sightings
	Crewe	02/10/66	09/10/66-18/12/66	07/01/67	?	?	Sightings
D5719	Derby		12/12/59-18/12/59		NC	9963	EHC
	Dukinfield		13/05/61-21/12/61		HC	22757/23521*	EHC
	Crewe		07/03/64-04/09/64		Unscheduled	Not recorded	EHC
	Crewe	19/06/66	26/06/66	24/07/66	?	?	Sightings
	Crewe	19/05/68	09/06/68-23/06/68	21/07/68	?	?	Sightings

Notes:

1. EHC 'Period in works' information is exactly as recorded on the Cards.
2. 'Period in works' information based on Sightings reflects the first and last dates locomotives were noted in Works. Most dates quoted are Sundays (far and away the most common day for Crewe Works visits).
    Underlined 'Pre-Dates' represent the previous Crewe Works visit report where the locomotive was NOT seen; similarly underlined 'Post Dates' represent the subsequent Crewe visit date where the locomotive was NOT seen.
    Non-underlined 'Pre Dates' and 'Post Dates' are (non-Crewe Works) dates when the locomotives were seen before and after the Crewe Works visit respectively.
    The 'Period in works' sighting information listed above will *always* be understated as locomotives will have arrived at Crewe during the period since the 'Pre Date' up to the first Works sighting, and will have departed in the period after the last Works sighting up to the 'Post Date'.
3. Mileages were not recorded for D5702/11 on entry to Dukinfield on the 'Classified Repairs' section of Engine History Cards; mileages given above for these two locomotives were calculated from the EHC 'Annual Statistics'.
4. D5715/6 'Gorton' entries on the EHCs are assumed to be errors for Dukinfield. The EHC for D5719 shows a Gorton entry crossed out and Dukinfield inserted in its place. Dukinfield and Gorton are only 4 miles apart geographically!
5. The EHC record for the Dukinfield start-of-repair period for D5716 is incorrect (18/10/62); based on mileages, the entry should presumably read 18/10/61.

6. EHC records for mileages on arrival at Dukinfield for D5707/8/12/9 are understated (see Section 8).
7. * D5700/3/4/9/10/3/5 were despatched from their final visit to Crewe without repairs being undertaken.
8. From the above table, D5707/8/12 appear to have operated for circa 5 years up to their first Crewe Works visit. However, given that all three locomotives received pairs of 25kV signs on their front ends (very much a Crewe Works feature during the 1963-68 period - see Section 18), it is entirely possible that these three locomotives visited Crewe during this period.

Based on the 25kV sign information D5707 could possibly have visited Crewe between 30/08/65 and 02/04/66, D5708 between 17/09/66 and 23/03/67 and D5712 between 08/10/66 and 01/04/67. However, for D5712, of the twenty-seven weekends between 15/10/66 and 01/04/67, Works reports have been seen for eighteen and none with D5712 present.

D5717 and D6843, Crewe Works, 1964. Presumably during the period 27/01/64-02/05/64 based on EHC information. *(Rail-Online)*

54 • THE METROPOLITAN-VICKERS TYPE 2 CO-BO DIESEL-ELECTRIC LOCOMOTIVES

D5717, Crewe Works (Paint Shop Yard), Undated. The adjacent English Electric Type 3 D6775 helps date the photograph as 3 May 1964; an LCGB visit to the Works on this date revealed both D5717 and D6775 resident in the Paint Shop Yard. Single 25kV sign retained despite a front-end clean up. Note the open door and associated steps on the body side used to allow steam-era water hoses to be used to fill the boiler water tank.
(*Transport Treasury*)

D5716, Crewe Works, May 1965 (sic?). The date doesn't fit with sighting information for this locomotive; the date is more likely to be November 1964, particularly given its ex-works condition. See also photographs on pages 112 and 211 for comparison.
(*C. Whitfield [Rail-Photoprints]*)

Overhaul History • 55

D5702 (sic?), Crewe Works, May 1965 (sic?). It is highly doubtful that this is D5702 given the position of the 25kV signs. Given the date discrepancy with the photograph on page 54 (same photographer and supplier), is this perhaps also a November 1964 photograph? D5700/6/14/6 were in Crewe Works during November 1964; if so, this locomotive could be D5700 based on the position of the front-end and bodyside 25kV signs. Carrying defunct 12E Barrow depot code on the buffer beam.(*C. Whitfield [Rail-Photoprints]*)

56 • THE METROPOLITAN-VICKERS TYPE 2 CO-BO DIESEL-ELECTRIC LOCOMOTIVES

D5716, Crewe Works, 15 November 1964. Fowler 4F 0-6-0 44450 alongside Metrovick D5716 and English Electric Type 4 D369 outside the Paint Shop at Crewe. (*Author's Collection*)

D5718 and D1585, Crewe Works, 1966. Possibly around December 1966. An RCTS visit to Crewe Works on 18 December 1966 revealed D5718 on the Diesel Test Roads (where this photograph was taken) and D1585 in the Erecting Shop. The Metrovick exhibits body cleaning but no obvious repainting work. (*Colour-Rail*)

Chapter 7
INDIVIDUAL LOCOMOTIVE HISTORIES

7.1 Sightings – Primary and Secondary Sources.
This section is deliberately based on Primary (personal observations and photographs) and Secondary sources (magazine reports, archive depot/works visit sightings and listings which provide fully dated information). There are, on average, 145 sightings per locomotive giving a total of over 2,900 individual locomotive observations overall.

7.2 Works Information from EHCs.
Information from the Engine History Cards have been added to fill out the locomotive histories. Ian Sixsmith, author of many of the Irwell Press locomotive histories, explains:

> 'Dates of leaving and entry to works were of course to some extent nominal and a day or two . . . either side should always be assumed. The works were not above "fiddling" dates at the beginning or the end of a month to enhance the monthly figures . . . It was thus not entirely unknown for a locomotive to be out on the road with the figures still showing it still in works and vice versa – for a few days at least.'

7.3 Information from BR 'Fires on Diesel Train Locomotives' Reports (1961-68).
These reports provide an invaluable context to the sighting information and explain the reason for some of the extended periods in storage suffered by the Metrovicks (see Section 14).

7.4 Data Presentation.
The date format in the locomotives logs is 'mmyy' or 'ddmmyy', as opposed to 'mm/yy' or 'dd/mm/yy', for clarity. The more conventional 'dd/mm/yy' format is, however, used in the 'Additional Comments' for each locomotive (excepting quotes where the original published format is retained).

Text colour coding used is as follows:
Black   Locomotive sightings.
Purple   Dates when locomotives were *not* seen at a particular depot or works.
Blue   Key dates (e.g. delivery, major depot transfers, Works data (prefixed by 'EHC'), fire damage (suffixed by 'FTDL'), withdrawal, disposal (Sources: *Railway Observer*, and *Diesel & Electric Locomotives for Scrap* (A. Butlin).

N.B. Some of the disposal information conflicts with the sightings – see Section 22.
Red   Sightings conflicting with works information, or, duplicated sightings on specified dates.

Depot codes used are as follows:

9C Reddish, 9E Trafford Park
10A Carnforth (from 09/09/63)
12A Carlisle Kingmoor (Steam or Diesel, as specified),
12B Carlisle Upperby, 12C Barrow (from 09/09/63), 12D Workington (from 09/09/63),
12E Barrow (up to 08/09/63),
12F Workington (up to 08/09/63)
14A Cricklewood
16C Derby Etches Park (from 09/09/63)
17A Derby (up to 08/09/63)
24L Carnforth (up to 08/09/63)

66A Polmadie (Glasgow)
D10 Preston Division

The EHC references in the following logs (e.g. EHC: Derby: 070859-180959 LC [33446]) specify 'Works', 'Date in Works' to 'Date out of works', 'Class of Repair' and 'Accumulated Mileage'.

Other abbreviations (Bowesfield/Horwich/Crewe Works sightings):

E.Shop: Erecting Shop, P.Shop: Paint Shop, Arr.Sdgs: Arrival Sidings.

And finally, 'Nil' refers to no observations at the specified location.

Abbreviations for the 'Comments' information sources are explained in the Bibliography.

7.5 Locomotive Histories.
Locomotive histories are provided below for each of the twenty Metrovicks.

Individual Locomotive Histories • 59

D5700

D5700, 17A Derby, 9 May 1959. *(Colour-Rail)*

60 • THE METROPOLITAN-VICKERS TYPE 2 CO-BO DIESEL-ELECTRIC LOCOMOTIVES

D5700, 17A Derby, 30 April 1961. Revised cab front windows. (*Colour-Rail*)

D5700, Crewe Works (Paint Shop Yard), Undated. (*Colour-Rail*)

51L Thornaby: 020758 (with D5701)
Leeds: 070758 (test train)
Leeds: 140758 (Bowesfield-Leeds & return test train)
Pelaw: 150758 (test train; to Tyneside via the Team Valley line and return via Sunderland)

New: 250758

Dronfield: 250758 (light engine)
Derby/Churnet Valley: 280758 (trials/driver-training)
Derby Works: 300858 (Open-Day exhibit)
Derby: 010958
Hendon-Gushetfaulds: 011058 (pre-'Condor' test train) (with D5701)
Gushetfaulds-Hendon: 021058 (pre-'Condor' test train) (with D5701)
Hendon-Chaddesden: 051058 (pre-'Condor' test train) (with D5701)
Manchester Central: 091058 (12.05 Manchester Central-St Pancras)
Derby: 131058 (10.25 Manchester Central-St Pancras) (with D5701)
Chaddesden-Bedford/Bedford-Chaddesden: 261058 (pre-'Condor' test train) (with D5701)
Chaddesden-Bedford/Bedford-Chaddesden: 091158 (pre-'Condor' test train) (with D5701)
Marylebone (exhibition): 131158
St Pancras: 271258 (Manchester Central-St Pancras passenger) (with D5705)
St Pancras: 170459 (16.25 St Pancras-Manchester Central) (with D5713)
17A Derby: 090559
St Pancras: 130559 (16.25 St Pancras-Manchester Central) (with D5706)
17A Derby: 310559
Derby Works: 100659/ 210659 (Diesel Finishing Shop)
Radlett: 130759 (up 'Condor') (with D5709)
Derby Works: 160859/ 170859 (Works Yard)/ 200859. EHC: Derby: 070859-180959 LC (33446). Not listed 190959.
Derby: 161059 (04.20 St Pancras-Manchester Central) (with D5711)
Leicester: 171059 (16.35 St Pancras-Manchester Central) (with D5711)
Derby: 031159 (07.25 Manchester Central-St Pancras) (with D5719)
17A Derby: 170160
Derby: 240260 (04.25 St Pancras-Manchester Central) (with D5705)

17A Derby: 280260
XX: 040360 (10.25 Manchester Central-St Pancras) (with D5705)
XX: 230360 (Cross-London transfer freight trials)
Derby Works: 240460/ 160560/ 290560. EHC: Derby: 240360-100660 LC (61380). Not listed 270360 and 030760.
Mill Hill: 040760 ('Condor') (with D5715)
Leicester: 130760 ('Condor', failed at 22.30, to depot)
15A Leicester: 140760 (returned to Derby at 21.00)
66A Polmadie: 310760/ 190860
XX (Midland Division): 161060 (coal train inc. dynamometer car)
17A Derby: 120261
14A Cricklewood: 260261
XX: 270261 (up 'Condor') (with D5705)
17A Derby: 300461/ 070561/ 140561/ 250661/ 240961. Not listed 130861.
Hauled from Derby to Dukinfield: 191061

Metro-Vick, Dukinfield: 201061. EHC: Dukinfield: 191061-300862 HC (99251).

To 12B: 030262.

9G Gorton: 250862
Preston: 200463 (21.05 Manchester Victoria-Heysham ['Belfast Boat Express'])
Lancaster Green Ayre: 210463 (up 'Royal Scot' [diverted via Morecambe])
XX: 100663 (despatched Barrow to Trafford Park)
XX: 11-140663 (Tunstead-Northwich ICI limestone train trials)
12E Barrow: 160863
12C Barrow: 290963
Carnforth: 050564 (13.45 Barrow-Carnforth parcels) (with D5711)
Ravenglass: 060664 (passenger)
12D Workington: 050764
Preston: 220864 (09.50 Manchester Victoria-Workington)
12C Barrow: 270864
Lancaster: 300864 (passenger)
12C Barrow: 111064
Crewe Works: 011164/ 151164 (E.Shop)/ 291164 (E.Shop)/ 131264 (E.Shop)/ 201264 (E.Shop)/ 030165 (Test Roads)/ 070165/ 230165 (Outside)/ 240165/ 070265/ 080265. Not listed 181064.
12C Barrow: 200265
Preston: 130365 (11.20 Euston-Barrow/Workington)

12C Barrow: 010565/ 110665
12D Workington: 060765
Bolton: 170765 (passenger)
12C Barrow: 010865
Lancaster: 070865
10A Carnforth: 070865/ 220865
Preston: 040965 (passenger)
10A Carnforth: 171065/ 280266
Crewe Works: 060366 (Test Roads)/ 130366/ 200366 (Works Yard). Not listed 270366.
12B Carlisle Upperby: 020466/ 090466/ 100466/ 300466/ 010566/ 070566/ 080766/ 090766/ 100766/ 060866/ 070866/ 140866/ 100966/ 121166/ 151166/ 060167/ 070167/ 080167/ 290167 (cannibalised)/ 110267/ 260367/ 290367/ 090467/ 220467/ 200567/ 100667/ 160667/ 180667/ 280667/ 290767/ 020867/ 030867/ 080867/ 190867/ 230967/ 071067/ 081067/ 211067/ 261067/ 281067/ 291067/ 191167. Not listed 081267/ 101267/ 181267/ 060168/ 280168.

Withdrawn: w/e 301267 (12B).

12A Carlisle Kingmoor (Steam): 100268/ 250268/ 170368/ 110468/ 130468/ 150468/ 180468/ 110568/ 060668/ 150668/ 210668/ 200768/ 270768/ 100868/ 250868. Not listed 060168/ 270168/ 280168.
Despatched from Carlisle to Shettleston: 280868 (with D5703/4)
J. MacWilliam, Shettleston: 310868 (intact)/ 061068 (intact)

Disposal: J. MacWilliam, Shettleston 0768-1168 (D&ELfS).

Annual mileages (EHC):

	1958	1959	1960	1961	1962	1963	Total
D5700	12172	39820	39357	7902	19758	45254	164,263

Notes:
1. 'On January 18th (*1959*) all of the class delivered by that date were congregated at Derby depot and there was a rumour that they had been temporarily withdrawn from service.' (TI0359)
2. 'Derby Works on February 5th [1961] . . . Yet more of the Metrovick Type 2 Co-Bos, Nos. D5701/6/15/7, were stored outside Derby depot, making a total of 13 of this class inactive, but Nos. D5700/5/14/8 were observed at work.' (TI0461)
3. 'In June 1963 it (*D5700*) was loaned to Trafford Park depot, from where it undertook trial running on the ICI limestone hopper trains from Tunstead to Northwich . . . D5700 is seen with a rake of ICI vacuum braked hoppers in August 1963. The trials were not conclusive and in September 1963 the loco was returned to Barrow.' (MLI226)
4. S(u): 06/06/66 (with no reinstatement date) (EHC).
5. D5700 presumably held at 12B Carlisle Upperby during 1966/7 (whilst others were congregating at Crewe Works) to act as a local source of spares.

Individual Locomotive Histories • 63

D5701

D5701, 66A Polmadie, 17 July 1959. (Rail-Online)

64 • THE METROPOLITAN-VICKERS TYPE 2 CO-BO DIESEL-ELECTRIC LOCOMOTIVES

D5701, 12B Carlisle Upperby, 2 July 1967.
(*Colour-Rail*)

D5701, 12C Barrow, Undated. Blue livery, full yellow ends.
(*Transport Topics*)

51L Thornaby: 020758 (with D5700)
Harrogate: 210858 (test train)
Metropolitan-Vickers, Bowesfield Works, Stockton: 310858

New: 010958

Dronfield: 010958 (light engine)
Derby Works: Nil. EHC: Derby: 190958-220958 NC (244).
Hendon-Gushetfaulds: 011058 (pre-'Condor' test train) (with D5700)
Gushetfaulds-Hendon: 021058 (pre-'Condor' test train) (with D5700)
Hendon-Chaddesden: 051058 (pre-'Condor' test train) (with D5700)
Manchester Central: 091058 (12.05 Manchester Central-St Pancras) (with D5700)
Derby: 131058 (10.25 Manchester Central-St Pancras) (with D5700)
Chaddesden-Bedford/Bedford-Chaddesden: 261058 (pre-'Condor' test train) (with D5700)
Chaddesden-Bedford/Bedford-Chaddesden: 091158 (pre-'Condor' test train) (with D5700)
XX: 150159 (09.00 Nottingham-Liverpool passenger [to Manchester])
Wellingborough: 140559 (17.30 St Pancras-Manchester Central) (with D5710)
St Pancras: 220559 (16.25 St Pancras-Manchester Central) (with D5716)
66A Polmadie: 300559
Kilnhurst: 040659
Derby Works: 100659/ 210659 (Diesel Finishing Shop)
Hendon: 070759 (with D5704, light engines for 'Condor')
66A Polmadie: 170759
Stirling: 180759 (southbound empty stock)
St Pancras: 040959 (16.25 St Pancras-Manchester Central) (with D5716)
St Pancras: 271059 (16.25 St Pancras-Manchester Central) (with D5712)
St Pancras: 281059 (St Pancras-Manchester Central relief) (with D5712)
St Pancras: 031159 (16.25 St Pancras-Manchester Central) (with D5715)
Derby Works: 130360 (Yard)
17A Derby: 270360 (SMA)/ 290560
Derby: 050760 (07.25 Manchester Central-St Pancras) (with D5710)
66A Polmadie: 310760/ 140860

Derby Works: 250960/ 181060/ 231060.
EHC: Derby: 220860-121160 LC (69800).
Derby Works: 271160 (Outside Diesel Test House).
EHC: Derby: 151160-291160 NC (Rect) (-).
Leicester: 031260 (07.25 Manchester Central-St Pancras) (with D5704)
Leicester: 121260 (07.25 Manchester Central-St Pancras) (with D5718)
Ampthill: 241260 (up special) (with D5715)
17A Derby: 050261/ 260261
Luton: 250361 (down l/e hauled by 42522)
Derby Works: 130461 (Works Sidings)
17A Derby: 140561/ 250661/ 130861/ 240961
Hauled from Derby to Dukinfield: 191061

Metro-Vick, Dukinfield: 201061
Gorton Works: 290762 (Paint Shop)
EHC: Dukinfield: 191061-170862 HC (86299).

To 12B: 030262.

Horwich Works: 240363/ 310363 (Works Yard)/ 060463 (E.Shop)/ 190463 (E.Shop)/ 210463 (E.Shop)/ 050563/ 120563 (E.Shop)/ 190563 (E.Shop Yard). EHC: Horwich: 250363-310563 HC (117675).
Skew Bridge, Preston: 010663 (Barrow-Manchester passenger)
12C Barrow: 290963
XX: 230164 (damaged by fire, location unknown) (FDTL)
XX: 260264 (damaged by fire, location unknown) (FDTL)
Preston: 200464 (13.03 Workington-Manchester Victoria)
Preston: 200664 (13.03 Workington-Manchester Victoria/ 21.05 Manchester Victoria-Heysham)
12D Workington: 050764
Preston: 180764 (09.50 Manchester Victoria-Workington)
Parton: 080864 (08.25 Carnforth-Workington)
Hest Bank: 080864 (13.03 Workington-Manchester Victoria)
Preston: 180864 (13.03 Workington-Manchester Victoria)
10D Lostock Hall: 060964
Preston: 120964 (09.50 Manchester Victoria-Workington)
12C Barrow: 111064
10A Carnforth: 061264
12C Barrow: 200265
Lancaster: 130365 (13.03 Workington-Manchester Victoria)
10A Carnforth: 160465
Carnforth: 300765 (13.03 Workington-Manchester Victoria) (with D5716)

12D Workington: 110865
12C Barrow: 171065
12D Workington: 270266
12B Carlisle Upperby: 070566/ 250566
Carlisle (London Road Bridge): 080766 (freight)
12B Carlisle Upperby: 090766
10A Carnforth: 140766
12B Carlisle Upperby: 060866/ 070866/ 100966
Dalston Road: 100966 (freight, with D5715)
9A Longsight: 221066
12C Barrow: 090167
12B Carlisle Upperby: 110267
10A Carnforth: 190367/ 260367 /290367
12B Carlisle Upperby: 100667/ 160667/ 180667/ 020767/ 070867/ 190867
12D Workington: 310867
10A Carnforth: 070967
12B Carlisle Upperby: 230967
5B Crewe South: 290967
Crewe Works: 300967/ 011067 (Arr.Sdgs)/ 291067 (E.Shop Yard)/ 051167/ 111167/ 191167/ 261167 (Test Roads). Not listed 121167.
12D Workington: 091267/ 101267/ 060168
12C Barrow: 250268

Crewe Works: 070468/ 210468. Not listed 310368 and 280468.
Kirkby-in-Furness: 060668 (16.10 Corkickle-Heysham tanks)
10A Carnforth: 150668
Grange-over-Sands: 210668 (tanks)
10A Carnforth: 230668/ 250668/ 290668
12A Carlisle Kingmoor (Diesel): 270768/ 280768/ 290768
10A Carnforth: 240868
XX: 050968 (failed)

Withdrawn: w/e 070968 (D10).

12A Carlisle Kingmoor (Steam): 060968 (stored)/ 080968/ 300968/ 241068/ 071268/ 311268/ 040169/ 110169
Carlisle Kingmoor Yard: 020469/ 120569/ 260569/ 060769/ 050869/ 200869/ 210869/ 230869/ 240869/ 040969
Blackburn (en route from Carlisle Yard to Great Bridge): 150969 (with D5702/6, hauled by D1795)
J.Cashmore Ltd, Great Bridge: Nil. Not noted xx1169.

Disposal: J.Cashmore Ltd, Great Bridge - 0969 (D&ELfS). Not proven.

Annual mileages (EHC):

	1958	1959	1960	1961	1962	1963	Total
D5701	14189	36348	24036	11726	20823	38948	146,070

Notes:
1. See 'Additional Note' No.1 for D5700.
2. S(u): 19/06/61-w/e 21/10/61 (EHC).
3. 'A visitor to Derby Works on February 5th [1961] . . . Yet more of the Metrovick Type 2 Co-Bos, Nos. D5701/6/15/7, were stored outside Derby depot, making a total of 13 of this class inactive, but Nos. D5700/5/14/8 were observed at work.' (TI0461)
4. 'When it (*D5701*) failed on 5 September 1968 it was agreed to withdraw it and withdrawal came on 7 September.' (MLI226)
5. Dragged Carlisle Kingmoor (steam) depot to Carlisle Marshalling Yard February 1969. (A. Whitaker)

Individual Locomotive Histories • 67

D5702

D5702, Crewe Works (Paint Shop Yard), 16 May 1965. Serif numbers. Note the small square 'window' cutting into the grey body side stripe; this housed the trigger for the fire extinguisher equipment and allowed the equipment to be operated from outside of the locomotive.
(*Noel A. Machell*)

D5702, 10A Carnforth, 22 June 1968.
(*Transport Topics*)

East Bolden: 160858 (test train)

New: 290958

XX: 241258 (Liverpool-Nottingham passenger [from Manchester])
14A Cricklewood: 150359
Derby Works: 110559 (Diesel Shop, under repair)/ 130559 (Diesel Erecting Shop). EHC: Derby: 270459-210559 HC (16782).
66A Polmadie: 300559
Manchester Central: 110659
Derby: 140759 (10.25 Manchester Central-St Pancras) (with D5717)
St Pancras: 280859 (16.25 St Pancras-Manchester Central) (with D5718)
St Pancras: 250959 (16.25 St Pancras-Manchester Central) (with D5711)
St Pancras: 300959 (16.25 St Pancras-Manchester Central) (with D5710)
17A Derby: 170160. Not listed 280260.
14A Cricklewood: 120360/ 130360
St Pancras: 230560 (14.25 St Pancras-Manchester Central) (with D5704)
Derby: 060660 (14.25 St Pancras-Manchester Central) (with D5705)
66A Polmadie: 030760
Leicester: 130760 ('Condor', failed at 22.30, to depot)
15A Leicester: 140760 (returned to Derby at 21.00)
Derby Works: 070860/ 040960 (Yard)/ 150960/ 250960/ 231060. Not listed 130860 and 270860/ 280860. EHC: Derby: 200860-251060 LC (74832).
17A Derby: 260261/ 140561/ 040661/ 130861/ 240961. Not listed 300461/ 070561/ 250661.
Hauled from Derby to Dukinfield: 181061

Metro-Vick, Dukinfield: 201061. EHC: Dukinfield: 161061-191262 HC (-).

To 12B: 030262.

Carlisle: 130463
12F Workington: 130463
Hest Bank: 180463 (10.55 Workington-Preston passenger)
Lancaster: 210463 (06.38 Workington-Euston)
12E Barrow: 150663

Manchester Victoria: 040763 (09.50 Manchester Victoria-Workington passenger)
Lakeside: 060763 (passenger)
Southport: 070863 (passenger)
12E Barrow: 160863
12C Barrow: 290963
Broughton: 260364 (Euston-Barrow passenger)
Preston: 230564 (13.03 Workington-Manchester Victoria/ 21.05 Manchester Victoria-Heysham)
Hest Bank: 100664 (18.50 Heysham-Corkickle fuel oil)
12C Barrow: 110764
Lancaster: 180764 (10.53 Workington-Euston) (to Preston)
Preston: 030864 (10.53 Workington-Euston) (to Preston)
Parton/Hest Bank: 080864 (10.53 Workington-Euston) (to Preston)
10A Carnforth: 061264
Crewe Works: 030165 (Arrival Sidings)
XX: 210165 (damaged by fire, location unknown) (FDTL)
Crewe Works: 070265/ 080265/ 190265/ 210265 (E.Shop)/ 280265 (E.Shop)/ 140365 (E.Shop)/ 210365 (E.Shop)/ 280365/ 110465 (E.Shop)/ 250465/ 090565/ 160565 (P.Shop Yard, repainted)/ 230565 (Works Yard). Not listed 240165 and 300565.
12D Workington: 110665
12C Barrow: 200665 (ex-works)/ 110865
12B Carlisle Upperby: 020965/ 060965/ 120965/ 250965/ 021065/ 031065
12D Workington: 270266
Crewe Works: 060366 (Arr.Sdgs)/ 130366/ 200366 (Works Yard)/ 270366 (Arr.Sdgs)/ 030466 (Works Yard)/ 240466 (Arr.Sdgs)/ 080566 (Works Yard)/ 210566 (Arr.Sdgs)/ 290566 (Arr.Sdgs)/ 050666/120666
5A Crewe North: 190666
12C Barrow: 220666
Grange-over-Sands: 260666 (pw train)
12B Carlisle Upperby: 080766/ 090766/ 100766/ 020866/ 060866/ 070866
Dalton: 120866 (Carnforth-Barrow freight)
12B Carlisle Upperby: 100966
12C Barrow: 121166
12D Workington: 090167
Carlisle Kingmoor (passing site of new diesel depot): 230367 (8P73 12.30 Carlisle-Preston freight, via Barrow) (with D5708)
9C Reddish: 090467
12B Carlisle Upperby: 200567
12C Barrow: 220667/ 240667

Individual Locomotive Histories • 69

10A Carnforth: 150767
Shap: 220767 (Carlisle-Blackpool passenger)
Crewe Works: 200867 (Works Yard)/ 230867/ 270867 (Arr.Sdgs)/ 100967/ 240967/ 011067 (Test Roads). Not listed 060867.
10A Carnforth: 171067
12B Carlisle Upperby: 191167/ 081267
12C Barrow: 101267
12A Carlisle Kingmoor (Diesel): 020168/ 060168
9C Reddish: 020268/ 150268/ 170268
Hazel Grove: 240268 (heading towards Cheadle Heath from Chinley)
10A Carnforth: 170368
Parton: 050668 (Up empty minerals)
10A Carnforth: 150668/ 220668/ 270768/ 280768/ 030868
Grange-over-Sands: 030868 (vans)
10A Carnforth: 240868

Withdrawn: w/e 070968 (D10).

12A Carlisle Kingmoor (Steam): 300968/ 241068/ 071268/ 311268/ 040169/ 110169. Not listed 060968.
Carlisle Kingmoor Yard: 020469/ 120569/ 260569/ 060769/ 050869/ 200869/ 210869/ 230869/ 240869/ 040969. Not listed 250869.
Blackburn (en route from Carlisle Yard to Great Bridge): 150969 (with D5701/6, hauled by D1795)
J.Cashmore Ltd, Great Bridge: Nil. Not noted xx1169.

Disposal: J. Cashmore Ltd, Great Bridge - 0969-1169 (D&ELfS). Not proven.

Annual mileages (EHC):

	1958	1959	1960	1961	1962	1963	Total
D5702	9176	39071	37428	539	572	45168	131,954

Notes:
1. See 'Additional Note' No.1 for D5700.
2. Dragged Carlisle Kingmoor (steam) depot to Carlisle Marshalling Yard February 1969. (A. Whitaker)

70 • THE METROPOLITAN-VICKERS TYPE 2 CO-BO DIESEL-ELECTRIC LOCOMOTIVES

D5703

D5703, 66A Polmadie, 16 August 1959. *(RCTS Archive)*

Individual Locomotive Histories • 71

D5703, Carnforth F&M Junction, Undated.
(RCTS Archive)

Leeds: 071058 (Stockton-Leeds & return test train)

New: 201058

Kilnhurst: 201058
Leicester: 141158 (XX-St Pancras (12.36 ex-Leicester) (with D5704)
Derby Works: Nil. EHC: Derby: 030459-040559 LC (7984).
66A Polmadie: 160859/ 190859/ 270859
St Rollox Works: Nil. EHC: St Rollox: 120959-260959 LC (21059).
Derby Works: 251059 (under repair)
Derby Midland: 020460 (with D5708)
Derby: 040460 (07.25 Manchester Central-St Pancras) (with D5708)

17A Derby: 290560
66A Polmadie: 030760
17A Derby: 270860/ 280860. Not listed 070860.
9B Stockport Edgeley: 041260 (with D5713)
9E Trafford Park: 260261/ 260361/ 090461/ 160461/ 180661/ 250661/ 130861/ 200861. Not listed 170961.

Metro-Vick, Dukinfield: Nil. EHC: Dukinfield: 180961-230562 HC (42914).

To 12B: 030262.

12E Barrow: 150762
Oxenholme: 280762 (Millom-Maryhill/Bridgeton (Glasgow) troop special)
12E Barrow: 290762

12F Workington: 130862
12E Barrow: 150663
12C Barrow: 290963
Lancaster: 261063
Carnforth: 271063
XX: 190364 (Trafford Park-Northwich light engine (with D5255), then Northwich-Peak Forest limestone empties (with D5255)
Lancaster: 060664 (10.53 Workington-Euston) (to Preston)
Preston: 160664 (1303 Workington-Manchester Victoria)
12C Barrow: 050764
Preston: 110764 13.03 Workington-Manchester Victoria)
Lancaster: 090864 (failed on 20.30 Preston-Barrow)
Carnforth: 290864 (Preston-Barrow)
12C Barrow: 111064
Preston: 281164 (09.50 Manchester Victoria-Workington)
Crewe Works: 030165 (E.Shop and Yard)/ 230165 (Traverser Area)/ 240165/ 080265/ 210265 (E.Shop)/ 280265 (E.Shop)/ 140365 (E.Shop)/ 210365 (E.Shop)/ 280365/ 110465 (E.Shop)/ 250465/ 090565/ 160565 (P.Shop Yard)/ 230565 (P.Shop Yard). Not listed 201264, 070265 and 060665.
12C Barrow: 110665
Crewe Works: 200665 (Works Yard) (rectification?). Not listed 270665.
Preston: 140765
Lancaster: 070865 (passenger)
Grange-over-Sands: 100865 (up passenger)
12C Barrow: 150865
12B Carlisle Upperby: 251065

12C Barrow: 280266
12A Carlisle Kingmoor: 090466
12D Workington: 100466
XX: 150466 (southbound parcels from Barrow) (with D1850)
12C Barrow: 060866/ 070866/ 180866/ 280866/ 121166/ 090167
Crewe Works: 090467 (Yard)/ 230467 (Yard)/ 300467/ 070567/ 210567 (Works Yard)/ 040667/ 110667 (Works Yard)/ 180667 (Works Yard)/ 020867/ 060867/ 160867/ 200867 (Works Yard)/ 230867/ 270867 (Arr.Sdgs)/ 100967. Not listed 190367 and 240967.
Greenholme: 250967 (D5703 being hauled north by D311)
12B Carlisle Upperby: 021067/ 071067/ 211067/ 241067/ 261067/ 281067/ 191167/ 081267/ 101267/ 181267. Not listed 300967.

Withdrawn: w/e 301267 (12B).

12B Carlisle Upperby: 020168/ 060168
12A Carlisle Kingmoor (Steam): 270168 (minus engine)/ 280168/ 100268/ 250268/ 170368/ 110468/ 130468/ 150468/ 180468/ 110568/ 060668/ 150668/ 210668/ 200768/ 270768
12A Carlisle Kingmoor (Diesel): 100868
Despatched from Carlisle to Shettleston: 280868 (with D5700/4)
J. MacWilliam, Shettleston: 310868 (cabs). Not listed 061068.

Disposal: J. MacWilliam, Shettleston 0768 (D&ELfS).

Annual mileages (EHC):

	1958	1959	1960	1961	1962	1963	Total
D5703	6047	25135	11732	0	32647	44981	120,542

Notes:
1. See 'Additional Note' No.1 for D5700.
2. S(u): 12/12/60 [Crossed out, with note 'See - W.E. 4/2/61 'Awaiting Works''] (EHC).
3. S(u): 20/03/61-18/09/61 (EHC).
4. S(u): 06/06/66 (with no reinstatement date) (EHC).

Individual Locomotive Histories • 73

D5704

D5704, 17A Derby, 9 May 1959. (*Colour-Rail*)

D5704, Cheadle Heath, 26 September 1960. Revised cab front windows. (*Colour-Rail*)

XX: 081058 (trial run from Stockton to Sunderland and return)

New: 051158

Leicester: 141158 (XX-St Pancras (12.36 ex-Leicester) (with D5703)
St Pancras: 181258 (16.25 St Pancras-Manchester Central) (with D5706)
St Pancras: 080159 (16.25 St Pancras-Manchester Central (with D5705)
14A Cricklewood: 220359
17A Derby: 090559/ 310559
Hendon: 070759 (with D5701, light engines for 'Condor')
St Pancras: 070859 (16.25 St Pancras-Manchester Central) (with D5712)
Silkstream Junction: 230859 ('Condor' Hendon-Gushetfaulds)
XX: 050959 (12.15 Brent-Wellingborough freight) (with D5705)
St Pancras: 061059 (16.25 St Pancras-Manchester Central) (with D5714)
Derby: 211059 (04.20 St Pancras-Manchester Central) (with D5719)
St Pancras: 010160 (16.25 St Pancras-Manchester Central) (with D5717)
Manchester Central: 030160 (19.40 Manchester Central-Derby)
Derby: 070160 (04.20 St Pancras-Manchester Central) (with D5714)
XX: 260160 (04.25 St Pancras-Manchester Central, changed at Derby) (with D5705)
Derby: 010260 (10.25 Manchester Central-St Pancras) (with D5708)
14A Cricklewood: 120360/ 130360
Baillieston: 090460 (Clydesmill power station-NCB Oakley coal empties)
Kilnhurst: 080560
St Pancras: 230560 (14.25 St Pancras-Manchester Central) (with D5702)
17A Derby: 290560

Derby Works: 070860/ 120860 (Diesel Shop)/ 130860/ 150860 (Diesel Shop)/ 270860/ 280860/ 040960 (Diesel Repair Shop). Not listed 030760 and 250960.
EHC: Derby: 080760-210960 LC (71460).
Cheadle Heath: 260960 (Manchester Central-St Pancras passenger)
Leicester: 031260 (07.20 Manchester Central-St Pancras) (with D5701)
9E Trafford Park: 260261/ 260361/ 090461/ 180661/ 250661/ 130861/ 200861. Not listed 160461 and 170961.

Metro-Vick, Dukinfield: Nil. EHC: Dukinfield: 180961-080662 HC (83737), and, 060862-140862 NC (Rect) (88442).

To 12B: 030262.

24L Carnforth: 150762
12E Barrow: 290762/ 150663
Brock: 220663 (Workington-London passenger)
Lakeside: 060763 (pass)
Preston: 210264 (10.53 Workington-Euston) (to Preston)
XX: 190564 (damaged by fire, location unknown) (FDTL)
Ulverston: 040864 (up freight)
Preston: 080864 (09.50 Manchester Victoria-Workington)
Carnforth: 290864 (Manchester-Workington)
12C Barrow: 111064
XX: 131164 (damaged by fire, location unknown) (FDTL)
12C Barrow: 200265/ 010565/ 110665/ 200665 (awaiting works and/or stored)/ 010865 (S[u])/ 110865/ 150865/ 171065/ 280266
Crewe Works: 060366/ 130366/ 200366 (E.Shop)/ 270366 (Stripping Shop)/ 030466 (Works Yard)/ 240466 (Stripping Shop)/ 080566 (Stripping Shop)/ 290566 (Stripping Shop)/ 050666/ 120666/ 190666/ 260666 (stored)/ 240766 (Stripping Shop)/ 310766/ 070866 (Stripping Shop)/ 140866/ 110966 (Stripping Shop)/ 180966/ 250966 (Stripping Shop)/ 021066/ 091066 (Stripping Shop)/ 161066 (Stripping Shop)/ 231066/ 301066 (Stripping Shop)/ 061166 (Stripping Shop)/ 131166 (Stripping Shop)/ 111266 (Stripping Shop)/ 181266 (Stripping Shop)/ 080167/ 220167 (Stripping Shop)/ 050267/ 120267 (Stripping Shop)/ 190267. Not listed 201166/ 080167 and 050367.
Warrington Dallam: xxxx67 (Stanier 5MT 45135 hauling D5713/10/04/09).
12B Carlisle Upperby: 260367/ 290367/ 090467/ 220467/ 200567/ 100667/ 160667/ 180667/ 250667/ 280667)/ 290767/ 020867/ 030867/ 080867/ 190867/ 230967/ 071067/ 081067/ 211067/ 241067/ 261067/ 281067/ 291067/ 191167/ 081267/ 101267/ 181267. Not listed 070867/ 300967/ 021067.

Withdrawn: w/e 301267 (12B).

12A Carlisle Kingmoor (Steam): 020168/ 060168/ 270168 (workshop)/ 280168
12A Carlisle Kingmoor (Diesel): 100268
12A Carlisle Kingmoor (Steam): 250268/ 170368
12A Carlisle Kingmoor (Diesel): 110468/ 130468/ 150468
12A Carlisle Kingmoor (Steam): 180468/ 110568/ 060668/ 150668/ 210668/ 200768/ 270768/ 100868/ 250868
Despatched from Carlisle to Shettleston: 280868 (with D5700/3)
J. MacWilliam, Shettleston: 310868 (intact)/ 061068 (intact)

Disposal: J. MacWilliam, Shettleston 0868 (D&ELfS).

Annual mileages (EHC):

	1958	1959	1960	1961	1962	1963	Total
D5704	6187	48436	29114	0	23224	48283	155,244

Notes:
1. 'On January 18th [1959] all of the class delivered by that date were congregated at Derby depot and there was a rumour that they had been temporarily withdrawn from service.' (TI0359)
2. S(u): 20/03/61-18/09/61 (EHC).
3. S(u): 30/01/65 (with no reinstatement date) (EHC).
4. 'On 27th January [1968] . . . Dumped at Kingmoor were . . . D5703/9/10/3 . . . In the adjacent workshop were D5704/15.' (RO0468)
5. Repeated movements between Kingmoor Steam and Diesel depots, presumably to facilitate spares recovery for other class members.

D5705/S15705/TDB968006

D5705, 17A Derby, 30 April 1960. *(Colour-Rail)*

Individual Locomotive Histories • 77

D5705, 17A Derby, 4 May 1961. Revised cab front windows. Serif 'D' on D5032; sans serif 'D' on D5705. (*Arnold W. Battson [Transport Treasury]*)

D5705, Crewe Works, October 1965.
(*Mike Jackson*)

Ripon: 131158 (first test train from Stockton)
Harrogate: 201158 (second trial run from Stockton)

New: 051258

St Pancras: 271258 (Manchester Central-St Pancras passenger) (with D5700)
St Pancras: 080159 (16.25 St Pancras-Manchester Central (with D5704)
Derby Works: 150359 (Yard)
66A Polmadie: 150559 (booked for 17.30 Glasgow St.Enoch-Carlisle pass (with D5709), but replaced by D5708/15)/ 160559 (with D5709)/ 300559
Derby: 180759 (passenger, with 'Crab' 42792)
XX: 050959 (12.15 Brent-Wellingborough freight) (with D5704)
XX: 080959 (16.25 Manchester-St Pancras passenger (assisting Stanier 5MT 44855)
XX: 140959/ 150959 (London suburban duties, both days)
St Pancras: 211159 (14.25 St Pancras-Manchester Central) (with D5719)
Derby Works: 141259 (Diesel Shop)/ 171259 (Diesel Erecting Shop)/ 110160. Not listed 140160. EHC: Derby: 041259-130160 NC (44051).
XX: 260160 (04.25 St Pancras-Manchester Central, changed at Derby) (with D5704)
Derby: 240260 (04.25 St Pancras-Manchester Central) (with D5700)
17A Derby: 280260/ 030360
XX: 040360 (10.25 Manchester Central-St Pancras) (with D5700)
17A Derby: 300460. Not listed 270360 (SMA).
XX: 090560 (07.25 Manchester Central-St Pancras) (with D5708)
17A Derby: 290560
Derby: 060660 (14.25 St Pancras-Manchester Central) (with D5702)
12A Carlisle Kingmoor: 100760
St Pancras: 120860 (18.30 St Pancras-XX) (with D5706)
Manchester Central: 170860
Derby Works: 271160 (Diesel Repair Shop)/ 091260/ 090161 (Diesel Erecting Shop)/ 220161 (Outside Test House) . EHC: Derby: 101160-240161 LC (96558).
17A Derby: 120261
14A Cricklewood: 260261
XX: 270261 (up 'Condor') (with D5700)
17A Derby: 040561/ 130861/ 240961. Not listed 140561/250661.

Hauled from Derby to Dukinfield: 191061
Metro-Vick, Dukinfield: 201061. EHC: Dukinfield: 161061-270662 HC (107484).

To 12B: 030262.

Lakeside: 010762 (passenger)
24L Carnforth: 150762
Farington Jct: 170762 (passenger)
12E Barrow: 290762
Preston: 220962 (passenger)
12F Workington: 130463
24L Carnforth: 110563
Bradkirk: 230763 (1Z44 Barrow-Blackpool Central)
Grange-over-Sands: 290763 (14.40 Preston-Barrow passenger)
24L Carnforth: 110863
12F Workington: 070963
12C Barrow: 290963
Preston: 180464 (13.03 Workington-Manchester Victoria)
Preston: 130664 (06.10 Heysham-Manchester Victoria)
Sellafield: 200864 (Sellafield-Workington workers' train)
Morecambe South Jct: 290864 (Lancaster-Barrow passenger)
Lancaster: 120964 (10.43 Workington-Euston, to Preston)
Silverdale: 240964 (Euston-Barrow passenger, presumably from Preston)
12C Barrow: 111064
Preston: 151064 (passenger)
Preston: 071164 (13.03 Workington-Manchester Victoria)
Ex-24K Preston: 010565
55A Leeds Holbeck: 090665
Barrow: 220665 (passenger)
Crewe Works: 250765 (E.Shop Yard)/ 050865/ 220865 (E.Shop)/ 120965 (E.Shop)/ 190965 (E.Shop)/ 260965/ 031065/ 101065 (Test Area)/ 171065 (Test Roads)/ 311065/ 011165/ 071165 (P.Shop Yard)/ 141165 (Test Area). Not listed 100765 and 051265.
Lancaster: 080166 (16.48 to Manchester Vic)
12C Barrow: 280266
12B Carlisle Upperby: 300466/010566
Whitehaven: 090666 (freight)
12D Workington: 060866
Carlisle: 220866
Crewe Works: 180966. Not listed 110966 and 021066.
Clifton & Lowther: 211066 (Hardendale-Motherwell limestone)
10A Carnforth: 071166

Individual Locomotive Histories • 79

12C Barrow: 121166/ 090167
12B Carlisle Upperby: 290167/ 110267/ 050367
10A Carnforth: 260367
12B Carlisle Upperby: 290367
Crewe Works: 090467 (E.Shop)/ 230467 (E.Shop)/ 300467/ 070567/ 210567 (E.Shop)/ 040667/ 110667 (E.Shop)/ 180667 (E.Shop)/ 020867/ 060867/ 160867 (Works Yard)/ 200867 (Works Yard & Test Area)/ 230867/ 270867 (Arr.Sdgs)/ 100967/ 240967 (Arr.Sdgs)/ 011067 (Arr.Sdgs)/ 151067/ 291067 (Test Roads)/ 051167/ 111167/ 121167
12C Barrow: 191167
12B Carlisle Upperby: 081267/ 101267
12A Carlisle Kingmoor (Diesel): 020168/ 060168

12D Workington: 280168
Carlisle: 050468 (hauled scrap 9Fs 92017 and 92125 from 12A Carlisle Kingmoor (Steam) to Bog Jct. triangle for turning)
Wigton: 050668 (down empty minerals)
12A Carlisle Kingmoor (Diesel): 140668/ 150668/ 210668
10A Carnforth: 210768
12A Carlisle Kingmoor (Diesel): 270768
10A Carnforth: 240868

Withdrawn: w/e 070968 (D10).

Disposal: Departmental S15705 (D&ELfS).

Annual mileages (EHC):

	1958	1959	1960	1961	1962	1963	Total
D5705	3606	40445	52507	10926	23874	38472	169,830

Notes:
1. See 'Additional Note' No.1 for D5700.
2. 'A visitor to Derby Works on February 5th [1961] . . . Yet more of the Metrovick Type 2 Co-Bos, Nos. D5701/6/15/7, were stored outside Derby depot, making a total of 13 of this class inactive, but Nos. D5700/5/14/8 were observed at work.' (TI0461)
3. S(u): 12/07/61-w/e 21/10/61 (EHC).
4. Received a modified Crossley engine during its 0467-1167 Crewe Works visit.

S15705

Derby RCD: by xx1268
Kirkby-in-Ashfield: 010269 (with D1992 hauling 3 brake vans)
Trowell Jct: 020269 (hauling dead D1992 and part of Derby mobile test unit)
Beeston: 230269 (S15705)
East Leake: xx0469 (light engine)
Derby RCD/Derby: 150669/ 100869/ 120969/ 051069/ 010370/ 080370
Derby Works: 100470 (Yard)
Derby RCD/Derby: 110470/ 260770/ 070970/ 250471
Kettering: 150871 (test train)
Derby RCD/16C Etches Park/Derby: 031171/ 051271/ 230172/ 060272/ 200272
St.Albans: 250272 (test train)

Egginton Jct-Mickleover: 150372 (trials with *Hermes* test coach)
Derby RCD: 120472/ 300572/ 030672/ 040672
Wolverhampton: 190672/ 260672 (both test trains, towards Stafford)
Derby RCD: 010772/ 090772
Wolverhampton: 100772 (test train, towards Stafford)
Derby RCD: 160772/ 230772
XX: 070872/ 090872/ 110872 (1T25 Tribometer train, Derby-Birmingham-Crewe-Derby all 3 days)
Derby Works: 260872/ 030972 (Klondyke Sidings)/ 100972
Derby RCD/16C Etches Park/Derby: 071072/ 121172/ 250173/ 240273/ 080473/ 200473/ 200573/ 230673/ 300773/ 250873/ 160973/ 091073/ 041173/ 041273/

050174/ 260174/ 100374/ 070474/ 270474/ 070574/ 160674/ 040874/ 310874
Derby RCD to Gloucester: 180974

Swansea Maliphant Carriage Sidings: 270974
Transfer: Swansea (High Street) Carriage Sidings to Danygraig (Swansea): early 1274 (but not seen 231274)

Notes:
1. Re-numbered S15705 in the Carriage stock numbering system in 12/68 (Rail524) or 02/69 (Locomotive Directory/ AHBRDE5).
2. 'Withdrawn Metrovick Co-Bo Type 2 diesel No. D5705, renumbered S15705 has been used almost daily by Derby Research Centre on runs to Toton, Market Harborough and Mansfield on plasma torch evaluation and adhesion tests.' (RW0669)

TDB968006

Danygraig Wagon Repair Shops, Swansea: 180575 (TDB968006)/ 250575/ 190775/ 210875/ 140975
Bristol: 100276 (hauled Danygraig-Bristol Bath Road by 37243)
BR Bristol Bath Road: Late-0276/ 260376/ 080476/ 270576/ 050676/ 270676/ 010876/ 260876/ 221076/050277/ 130377/ 101177/ 200578/ 250678/ 221078/ 251178/ 021278/ 050279/ 190579/ 300579/ 240679/ 280779/ 210879/281179/ 060280
Transferred to Swindon: 110680

Swindon CM&EE Yard: 300780/ 210880/ 051080/ 010181/ 060681/ 260981/ 290382/ 080582/ 160882/ 041082/ 261282/ 170284/ 160384/ 280485/ 161085
Swindon s.p.: 270286/ 120386
Swindon Cocklebury Yard: 190386
Transfer Swindon-Derby (for Matlock): 200386 (hauled by 56088)
Transfer Derby to Peak Rail, Matlock: 070486 (hauled by 37158, for preservation; 31116 also quoted)

Notes:
1. Variously quoted as re-numbered to TDB968006 in 1/75 and 2/75.
2. Withdrawn: 0977 (LocDir).
3. Fire-damaged whilst at Bristol 1976/77.

D5705 (Preservation)

Renumbered from TDB968006 to D5705 during May 1986.

Individual Locomotive Histories • 81

D5706

D5706, 17A Derby, 30 April 1960. (*Colour-Rail*)

D5706, Crewe Works, 8 November 1964.

(*Alec Swain [Transport Treasury]*)

Harrogate: 271158 (test run from Stockton)

New: 051258

St Pancras: 181258 (16.25 St Pancras-Manchester Central) (with D5704)
Derby Works: 210359
St Pancras: 130559 (16.25 St Pancras-Manchester Central) (with D5700)
17A Derby: 310559
Leicester: 110659 (XX-St Pancras, 14.36 ex-Leicester) (with D5709)
Auldgirth: 130659 (17.30 Glasgow St.Enoch-Carlisle passenger) (with D5709)
XX: 140759 (17.55 St Pancras-Manchester Central passenger (to Leicester) (piloting Stanier 5MT 44809)
St Pancras: 170759 (16.25 St Pancras-Manchester Central) (with D5708)
Motherwell: 250759 ('Condor' freight) (piloting Standard 5MT 73058)
Derby: 300759
Bedford: 290859 (08.45 Manchester Central-St Pancras)
Derby: 070959 (10.25 Manchester Central-St Pancras) (with D5711)
XX: 021159 (05.55 Manchester Central-St Pancras) (with D5707)
Kettering: 270160 (16.25 St Pancras-Manchester) (with D5711)
17A Derby: 300460
St Pancras: 180560 (passenger ex-Manchester) (with D5708)
17A Derby: 290560
St Pancras: 120860 (18.30 St Pancras-XX) (with D5705)
66A Polmadie: 140860
17A Derby: 270860/ 280860
Derby Works: 271160 (Sidings)
17A Derby: 050261/ 120261/ 260261
66A Polmadie: 020361
XX: 140461 ('Condor') (with D5715)
17A Derby: 250661/ 130861/ 240961. Not listed 140561.
Hauled from Derby to Dukinfield: 191061

Metro-Vick, Dukinfield: 201061
Gorton Works: 290762 (Paint Shop)
EHC: Dukinfield: 191061-300762 HC (81209).

To 12B: 030262.

12F Workington: 130862
Morecambe: 250862 (stabled)
12F Workington: 280763
12E Barrow: 160863
12C Barrow: 290963
XX: 051063 (09.50 Manchester Victoria-Workington)
12C Barrow: 090564
Lancaster: 120664 (passenger)
12D Workington: 050764
Preston: 160764 (13.03 Workington-Manchester Victoria)
Preston: 180764 (13.03 Workington-Manchester Victoria)
Preston: 210764 (09.50 Manchester Victoria-Workington)/ 270764
Crewe Works: 120864 (Works Yard)/ 150864/ 300864 (E.Shop)/ 010964/ 130964/ 200964 (E.Shop)/ 270964 (E.Shop)/ 041064 (E.Shop)/ 101064 (E.Shop)/ 181064/ 011164 (Test Roads)/ 081164. Not listed 160864 and 151164.
12D Workington: 061264
12C Barrow: 200265
10A Carnforth: 160465
12C Barrow: 010565
12D Workington: 110665
10A Carnforth: 120665/ 200665/ 070865
12C Barrow: 150865
12D Workington: 021065
Crewe Works: xx1265/ 020166 (Arr.Sdgs)/ 160166 (Works Yard)/ 130266 (Arr.Sdgs)/ 270266 (E.Shop)/ 060366 (Test Roads)/ 130366 (E.Shop)/ 200366 (E.Shop). Not listed 051265, 300166 and 270366.
Carlisle Kingmoor: 140566 (passing)
Carlisle: 150766 (freight)
12D Workington: 060866/ 130866
Carlisle Kingmoor (Depot/Yard?): 220866
10A Carnforth: 191166
12B Carlisle Upperby: 271166
10A Carnforth: 070167
12D Workington: 260367/ 300367
9C Reddish: 150467/ 200567
10A Carnforth: 170667
9C Reddish: 010867
12D Workington: 190867 (head-on collision with 9F 92093)/ 220867
10A Carnforth: 020967

Crewe Works: 100967/ 240967/ 011067 (Test Roads). Not listed 291067.
12C Barrow: 191167
10A Carnforth: 091267/ 101267
12D Workington: 060168
10A Carnforth: 210168
12A Carlisle Kingmoor (Diesel): 250268
Grange-over-Sands: 260368 (14.15 Carnforth-Barrow freight)
12A Carlisle Kingmoor (Diesel): 110468/ 130468/ 150468
9C Reddish: 140668/ 220668/ 210768/ 040868. Not listed 070668.
Carlisle New Yard (North): 250868

Withdrawn: w/e 070968 (D10).

12A Carlisle Kingmoor (Steam): 060968 (stored)/ 080968/ 300968/ 241068/ 071268/ 311268/ 040169/ 110169
Carlisle Kingmoor Yard: 020469/ 120569/ 260569/ 060769/ 050869/ 200869/ 210869/ 230869/ 240869/ 040969
Blackburn (en route from Carlisle Yard to Great Bridge): 150969 (with D5701/2, hauled by D1795)
J. Cashmore Ltd, Great Bridge: Nil. Not noted xx1169.

Disposal: J. Cashmore Ltd, Great Bridge - 0969-1169 (D&ELfS). Not proven.

Annual mileages (EHC):

	1958	1959	1960	1961	1962	1963	Total
D5706	4824	33871	28697	13817	21668	39030	141,907

Notes:
1. See 'Additional Note' No.1 for D5700.
2. S(u): 12/06/61-we 21/10/61 (EHC).
3. 'A visitor to Derby Works on February 5th [1961] . . . Yet more of the Metrovick Type 2 Co-Bos, Nos. D5701/6/15/7, were stored outside Derby depot, making a total of 13 of this class inactive, but Nos. D5700/5/14/8 were observed at work.' (TI0461)
4. Dragged Carlisle Kingmoor (steam) depot to Carlisle Marshalling Yard February 1969. (A. Whitaker)

D5707

D5707, 17A Derby, 9 May 1959. (*Colour-Rail*)

D5707, 10A Carnforth, 1 July 1966. (*Noel A. Machell*)

D5707, 10A Carnforth, March 1967. (*Clifford Essex [Transport Topics]*)

Harrogate: 111258 (test run from Stockton)

New: 191258

Wilstead (Bedford): 130159 (freight)
Derby Works: 150359 (Yard)
St Pancras: 250459 (16.25 St Pancras-Manchester Central) (with D5712)
17A Derby: 090559/ 100859/ 311059
XX: 021159 (05.55 Manchester Central-St Pancras) (with D5706)
Manchester Central: 091159 (10.25 Manchester Central-St Pancras) (with D5714)
Derby Works: 160560 (Klondyke Sidings)/ 290560/ 140660/ 030760/ 070860/ 280860/ 040960 (under covers at side of Derby station)/ 250960/ 231060/ 061160 (Works Sidings)/ 131160 (Works Sidings, sheeted cabs)/ 271160 (Works Sidings). Not listed 270360/240460, 080760/ 130860/ 270860 and 091260/ 120261
9E Trafford Park: 260261/ 260361/ 160461. Not listed 090461 and 180661.

Metro-Vick, Dukinfield: Nil. EHC: Dukinfield: 190661-290362 HC (42887).

To 12B: 030262.

12E Barrow: 150762/ 290762
Lancaster Castle: 060862 (passenger)
Morecambe South Junction: 090263 (10.53 Workington-Euston)
12F Workington: 150663
Leyland: 130763 (13.03 Workington-Manchester Victoria passenger)

12F Workington: 070963
12D Workington: 150963
10A Carnforth: 240963
Lancaster: 161263 (XX-Preston (14.19 ex-Lancaster)
Preston: 110164 (10.53 Workington-Euston, to Preston)
9E Trafford Park: 090264
Garstang: 150264 (10.53 Workington-Euston) (to Preston)
Preston: 180564 (09.50 Manchester Victoria-Workington)
12C Barrow: 050764/ 110764
12D Workington: 270864
Preston: 300864 (14.55 Preston-Barrow passenger)
12C Barrow: 300864
12D Workington: 111064/ 200665
XX: 050765 (damaged by fire, location unknown) (FDTL)
12D Workington: 060765/ 070865/ 120865
Lancaster/Preston: 300865 (10.53 Workington-Euston, to Preston)
9C Reddish: 110965/171065
Preston (stabled): 080166
Carlisle New Yard: 020466 (Tyne Yard-Workington coke train)
Sellafield: 070466 (freight)
12D Workington: 100466
Dalton Jct 130466 (11.25 Euston-Workington passenger)
12B Carlisle Upperby: 300466/010566
Carlisle: 150666 (freight)
10A Carnforth: 010766
12B Carlisle Upperby: 100766/ 020866
12D Workington: 060866
Carlisle: 120866 (freight, piloting 'Britannia' 70041)
12B Carlisle Upperby: 180866/ 100966
Haydon Bridge: 300966 (Heads of Ayr-Newcastle relief)
12C Barrow: 121166
12B Carlisle Upperby: 060167
12D Workington: 090167
12A Carlisle Kingmoor: 260367 /270367

12B Carlisle Upperby: 290367
12D Workington: 290367
Crewe Works: 090467 (E.Shop)/ 230467 (E.Shop)/ 300467/ 070567/ 210567 (E.Shop)/ 040667 (Test Area) (touched-up green (GFY)/ 110667 (Works Yard)
12B Carlisle Upperby: 160667/ 180667/ 020867
Carlisle Citadel/Oxenholme: 050867 (10.30 Carlisle-Euston, presumably to Preston)
10A Carnforth: 190867
Workington: 030967 (passenger)
Carnforth (Depot/Station?): 070967
12B Carlisle Upperby: 230967/ 281067/ 191167
10A Carnforth: 060168
12A Carlisle Kingmoor (Diesel): 250268
10A Carnforth: 250368
12D Workington: 160468
10A Carnforth: 110568/ 220668
Windermere: 270668 (on Windermere services due to d.m.u. failure)
10A Carnforth: 290668
12A Carlisle Kingmoor (Diesel): 200768/ 270768
10A Carnforth: 300768 (out of use)/ 010868
9C Reddish: 040868/ 310868

Withdrawn: w/e 070968 (D10).

12A Carlisle Kingmoor (Steam): 300968/ 241068/ 071268/ 311268/ 040169/ 110169. Not listed 060968.
Carlisle Kingmoor Yard: 020469/ 120569/ 260569/ 060769/ 050869/ 200869/ 210869/ 230869/ 240869/ 040969
Carlisle Yard to Great Bridge (booked transfer): 160969 (with D5708/11)
J. Cashmore Ltd, Great Bridge: Nil. Not noted xx1169.

Disposal: J. Cashmore Ltd, Great Bridge - 0969 (D&ELfS). Not proven.

Annual mileages (EHC):

	1958	1959	1960	1961	1962	1963	Total
D5707	574	34349	7964	69	32535	56819	132,310

Notes:
1. See 'Additional Note' No.1 for D5700.
2. S(u): 12/12/60 (*Crossed out, with note* 'See - W.E. 4/2/61 'Awaiting Works'') (EHC).
3. S(u): 20/03/61-19/06/61 (EHC).
4. Dragged Carlisle Kingmoor (steam) depot to Carlisle Marshalling Yard February 1969. (A.Whitaker)

Individual Locomotive Histories • 87

D5708

D5708, 66A Polmadie, 17 May 1959. Fickle modernity alongside trusted antiquity! (*Author's Collection*)

Harrogate: 181258 (test train)/ 311258 (test train)

New: 070159

Kilnhurst: 060359
Skipton: 160359 (Down 'Condor') (with D5710)
66A Polmadie: 150559 (booked for 17.30 Glasgow St.Enoch-Carlisle pass) (with D5715)/ 170559 (with D57xx)
17A Derby: 310559
XX: 140659 (Leeds-Carlisle light engine)
Killamarsh: 170659 (being towed by 4F 0-6-0 43902, light engines)
St Pancras: 170759 (16.25 St Pancras-Manchester Central) (with D5706)
17A Derby: 221059/ 201259
XX: 211259 (04.20 St Pancras-Manchester Central) (with D5713)
Derby: 010260 (10.25 Manchester Central-St Pancras) (with D5704)
17A Derby: 270360
Derby Midland: 020460 (with D5703)
Derby: 040460 (07.25 Manchester Central-St Pancras) (with D5703)
17A Derby: 080560
XX: 090560 (07.25 Manchester Central-St Pancras) (with D5705)
St Pancras: 180560 (passenger ex-Manchester) (with D5706)
17A Derby: 290560
Derby Works: 030760/ 080760/ 070860/ 270860/ 280860/ 040960 (under covers at side of Derby station)/ 250960/ 231060/ 061160 (Works Sidings)/ 271160 (Works Sidings). Not listed 140660, 130860/ 150860 and 091260/ 120261.
9E Trafford Park: 260261/ 260361/ 090461/ 160461/ 180661/ 250661

Metro-Vick, Dukinfield: Nil. EHC: Dukinfield: 100761-190462 HC (62508).

To 12B: 030262.

9G Gorton: 140462
12E Barrow: 150762
24L Carnforth: 290762
Manchester Victoria: 180862 (09.55 Manchester Victoria-Barrow/Workington passenger)

XX: 060563 (banking 10.15 Carnforth-Barrow freight between Plumpton Jct and Lindal ore sidings)
Lancaster: 040663
24L Carnforth: 150663
Seascale: 310763 (Workington-Carnforth passenger)
Lakeside: 210963 (passenger)
9C Reddish: 211063 (undergoing modifications by Crossley staff)/ xx1163
9E Trafford Park: 021163
8K Bank Hall: 020264
10D Lostock Hall: 230264
Preston: 200364 (09.50 Manchester Victoria-Workington)
Morecambe: 300364 (excursion ex-Barrow)
12C Barrow: 090564)
Preston: 180564 (09.50 Manchester Victoria-Workington)
Hest Bank: 190564 (10.53 Workington-Euston) (to Preston)
Preston: 230564 (09.50 Manchester Victoria-Workington)
Preston: 150664 (09.50 Manchester Victoria-Workington)
Preston: 270664 (13.03 Workington-Manchester Victoria)
Hest Bank: 150864 (10.53 Workington-Euston) (to Preston)
Preston: 270864 (09.50 Manchester Victoria-Workington)
12C Barrow: 111064
12D Workington: 061264
12C Barrow: 200265
XX: xx0365 (cross-London freight trials)
Feltham: 050365 (cross-London freight trials involving 10.45 Purfleet-Southampton (to Feltham) and 13.47 Feltham-Ripple Lane)
9C Reddish: 090565/ 220565
Barrow: 090665 (17.08 Workington-St Pancras sleeper)
12D Workington: 200665
12C Barrow: 010865/ 150865/ 010965
10A Carnforth: 171065
12B Carlisle Upperby: 020466
Carlisle Kingmoor: 140566 (passing)
12C Barrow: 060866/ 070866
12D Workington: 180866
12B Carlisle Upperby: 100966/ 170966
12C Barrow: 121166
12B Carlisle Upperby: 121166
12D Workington: 090167
Glasgow-Workington: 110267 (seen on journey)
9C Reddish: 190367
Carlisle Kingmoor (passing site of new diesel depot): 230367 (8P73 1230 Carlisle-Preston freight, via Barrow) (with D5702)
12B Carlisle Upperby: 260367/ 290367/ 090467/ 100667

12D Workington: 240667/270667
XX: 290667 (11.30 Workington-Carlisle freight, failed, rescued by Ivatt 4MT 43049)
10A Carnforth: 020767
Ravenglass: 130767 (freight)
12B Carlisle Upperby: 020867
Carnforth: 070867 (up passenger)
12D Workington: 190867
12C Barrow: 310867 (engine problems)
12B Carlisle Upperby: 230967
5B Crewe South: 290967
Crewe Works: 011067 (Arrival Sidings)/ 291067 (E.Shop Yard)/ 051167/ 111167/ 121167/ 191167/ 261167 (E.Shop)
10A Carnforth: 280168
12A Carlisle Kingmoor (Diesel): 250268/ 130468
Carlisle Kingmoor Yard: 150468
Workington Yard: 160468
9C Reddish: 140668. Not listed 070668.

12A Carlisle Kingmoor (Diesel): 200768/ 270768/ 290768/ 100868
Carlisle Kingmoor Yard (North): 250868
10A Carnforth: 310868

Withdrawn: w/e 070968 (D10).

12A Carlisle Kingmoor (Steam): 300968/ 241068/ 071268/ 311268/ 040169/ 110169. Not listed 060968.
Carlisle Kingmoor Yard: 020469/ 030569/ 120569/ 260569/ 060769/ 050869/ 200869/ 210869/ 230869/ 240869/ 040969
Carlisle Yard to Great Bridge (booked transfer): 160969 (with D5707/11)
J. Cashmore Ltd, Great Bridge: xx1169

Disposal: J. Cashmore Ltd, Great Bridge - 0969-1169 (D&ELfS).

Annual mileages (EHC):

	1958	1959	1960	1961	1962	1963	Total
D5708	-	48092	14416	49	31064	31506	125,127

Notes:
1. See 'Additional Note' No.1 for D5700.
2. S(u): 12/12/60 [Crossed out, with note 'See - W.E. 4/2/61 'Awaiting Works''] (EHC).
3. S(u): 20/03/61-17/07/61 (EHC).
4. Dragged Carlisle Kingmoor (steam) depot to Carlisle Marshalling Yard February 1969. (A. Whitaker)

D5709

D5709, 17A Derby, 9 January 1959. Very recently delivered. (*Mick Mobley*)

D5709, near Barrow, Undated. Note the repair to accident damage on the right corner of the cab reducing the size of the yellow warning panel. (*RCTS Archive*)

Harrogate: 010159 (test run from Stockton)

New: 070159

17A Derby: 090159
XX: 120159 (16.00 Derby-Manchester Central passenger)
St Pancras: 200259 (16.25 St Pancras-Manchester Central) (with D5711)
Glasgow St Enoch: 180459 (17.30 Glasgow St Enoch-Carlisle pass) (with D5710)
Elvanfoot: 190459 (Euston-Glasgow sleeper (from Carlisle), with D5710)
66A Polmadie: 150559 (booked for 17.30 Glasgow St.Enoch-Carlisle pass (with D5705), but replaced by D5708/15)/ 160559 (with D5705)
Leicester: 110659 (XX-St Pancras, 14.36 ex-Leicester) (with D5706)
Auldgirth: 130659 (17.30 Glasgow St.Enoch-Carlisle passenger) (with D5706)
Radlett: 130759 (up 'Condor') (with D5700)
Birmingham New Street: 270759 (piloted 73069 on 08.15 Newcastle-Cardiff, came off at Birmingham NS, believed piloted 09.14 Paignton-Sheffield back to Derby)
Derby: 231059 (04.20 St Pancras-Manchester Central) (with D5715)
Manchester Central: 071159 (10.25 Manchester Central-St Pancras) (with D5715)
Manchester Central: 101159 (14.30 Liverpool Central-Nottingham)
17A Derby: 170160
14A Cricklewood: 140260
Manchester Central: 060660 (10.25 Manchester Central-St Pancras) (with D5714)
17A Derby: 270860/ 280860. Not listed 070860 and 120261.
9E Trafford Park: 260261/ 260361/ 090461/ 160461

Metro-Vick, Dukinfield: Nil
Gorton Works: 220262 (Paint Shop Yard)
EHC: Dukinfield: 050661-230262 HC (63171).

To 12B: 030262.

Bilsbarrow: 010662 (Barrow-Liverpool passenger)
12E Barrow: 150762
Lancaster: 291262 (down passenger)
12F Workington: 070963
Whitehaven: 130963 (06.40 Euston-Workington passenger)

Broughton: 070464 (Barrow-Euston passenger)
Preston: 180464 (06.10 Heysham-Manchester Victoria)
Preston: 150864 (09.50 Manchester Victoria-Workington)
12D Workington: 111064
10A Carnforth: 061264
12C Barrow: 200265
Crewe Works: 200665 (E.Shop)/ 270665 (E.Shop)/ 250765 (P.Shop)/ 050865/ 220865 (P.Shop)/ 120965 (P.Shop)/ 190965 (P.Shop)/ 101065/ 171065 (P.Shop)/ 311065/ 071165 (P.Shop)/ 141165 (P.Shop)/ 051265 (P.Shop, stored)/ 020166 (P.Shop, stored)/ 160166 (P.Shop)/ 300166 (P.Shop, stored)/ 130266 (P.Shop, stored)/ 270266 (P.Shop, stored)/ 060366 (P.Shop, stored)/ 130366 (P.Shop)/ 200366 (P.Shop)/ 270366 (P.Shop, stored)/ 030466 (P.Shop)/ 240466 (P.Shop, stored)/ 080566 (P.Shop)/ 290566 (P.Shop, stored)/ 050666/ 120666/ 190666/ 260666 (stored)/ 240766 (P.Shop, stored)/ 310766/ 070866 (P.Shop)/ 140866/ 110966 (P.Shop, stored)/ 180966/ 021066/ 091066 (P.Shop, stored)/ 161066 (P.Shop)/ 231066/ 301066 (P.Shop)/ 061166 (P.Shop, stored)/ 131166 (P.Shop)/ 201166 (P.Shop, stored)/ 111266 (P.Shop)/ 181266 (P.Shop, stored)/ 080167 (Old P.Shop)/ 220167 (P.Shop, stored)/ 050267/ 120267 (P.Shop)/ 190267. Not listed 060665, 100765/ 250765/ 260965/ 011165/ 060366 and 050367.
Warrington Dallam: xxxx67 (Stanier 5MT 45135 hauling D5713/10/04/09).
12B Carlisle Upperby: 260367/ 290367/ 090467/ 220467/ 200567/ 100667/ 160667/ 180667/ 250667/ 280667/ 290767/ 020867/ 030867/ 080867/ 190867/ 230967/ 071067/ 081067/ 211067/ 241067/ 261067/ 281067/ 291067/ 191167/ 081267/ 181267. Not listed 070867/ 300967/ 021067/ 101267.

Withdrawn: w/e 301267 (12B).

12B Carlisle Upperby: 020168/ 060168
12A Carlisle Kingmoor (Steam): 270168 (minus engine)/ 280168/ 100268/ 250268/ 170368/ 110468/ 130468/ 150468/ 180468/ 110568/ 060668/ 150668/ 210668/ 200768/ 270768/ 100868/ 250868/ 060968 (stored)/ 080968
Despatched from Carlisle to Shettleston: 110968 (with D5710/3)
J. MacWilliam, Shettleston: 061068 (intact)

Disposal: J. MacWilliam, Shettleston 0968 (D&ELfS).

Annual mileages (EHC):

	1958	1959	1960	1961	1962	1963	Total
D5709	-	46299	16872	0	35495	54075	152,741

Notes:
1. See 'Additional Note' No.1 for D5700.
2. S(u): 12/12/60 [Crossed out, with note 'See - W.E. 4/2/61 'Awaiting Works''] EHC).
3. S(u): 20/03/61-15/05/61 (EHC).
4. S(u): 03/09/65 (with no reinstatement date) (EHC). N.B. Might be 03/04/65; poor hand writing.
5. Disproportionately large number of 'Not listed' reports whilst at Crewe Works from 1965, probably due to its 'unusual' storage location at Crewe Works. 'Railway Locomotives' visit reports for 071165 and 131166 mention 'Shop adjoining Paint Shop'.
6. Sold for scrap (September 1968): J. MacWilliam, Shettleston: D5709/10/3 (from Carlisle). (RO1168)

D5710

D5710, 17A Derby, Undated. *(Colour-Rail)*

D5710, Crewe Works, Arrival Sidings, 25 June 1966. *(David Birt [Transport Treasury])*

New: 100259

Kilnhurst: 060359
Skipton: 160359 (Down 'Condor') (with D5708)
Glasgow St Enoch: 180459 (17.30 Glasgow St Enoch-Carlisle pass) (with D5709)
Elvanfoot: 190459 (Euston-Glasgow sleeper (from Carlisle), with D5708 (sic D5709?)
Wellingborough: 140559 (17.30 St Pancras-Manchester Central) (with D5701)
66A Polmadie: 300559
Cricklewood: 210659
Manningham: 070859 (failed at Bingley on previous night's 'Condor')
St Pancras: 280859 (07.25 Manchester-St Pancras passenger) (assisting 'Jubilee' 45585), 12.15 St Pancras-Bradford passenger (assisting 'Royal Scot' 46103)
St Pancras: 110959 (16.25 St Pancras-Manchester Central) (with D57xx)
St Pancras: 300959 (16.25 St Pancras-Manchester Central) (with D5702)
Elstree: 031059 (passenger, with D57xx)
17A Derby: 041059
Derby Works: 141259 (Diesel Shop)
17A Derby: 170160
Derby Works: 130360 (Diesel Finishing Shop)/ 160360. EHC: Derby: 260160-280360 NC (57606).
17A Derby: 270360
St Pancras: 090560 (St Pancras-Manchester Central) (with D5718)
St Pancras: 100560 (16.25 St Pancras-Manchester Central) (with D5718)
Derby: 050760 (07.25 Manchester Central-St Pancras) (with D5701)
Derby Works: 070860/ 120860 (Diesel Test House)/ 130860/ 150860 (Test House). EHC: Derby: 260760-150860 NC (77303).
17A Derby: 270860/ 280860
Harpenden: 240960 (10.25 Manchester Central-St Pancras passenger) (with D5711)
Derby: 260960 (10.25 Manchester Central-St Pancras) (with D5711)
Trowell: 091060 (freight test train with 16t mineral wagons to Brent) (with D5716)
Derby Works: 061160 (Diesel Repair Shop)/ 141160/ 271160 (Diesel Repair Shop). EHC: Derby: 181060-020161 LC (86984).
17A Derby: Nil. Not listed 120261 (SMA).

9E Trafford Park: 260261/ 260361/ 030461/ 090461/ 160461/ 180661/ 250661/ 130861. Not listed 200861/ 170961.

Metro-Vick, Dukinfield: Nil. EHC: Dukinfield: 180961-080662 HC (88561).

To 12B: 030262.

12F Workington: 150762
Grange-over-Sands: 030962 (crew-training)
Bare Lane: 050563 (Barrow-Preston passenger)
24L Carnforth: 160863
12C Barrow: 290963
XX: 210164 (damaged by fire, location unknown) (FDTL)
Preston: 190564 (13.03 Workington-Manchester Victoria)
Preston: 160664 (09.50 Manchester Victoria-Workington)
Preston: 200664 (09.50 Manchester Victoria-Workington)
12C Barrow: 050764/ 110764
Crewe Works: 201264 (E.Shop)/ 030165 (E.Shop)/ 070165/ 230165 (E.Shop)/ 240165/ 070265 (P.ShopYard)/ 080265/ 210265 (E.Shop Yard)/ 280265 (Test Roads). Not listed 131264 and 140365.
Barrow: 050665 (empty stock) (with Stanier 8F 48125)
12C Barrow: 110665
12D Workington: 070865/ 110865/ 120865
12C Barrow: 150865
10A Carnforth: 220865
12D Workington: 240865
Lancaster: 300865 (stabled)
XX: 080965 (damaged by fire, location unknown) (FDTL)
Crewe Works: 260965/ 101065 (Outside E.Shop)/ 171065 (Arr.Sdgs)/ 311065/ 011165/ 071165 (P.Shop)/ 141165 (P.Shop Yard). Not listed 190965 and 051265.
12C Barrow: 280266
Crewe Works: 240466 (Arr.Sdgs)/ 080566 (Arr.Sdgs)/ 290566 (Arr.Sdgs)/ 050666/ 120666/ 190666/ 250666 (Arr.Sdgs)/ 260666 (stored)/ 240766 (Arr.Sdgs)/ 310766/ 140866/ 110966 (Arr.Sdgs)/ 180966/ 250966/ 021066/ 031066/ 091066 (Arr.Sdgs)/ 161066 (Works Yard)/ 231066/ 301066 (Yards)/ 061166 (Arr.Sdgs)/ 131166 (Arr.Sdgs)/ 201166 (Arr.Sdgs)/111266 (Side of Works)/ 181266 (Arr.Sdgs)/ 080167 (Side of Works)/ 220167/ 050267/ 120267/ 190267. Not listed 030466, 070866 and 050367.
Warrington Dallam: xxxx67 (Stanier 5MT 45135 hauling D5713/10/04/09).

12B Carlisle Upperby: 260367/ 290367/ 090467/ 220467/ 200567/ 100667/ 160667/ 180667/ 280667/ 290767/ 020867/ 030867/ 080867/ 190867/ 230967/ 021067/ 071067/ 081067/ 211067/ 241067/ 261067/ 281067/ 291067/ 191167/ 081267/ 101267/ 181267.
Not listed 250667/ 070867/ 300967.

Withdrawn: w/e 301267 (12B).

12B Carlisle Upperby: 020168/ 060168

12A Carlisle Kingmoor (Steam): 270168 (minus engine)/ 280168/ 100268/ 250268/ 170368/ 110468/ 130468/ 150468/ 180468/ 110568/ 060668/ 150668/ 210668/ 200768/ 270768/ 100868/ 250868/ 060968/ 080968
Despatched from Carlisle to Shettleston: 110968 (with D5709/13)
J. MacWilliam, Shettleston: 061068 (intact)

Disposal: J. MacWilliam, Shettleston 0968 (D&ELfS).

Annual mileages (EHC):

	1958	1959	1960	1961	1962	1963	Total
D5710	-	57478	29506	1577	27021	50895	166,477

Notes:
1. S(u): 27/03/61-18/09/61 (EHC).
2. S(u): 18/10/65 (with no reinstatement date) (EHC).
3. Sold for scrap (September 1968): J. MacWilliam, Shettleston: D5709/10/3 (from Carlisle). (RO1168)

D5711

D5711, 17A Derby, 30 April 1960. *(Colour-Rail)*

Individual Locomotive Histories • 97

D5711, 17A Derby, 1961. Revised cab front windows. Single 25kV warning sign. *(Peter Sedge)*

D5711, Carnforth, 24 May 1968. Serif numbers. *(Author's Collection)*

New: 100259

St Pancras: 200259 (16.25 St Pancras-Manchester Central) (with D5709)
Glasgow Central: 130359 (08.23 Glasgow Central-Gourock pass)
Derby Works: Nil. EHC: Derby: 110459-280459 LC (6988).
17A Derby: 310559
St Pancras: 140859 (St Pancras-XX) (with D5714)
St Pancras: 210859 (16.25 St Pancras-Manchester Central) (with D5714)
Derby: 070959 (1.025 Manchester Central-St Pancras) (with D5706)
St Pancras: 250959 (16.25 St Pancras-Manchester Central) (with D5702)
Derby: 161059 (04.20 St Pancras-Manchester Central) (with D5700)
Leicester: 171059 (16.35 St Pancras-Manchester Central) (with D5700)
14E Bedford: 100160
Kettering: 270160 (16.25 St Pancras-Manchester) (with D5706)
17A Derby: 270360/ 300460/ 290560. Not listed 280260.
Derby Works: 120860 (Diesel Finishing Shop)/ 130860/ 150860 (Diesel Finishing Shop)/ 270860/ 280860/ 040960 (Works Yard). EHC: Derby: 220660-160960 NC (56251). Not listed 030760 and 070860.
Harpenden: 240960 (10.25 Manchester Central-St Pancras passenger) (with D5710)
Derby: 260960 (10.25 Manchester Central-St Pancras) (with D5710)
Wellingborough-Brent: 171060 (trials with coal and empty wagon trains)
Leicester: 311060 (07.25 Manchester Central St Pancras/ 14.25 St Pancras-Manchester passenger) (with D5717)
Derby Works: 091260/ 090161 (Diesel Erecting Shop)/ 220161 (Works Sidings). EHC: Derby: 111160-030261 LC (66081).
Glendon South Jct: 100261
XX: 130261 ('Condor')
Glendon South Jct: 140261
17A Derby: 260261/ 140561/ 040661/ 250661/ 130861/ 240961
Hauled from Derby to Dukinfield: 201061

Metro-Vick, Dukinfield: 201061. EHC: Dukinfield: 231061-071262 HC (-).

To 12B: 030262.

Lancaster Castle: 240363 (10.15 Barrow-Preston passenger (diverted via Morecambe)
XX: 21-230563 (Tunstead-Northwich ICI limestone train trials) (with D5714)
Carnforth: 271063 (southbound passenger, 13.53 ex-Carnforth)
10D Lostock Hall: 010364
Preston: 140364 (09.50 Manchester Victoria-Workington)
Preston: 280364 (09.50 Manchester Victoria-Workington)
Preston: 020564 (06.10 Heysham-Manchester Victoria)
Carnforth: 050564 (13.45 Barrow-Carnforth parcels, with D5700)
12C Barrow: 090564
Preston: 040764 (09.50 Manchester Victoria-Workington)
Seascale: 080864 (06.37 Lancaster-Workington)
9C Reddish: 010964
12D Workington: 061264
Shaw: 190665 (passenger to Morecambe)
10A Carnforth: 220665/ 190765
Grange-over-Sands: 100865 (up freight, dead in train, behind Stanier 5MT 45138)
12D Workington: 110865/ 120865
Preston: 220865
Lancaster Castle: 230865
Preston: 270865 (northbound passenger, piloting Stanier 5MT 45156)
Journey Preston-Crewe: 300865
12C Barrow: 171065
10A Carnforth: 280266
12B Carlisle Upperby: 080766/ 100766
XX: 200766 (damaged by fire, location unknown) (FDTL)
Crewe Works: 310766/ 140866/ 110966 (E.Shop)/ 180966/ 021066/ 091066 (E.Shop)/ 161066 (E.Shop)/ 231066/ 301066 (E.Shop)/ 061166 (E.Shop)/ 131166 (E.Shop)/ 201166 (E.Shop)/ 181266 (Test Roads)/ 080167 (E.Shop)/ 150167 (Works Yard, repainted). Not listed 240766 and 070866/ 111266.
Crewe North Yard: 220167
12B Carlisle Upperby: 110267/ 050367
Carnforth: 190467 (parcels)
12D Workington: 110667
12B Carlisle Upperby: 160667/ 180667
12C Barrow: 240667
10A Carnforth: 260667/ 020767
Hest Bank: 010867 (Workington-Morecambe excursion)
Carnforth: 030867 (10.40 Barrow-Manchester)
9C Reddish: 220967
10A Carnforth: 071067

12B Carlisle Upperby: 081067
9C Reddish: 151067
12B Carlisle Upperby: 281067/291067
12D Workington: 191167
12C Barrow: 101267
10A Carnforth: 060168
12A Carlisle Kingmoor (Diesel): 100268
10A Carnforth: 240268
12A Carlisle Kingmoor (Diesel): 180468
10A Carnforth: 220468
12A Carlisle Kingmoor (Diesel): 110568
10A Carnforth: 240568
Carlisle Upperby s.p.: 150668
10A Carnforth: 260768/ 270768/ 280768/ 300768 (engine problems)
12A Carlisle Kingmoor (Diesel): 100868
12E Tebay: 110868

Withdrawn: w/e 070968 (D10).

12A Carlisle Kingmoor (Steam): 060968 (stored)/ 080968/ 300968/ 241068/ 071268/ 311268/ 040169/ 110169
Carlisle Kingmoor Yard: 020469/ 120569/ 260569/ 060769/ 050869/ 200869/ 210869/ 230869/ 240869/ 040969
Carlisle Yard to Great Bridge (booked transfer): 160969 (with D5707/8)
J. Cashmore Ltd, Great Bridge: xx1169

Disposal: J. Cashmore Ltd, Great Bridge - 0969-1169 (D&ELfS).

Annual mileages (EHC):

	1958	1959	1960	1961	1962	1963	Total
D5711	-	37952	28129	2060	1789	53522	123,452

Notes:
1. S(u): 27/03/61-28/10/61 (EHC).
2. Dragged Carlisle Kingmoor (steam) depot to Carlisle Marshalling Yard February 1969. (A. Whitaker)

100 • THE METROPOLITAN-VICKERS TYPE 2 CO-BO DIESEL-ELECTRIC LOCOMOTIVES

D5712

D5712, 10A Carnforth, 8 October 1966. Single centrally positioned 25kV sign. (*John Grey Turner*)

D5712, Carlisle Bog Junction, Date unknown. Double 25kV safety signs, plus the scar of the old centrally positioned sign now removed. (*Regional Bus Photos*)

Bowesfield Works: 100259 (P.Shop)

New: 040359

St Pancras: 250459 (16.25 St Pancras-Manchester Central) (with D5707)
Leicester: 220559 (XX-St Pancras, 12.36 ex-Leicester) (with D5713)
17A Derby: 310559
St Pancras: 070859 (16.25 St Pancras-Manchester Central) (with D5704)
Elstree & Boreham Wood: 120959 (12.25 Manchester-St Pancras, with D57xx)
St Pancras: 271059 (16.25 St Pancras-Manchester Central) (with D5701)
St Pancras: 281059 (St Pancras-Manchester Central [relief]) (with D5701)
Derby Works: Nil. EHC: Derby: 081259-151259 NC (34891).
Farringdon: 290160 (17.20 Moorgate-?) (failed)
Moorgate: 170560/ 180560 (17.21 ex-Moorgate, both days)
17A Derby: 290560/ 270860/ 280860. Not listed 070860/ 120261.
9E Trafford Park: 260261/ 260361/ 090461/ 160461/ 180661/ 250661

Metro-Vick, Dukinfield: Nil. EHC: Dukinfield: 100761-180562 HC (38347).

To 12B: 030262.

12E Barrow: 150762
Preston: 280762 (10.15 Manchester Victoria-Barrow)
24L Carnforth: 290762
Skew Bridge, Preston: 010862 (Manchester-Barrow/ Workington)
24L Carnforth: 120862
Carnforth: 101062 (06.45 Euston-Workington [from Preston])
Green Road: 060563 (Manchester Victoria-Workington passenger)
Whitehaven: 010863 (passenger)
Horwich Works: Nil. EHC: Horwich: 030863-200863 LC (101567).
12C Barrow: 290963
8K Bank Hall: 020264
Preston: 090564 (09.50 Manchester Victoria-Workington)
12C Barrow: 090564
Preston: 080664 (13.03 Workington-Manchester Victoria)
Preston: 270664 (09.50 Manchester Victoria-Workington)
Preston: 290664 (06.10 Heysham-Manchester Victoria)
12D Workington: 050764
12C Barrow: 110764
Preston: 120964 (13.03 Workington-Manchester Victoria)
Preston: 190964 (09.50 Manchester Victoria-Workington)
12D Workington: 061264
Preston: 050165 (damaged by fire) (FDTL)
Silverdale: 290165 (damaged by fire) (FDTL)
XX: 120265 (damaged by fire, location unknown) (FDTL)
12C Barrow: 010565/ 110665
Carnforth: 240865 (13.03 Workington-Manchester Victoria)
Newton Heath: 031065
12C Barrow: 171065
12B Carlisle Upperby: 020466
9A Longsight: 310766/ 070866
10A Carnforth: 081066/ 151066
12D Workington: 121166
Carnforth: 281266 (down freight)
12B Carlisle Upperby: 060167/ 070167/ 080167
12D Workington: 110267/ 260367
Carlisle: 010467
Shap: 010467 (freight)
12B Carlisle Upperby: 090467/ 200567
9C Reddish: 250667
10A Carnforth: 040867
12D Workington: 190867
Shap: 260867 (Newcastle-Blackpool)
10A Carnforth: 160967
12B Carlisle Upperby: 071067/ 081067/ 211067/ 241067/ 281067/ 291067
12D Workington: 191167
10A Carnforth: 031267
12C Barrow: 101267
Workington: 161267 (freight)
9C Reddish: Late-1267
12A Carlisle Kingmoor (Diesel): 100268 (D5712/9 towed in by Stanier 8F 48272)/ 110468/ 130468/ 150468/ 180468. Not listed 250268.
9C Reddish: 280468/ 030568/ 050568/ 120568/ 260568/ 300568/ 020668. Not listed 070668.
Crewe Works: 090668 (Arrival Sidings)
Dillicar: 150668 (ballast train for Carlisle)
12A Carlisle Kingmoor (Diesel): 100868/ 250868

Withdrawn: w/e 070968 (D10).

12A Carlisle Kingmoor (Diesel): 060968 (Etterby Road)/ 080968
12A Carlisle Kingmoor (unspecified): 091068. Not listed 300968.
12A Carlisle Kingmoor (Steam): 241068/ 071268/ 311268/ 040169/ 110169

Carlisle Kingmoor Yard: 020469/ 030569/ 120569/ 260569/ 060769/ 050869/ 200869/ 210869/ 230869/ 240869/ 040969/ 190969/ 200969/ 221069
Carlisle Yard to Great Bridge: 171169
J. Cashmore Ltd, Great Bridge: xx1169

Disposal: J. Cashmore Ltd, Great Bridge - 1169 (D&ELfS).

Annual mileages (EHC):

	1958	1959	1960	1961	1962	1963	Total
D5712	-	34891	3456	17	31736	44795	114,895

Notes:
1. 'On a recent visit to Bowesfield works D5712/3 were in the paint shop, D5714-8 were in the erecting shop and the body of D5719 was outside.' (RO0359)
2. S(u): 12/12/60 [Crossed out, with note 'See - W.E. 4/2/61 'Awaiting Works''] (EHC).
3. S(u): 20/03/61-17/07/61 (EHC).
4. Dragged Carlisle Kingmoor (steam) depot to Carlisle Marshalling Yard February 1969. (A. Whitaker)
5. 'Disposal details of the following locomotives are still not known . . . Preston Division (Carlisle): D5712 (9/68)' (RO0471)
6. Why was D5712's transfer to J. Cashmore, Great Bridge delayed by two months compared with D5701/2/6-8/11/4/6/7/9.

D5713

D5713, Morecambe, 25 August 1962.
(Author's Collection)

Bowesfield Works: 100259 (P.Shop)

New: 040359

St Pancras: 170459 (16.25 St Pancras-Manchester Central) (with D5700)
Leicester: 220559 (XX-St Pancras, 12.36 ex-Leicester) (with D5712)
66A Polmadie: 300559
Stirling: 080859 (southbound passenger)
St Pancras: 030959 (passenger) (with D57xx)

XX: 211259 (04.20 St Pancras-Manchester Central) (with D5708)
Derby Works: Nil. EHC: Derby: 291259-010160 NC (34739).
Derby Works: 110160
Derby Works: 160360 (Klondyke Sidings)/ 270360/ 130460 (Paint Shop)/ 160560/ 290560. Not listed 130260/ 280260, 240460 and 140660. EHC: Derby: 110360-100660 NC (38363).
66A Polmadie: 030760
17A Derby: 270860/ 280860. Not listed 070860.

9B Stockport Edgeley: 041260 (with D5703)
9E Trafford Park: 260261/ 260361/ 090461/ 160461.
Not listed 180661.

Metro-Vick, Dukinfield: Nil. EHC: Dukinfield: 190661-150362 HC (41005).

To 12B: 030262.

12E Barrow: 150762/ 290762
Morecambe: 250862
24L Carnforth: 110563
12E Barrow: 150663
12F Workington: 280763
Chinley South Jct: 040164 (Northwich-Tunstead empty ICI limestone hoppers)
Preston: 290264 (13.03 Workington-Manchester Victoria)
Preston: 070364 (09.50 Manchester Victoria-Workington)
Preston: 200364 (13.03 Workington-Manchester Victoria)
Preston: 100464 (09.50 Manchester Victoria-Workington)
12C Barrow: 090564
Preston: 300564 (09.50 Manchester Victoria-Workington)
Preston: 150664 (13.03 Workington-Manchester Victoria)
12C Barrow: 050764
Preston: 110764 (09.50 Manchester Victoria-Workington)
Preston: 030864 (09.50 Manchester Victoria-Workington)
Preston: 040864 ('Lakes Express', piloting A1 60131, from Preston)
12C Barrow: 300864

Lancaster: 031064 (10.53 Workington-Euston passenger)
Preston: 101064 (09.50 Manchester Victoria-Workington)
12C Barrow: 200265/ 010565/ 110665/ 010865 (bodyside accident damage, S[u])/ 110865/ 150865/ 171065/ 280266/ 060866/ 070866/ 280866/ 300866/ 121166
Crewe Works: 080167 (Side of Works)/ 220167/ 050267/ 120267/ 190267. Not listed 181266, and 050367.
Warrington Dallam: xxxx67 (Stanier 5MT 45135 hauling D5713/10/04/09).
12B Carlisle Upperby: 260367/ 290367/ 090467/ 220467/ 200567/ 100667/ 160667/ 180667/ 250667/ 280667/ 290767/ 020867/ 030867/ 080867/ 190867/ 081067/ 211067/ 241067/ 261067/ 291067/ 191167/ 081267/ 101267/ 181267. Not listed 070867/ 300967/ 021067/ 281067.

Withdrawn: w/e 301267 (12B).

12B Carlisle Upperby: 020168/ 060168/ 270168 (minus engine)/ 280168/ 100268/ 250268/ 170368/ 110468/ 130468/ 150468/ 180468/ 110568/ 060668/ 150668/ 210668/ 200768/ 270768/ 100868/ 250868/ 060968/ 080968
Despatched from Carlisle to Shettleston: 110968 (with D5709/10)
J. MacWilliam, Shettleston: 061068 (intact)

Disposal: J. MacWilliam, Shettleston 0968-1168 (D&ELfS).

Annual mileages (EHC):

	1958	1959	1960	1961	1962	1963	Total
D5713	-	34739	6266	0	37484	35973	114,463

Notes:
1. See 'Additional Note' No.1 for D5712.
2. S(u): 12/12/60 [Crossed out, with note 'See - W.E. 4/2/61 'Awaiting Works''] (EHC).
3. S(u): 20/03/61-19/06/61 (EHC).
4. S(u): 30/11/64 (with no reinstatement date) (EHC).
5. Sold for scrap (September 1968): J. MacWilliam, Shettleston: D5709/10/3 (from Carlisle). (RO1168)

Individual Locomotive Histories • 105

D5714

D5714, 17A Derby, 30 April 1960. (*Colour-Rail*)

D5714, 10A Carnforth, 13 July 1968. Serif numbers. (*Clinton Shaw*)

Bowesfield Works: 100259 (E.Shop: under construction)

New: 110359

Derby Works: 150359 (Yard)/ 120459/ 140459 (Diesel Erecting Shop)/ 150459 (Diesel Shop, under repair).
EHC: Derby: 250359-200459 LC (3783).
XX: 240459 (London-Derby/Derby-London special)
Buxton: 280459 (11.47 Buxton-Manchester Central)
17A Derby: 310559
Great Rocks: 240659 (passenger)
St Pancras: 140859 (St Pancras-XX) (with D5711)
St Pancras: 210859 (16.25 St Pancras-Manchester Central) (with D5711)
St Pancras: 061059 (16.25 St Pancras-Manchester Central) (with D5704)
Manchester Central: 091159 (10.25 Manchester Central-St Pancras) (with D5707)
Derby Works: Nil. EHC: Derby: 181259-291259 NC (37761).
Derby: 070160 (04.20 St Pancras-Manchester Central) (with D5704)
14A Cricklewood: 120360/ 130360
Cricklewood-Norwood (SR): 040460 (for trials)
Three Bridges/Balcombe Tunnel: 06-070460 (trials)
Three Bridges-Cricklewood: 070460
66A Polmadie: 170460
17A Derby: 300460/ 290560
Manchester Central: 060660 (10.25 Manchester Central-St Pancras) (with D5709)
14A Cricklewood: 210760
17A Derby: 280860
St Pancras: 010960 (16.35 St Pancras-Derby) (with D5716)
17A Derby: 120261/ 260261. Not listed 070860/ 270860.
XX (Midland lines, London area): 290361 (freight)
66A Polmadie: 020461
16A Toton: 140561
17A Derby: 250661/ 130861/ 240961.
Hauled from Derby to Dukinfield: 201061

Metro-Vick, Dukinfield: 201061. EHC: Dukinfield: 221061-081162 HC (88852).

To 12B: 030262.

12F Workington: 111162
XX: 21-230563 (Tunstead-Northwich ICI limestone train trials) (with D5711)
Preston: 070364 (13.03 Workington-Manchester Victoria)
Preston: 100464 (10.53 Workington-Euston) (to Preston)

12C Barrow: 090564
Carnforth: 050664 (18.50 Heysham-Whitehaven Fina tanks)
Preston: 100664 (09.50 Manchester Victoria-Workington)
Preston: 110664 (13.03 Workington-Manchester Victoria)
XX: 260764 (damaged by fire, location unknown) (FDTL)
12C Barrow: 300864
Crewe Works: 101064 (Traverser Area)/ 181064/ 011164/ 151164 (E.Shop)/ 131264 (E.Shop)/ 201264 (E.Shop) . Not listed 041064 and 291164.
5A Crewe: 030165(ex-works)
Crewe Works: 070165/ 230165 (P.Shop)/ 240165.
Not listed 070265.
Carnforth: 070665 (10.53 Workington-Euston)
Crewe Works: 161065/ 171065 (Arr. Sdgs)/ 311065/ 011165/ 071165 (P.Shop Yard)/ 141165 (Test Area).
Not listed 101065 and 051265.
12D Workington: 270266
10A Carnforth: 110466
12B Carlisle Upperby: 010566
12D Workington: 070566
12C Barrow: 310566 (damaged by fire in depot roof blaze)
12B Carlisle Upperby: 080766/ 090766/ 100766
Crewe Works: 240766 (E.Shop Yard)/ 310766/ 070866 (E.Shop)/ 140866/ 110966 (E.Shop)/ 180966. Not listed 021066.
10A Carnforth: 151066
Grange-over-Sands: 181066 (Carnforth-Barrow freight)
12D Workington: 121166
12B Carlisle Upperby: 080167
9C Reddish: 190367
Askam: 080667 (Barrow-Workington-Barrow freight)
12B Carlisle Upperby: 100667
12D Workington: 180667
XX: 260667 (05.20 Carlisle-Hardendale freight, failed, rescued by Britannia 70024)
12B Carlisle Upperby: 280667
10A Carnforth: 020767/ 150767/ 040867/ 050867
12C Barrow: 310867
12D Workington: 310867
10A Carnforth: 130967
12B Carlisle Upperby: 081067/ 281067/ 291067.
Not listed 071067.
10A Carnforth: 181167
12D Workington: 101267
12B Carlisle Upperby: 181267
Lancaster: 231267

10A Carnforth: 301267/ 210168
9C Reddish: 020268/ 150268
16A Toton: End-0368
12A Carlisle Kingmoor (Diesel): 120468
Carlisle New Yard: 150468
10A Carnforth: 150668/ 160668
Carnforth: 090768 (freight)/ 100768 (freight)
10A Carnforth: 130768/ 210768/ 270768/ 280768/ 290768/ 300768 (out of use)/ 010868
9C Reddish: 040868
10A Carnforth: 140868
12D Workington: 240868

Withdrawn: w/e 070968 (D10).

12A Carlisle Kingmoor (Steam): 300968/ 241068/ 071268/ 311268/ 040169/ 110169. Not listed 060968.
Carlisle Kingmoor Yard: 020469/ 120569/ 260569/ 060769/ 050869/ 200869/ 210869/ 230869/ 240869/ 040969
Carlisle Yard to Great Bridge (booked transfer): 180969 (with D5719)
J. Cashmore Ltd, Great Bridge: xx1169

Disposal: J. Cashmore Ltd, Great Bridge - 0969 (D&ELfS).

Annual mileages (EHC):

	1958	1959	1960	1961	1962	1963	Total
D5714	-	39230	40539	9083	5054	50464	144,370

Notes:
1. See 'Additional Note' No.1 for D5712.
2. 'A visitor to Derby Works on February 5th [1961] . . . Yet more of the Metrovick Type 2 Co-Bos, Nos. D5701/6/15/7, were stored outside Derby depot, making a total of 13 of this class inactive, but Nos. D5700/5/14/8 were observed at work.' (TI0461)
3. S(u): 19/05/61-28/10/61 (EHC).
4. S(u): 28/09/65-18/10/65 (EHC).
5. Dragged Carlisle Kingmoor (steam) depot to Carlisle Marshalling Yard February 1969. (A. Whitaker)

108 • THE METROPOLITAN-VICKERS TYPE 2 CO-BO DIESEL-ELECTRIC LOCOMOTIVES

D5715

D5715, 17A Derby, 30 April 1960. (*Colour-Rail*)

D5715, Crewe Works (Paint Shop Yard), 12 February 1967. (*Eric Sawford [Transport Treasury]*)

Bowesfield Works: 100259 (E.Shop: under construction)

New: 080459

Derby Works: Nil. EHC: Derby: 150459-010559 LC (651).
17A Derby: 150459
66A Polmadie: 150559 (booked for 17.30 Glasgow St.Enoch-Carlisle pass) (with D5708)
17A Derby: 310559
St Pancras: 140759 (16.25 St Pancras-Manchester Central) (with D5716)
Kilnhurst: 050859
Dore & Totley: 050859 (12.43 Newcastle-Bristol passenger)
Derby: 231059 (04.20 St Pancras-Manchester Central) (with D5709)
St Pancras: 031159 (16.25 St Pancras-Manchester Central) (with D5701)
Manchester Central: 071159 (10.25 Manchester Central-St Pancras) (with D5709)
Derby Works: Nil. EHC: Derby: 231259-261259 NC (34758).
14A Cricklewood: 120360/ 130360
Derby Works: 270360. Not listed 240460.
17A Derby: 300460
Derby Works: 140660
Mill Hill: 040760 ('Condor', with D5700)
66A Polmadie: 310760
Beattock: 020860
Ampthill: 241260 (up special) (with D5701)
XX: 170161 ('Condor')
17A Derby: 050261/ 120261/ 260261
XX: 140461 ('Condor') (with D5706)
17A Derby: 140561/ 250661/ 130861/ 240961. Not listed 070561.
Hauled from Derby to Dukinfield: 191061

Metro-Vick, Dukinfield: 201061 EHC: Dukinfield: 161061-280363 HC (73259).

To 12B: 030262.

Preston: 150463
Green Road : 030563 (Manchester Victoria-Workington passenger)
24L Carnforth: 110563
12F Workington: 150663
Penrith: 270763 (guards vans)
12F Workington: 280763
Preston: 110863 (stabled)

12C Barrow: 090564
Preston: 150564 (06.10 Heysham-Manchester Victoria)/ 09.50 Manchester Victoria-Workington)
Preston: 260664 (09.50 Manchester Victoria-Workington)
Carnforth/Preston: 150864 (13.03 Workington-Manchester Victoria)
Barrow: 270864 (10.53 Workington-Euston) (to Preston)
Silverdale: 240964 (Barrow-Manchester Victoria passenger)
Preston: 031064 (09.50 Manchester Victoria-Workington)
12D Workington: 111064
12C Barrow: 200265
Crewe Works: 090565/ 160565 (E.Shop)/ 230565 (E.Shop)/ 060665 (E.Shop)/ 200665 (E.Shop)/ 270665 (E.Shop)/ 250765 (E.Shop)/ 050865/ 220865 (Test Roads)/ 120965 (Test Roads). Not listed 250465, 100765 and 190965.
Lancaster: 091065 (13.03 Workington-Manchester Victoria)
10A Carnforth: 171065
Crewe Works: 160166 (Works Yard)/ 300166 (E.Shop Yard)/ 130266 (E.Shop Yard)/ 270266 (Traverser Area)/ 060366 (Minor Repair Roads)/ 130366 (Works Yard)/ 200366 (Works Yard)/ 270366 (Arr.Sidings)/ 030466 (E.Shop)/ 240466 (P.Shop Yard)/ 290566 (E.Shop). Not listed 020166, 080566 and 050666.
Carlisle: 020766 (13.55 (SO) Stranraer-Newcastle (from Carlisle)
12B Carlisle Upperby: 080766/ 090766
12C Barrow: 280866
Dalston Road: 100966 (freight, with D5701)
XX: 200966 (damaged by fire, location unknown) (FDTL)
12D Workington: 081066
XX: 281066 (damaged by fire, location unknown) (FDTL)
Crewe Works: 111266 (Traverser Area)/ 181266 (Electric Traction Shop Yard)/ 080167 (Traverser Area)/ 220167/ 050267/ 120267. Not listed 201166 and 190267.
12B Carlisle Upperby: 260367
Askam: 080667 (04.10 Corkickle-Heysham tanks)
10A Carnforth: 110667
Hay Fell (north of Oxenholme): 120667 (hauled by Standard 4MT 75024, with D5717)
12B Carlisle Upperby: 160667/ 180667/280667
9C Reddish: 160767/ 010867
Crewe Works: 020867/ 060867
12C Barrow: 190867
10A Carnforth: 171067
12B Carlisle Upperby: 081267/ 101267

12A Carlisle Kingmoor (Steam): 020168/ 060168
12A Carlisle Kingmoor (Diesel): 270168 (workshop)/ 280168/ 100268
Crewe Works: 070468/ 210468/ 280468 (Works Yard). Not listed 310368.
Crewe North Sidings: 040568

Withdrawn: w/e 040568 (12A).

12A Carlisle Kingmoor (Diesel): 110568
Crewe Works: 090668 (Arr.Sdgs). Not listed 190568.

12A Carlisle Kingmoor (Diesel): 150668 ('nearby')
Crewe North Sidings: 230668/ 100768/ 210768/ 040868/ 140868
Transfer Crewe DD to Carlisle: 150868
12A Carlisle Kingmoor (Diesel): 250868
12A Carlisle Kingmoor (Steam): 060968/080968/ 300968/ 241068
J. MacWilliam, Shettleston: Nil. Not listed 061068.

Disposal: J. MacWilliam, Shettleston 1168 (D&ELfS). Not proven.

Annual mileages (EHC):

	1958	1959	1960	1961	1962	1963	Total
D5715	-	35452	25995	11812	78	42509	115,846

Notes:
1. See 'Additional Note' No.1 for D5712.
2. A traction display was held in Great Howard Street Yard, Liverpool in mid-1959 organised by a railway trade group; D5715 attended .
3. 'A visitor to Derby Works on February 5th [1961] . . . Yet more of the Metrovick Type 2 Co-Bos, Nos. D5701/6/15/7, were stored outside Derby depot, making a total of 13 of this class inactive, but Nos. D5700/5/14/8 were observed at work.' (TI0461)
4. 'On 27th January [1968] . . . Dumped at Kingmoor were . . . D5703/9/10/3. In the adjacent workshop were D5704/15.' (RO0468)
5. 'Disposal details of the following locomotives are still not known . . . Preston Division (Carlisle): . . D5715 (5/68).' (RO0471)
6. 'Regarding the list in the April R.O., the following have been reported as sold: J. McWilliam, Shettleston: October 1968: 5715 [from Carlisle].' (RO1071)

Individual Locomotive Histories • 111

D5716

D5716, 66A Polmadie, 13 September 1959. (*Transport Treasury*)

112 • THE METROPOLITAN-VICKERS TYPE 2 CO-BO DIESEL-ELECTRIC LOCOMOTIVES

D5716, Crewe Works (Erecting Shop Yard), 1 November 1964. Serif numbers. (Arnold W. Battson [Transport Treasury])

D5716, Crewe Diesel Depot, 6 December 1964. (Mark Hoofe)

Bowesfield Works: 100259 (E.Shop: under construction)

New: 130559

Bedford: 180559 (St Pancras-Manchester Central passenger)
XX: 190559 (13.15 St Pancras-Bradford passenger [to Leicester]) (piloting 'Jubilee' 45694)
St Pancras: 220559 (16.25 St Pancras-Manchester Central) (with D5701)
17A Derby: 310559
Kilnhurst: 090759
St Pancras: 140759 (16.25 St Pancras-Manchester Central) (with D5715)
St Pancras: 040959 (16.25 St Pancras-Manchester Central) (with D5701)
66A Polmadie: 130959
Derby Works: 171259 (Diesel Erecting Shop). Not listed 141159 (SBUK). EHC: Derby: 101259-181259 NC (30149).
17A Derby: 170160
Derby Works: 110160/ 110260 (Diesel Finishing Shop)/ 270360/ 130460 (Works Yard). Not listed 130260 and 240460.
17A Derby: 290560
Mill Hill: 040760 (parcels)
14A Cricklewood: 210760
66A Polmadie: 140860
17A Derby: 280860. Not listed 270860.
St Pancras: 010960 (16.35 St Pancras-Derby) (with D5714)
Trowell: 091060 (freight test train with 16t mineral wagons to Brent) (with D5710)
Manchester Central: 181160 (14.25 Manchester Central-St Pancras) (with Jubilee 45568)
Derby Works: 220161 (Works Sidings)/ 120261 (Works Yard)/ 260261 (by station, in store)/ 260361
17A Derby: 140561/ 250661/ 130861/ 240961. Not listed 300461/ 070561.
Hauled from Derby to Dukinfield: 201061

Metro-Vick, Dukinfield: 201061. EHC: Dukinfield: 181061-051062 HC (63647).

To 12B: 030262.

Cark: 060563 (09.46 Lancaster-Barrow)
12F Workington: 280763
En route Carnforth-Lancaster: 110863

Bolton: 290963 (09.50 Manchester Victoria-Barrow)
Preston: 110164 (09.50 Manchester Victoria-Workington)
Preston: 290264 (09.50 Manchester Victoria-Workington)
Crewe Works: 250364 (Yard). Not listed 010364 and 310364.
Preston: 300564 (13.03 Workington-Manchester Victoria/ 21.05 Manchester Victoria-Heysham)
Preston: 040764 (13.03 Workington-Manchester Victoria)
12C Barrow: 110764
Crewe Works: 120864 (Works Yard)/ 150864/ 010964/ 270964 (E.Shop)/ 041064 (E.Shop)/ 101064 (E.Shop)/ 181064/ 011164 (E.Shop Yard, repainted)/ 081164 (P.Shop Yard, repainted)/ 151164 (P.Shop Area)/ 291164 (P.Shop Yard). Not listed 260764, 160864/ 300864/ 130964/ 200964.
Crewe Diesel Depot: 061264
Carnforth: 300765 (13.03 Workington-Manchester Victoria) (with D5701)
Grange-over-Sands: 100865 (down passenger)
12C Barrow: 150865
12B Carlisle Upperby: 251065
Crewe Works: 311065/ 011165/ 071165 (P.Shop Yard)/ 141165 (Traverser Area)/ 051265 (Arr.Sdgs)/ 020166 (Arr.Sdgs)/ 160166 (Works Yard)/ 300166 (Test Roads)/ 130266 (Test Roads).
Preston: 190266 (down light engine)
12B Carlisle Upperby: 090466/ 100466
Carlisle: 130466 (freight)
10A Carnforth: 280466
Barrow: 180666 (14.35 Barrow-Manchester Victoria)
Sandside Quarry: 200666
10A Carnforth: 060866
12C Barrow: 070866
12B Carlisle Upperby: 070866
12C Barrow: 121166
9A Longsight: 140167/ 220167
Carlisle Durranhill: 270567
12B Carlisle Upperby: 100667
Carnforth: 230667 (parcels)
10A Carnforth: 240667
Carlisle Citadel: 290767
Dillicar: 290767 (passenger)
XX: 110867 (damaged by fire, location unknown) (FDTL)
12D Workington: 190867
12B Carlisle Upperby: 230967/ 021067/ 071067/ 081067. Not listed 300967.
9C Reddish: 031167/ 251167
12B Carlisle Upperby: 181267

10A Carnforth: 060168
12A Carlisle Kingmoor (Diesel): 280168
9C Reddish: 150268
10A Carnforth: 060468/ 070468
Carlisle New Yard: 150468
Hest Bank: 050668 (parcels)
Carnforth: 060668 (Plumpton Jct-Heysham tanks)
10A Carnforth: 200768/ 210768
12A Carlisle Kingmoor (Diesel): 290768
12D Workington: 240868
10A Carnforth: 310868

Withdrawn: w/e 070968 (D10).

Annual mileages (EHC):

	1958	1959	1960	1961	1962	1963	Total
D5716	-	30149	33267	231	10709	49330	123,686

12A Carlisle Kingmoor (Steam): 060968 (stored)/ 080968/ 300968/ 241068
12A Carlisle Kingmoor (Diesel): 071268/ 081268
12A Carlisle Kingmoor (Steam): 311268/ 030169/ 040169/ 110169
Carlisle Kingmoor Yard: 020469/ 120569/ 260569/ 060769/ 050869/ 200869/ 210869/ 230869/ 240869/ 040969
Carlisle Yard to Great Bridge (booked transfer): 170969 (with D5717)
J. Cashmore Ltd, Great Bridge: Nil. Not noted xx1169.

Disposal: J. Cashmore Ltd, Great Bridge - 0969-1269 (D&ELfS). Not proven.

Notes:
1. See 'Additional Note' No.1 for D5712.
2. 'On Friday 3rd November, 1967 D5716 ran light to Reddish for a general overhaul.' (BWTE11)
3. Dragged Carlisle Kingmoor (steam) depot to Carlisle Marshalling Yard February 1969. (A. Whitaker)

Individual Locomotive Histories • 115

D5717

D5717, 17A Derby, Undated but presumably circa June 1959. Ex-works condition with the bogie frames and grilles still exhibiting the original light grey paintwork. Compare the condition of D5717 with D5702 behind which had been in traffic nine months by this time, or, with the photograph of D5717 below five months later!
(*T. Smith [Transport Treasury]*)

D5717, 17A Derby, 4 November 1959.
(*Author's Collection*)

116 • THE METROPOLITAN-VICKERS TYPE 2 CO-BO DIESEL-ELECTRIC LOCOMOTIVES

D5717, 12D Workington, June 1964 (*Rail Image Collections*).

Bowesfield Works: 100259 (E.Shop: under construction)

New: 080659

Suffolk Street Yard, Birmingham (exhibition): 170659
Derby: 140759 (10.25 Manchester Central-St Pancras) (with D5702)
Derby Works: 160859/ 170859 (Works Yard)/ 200859.
Not listed 190959.
14A Cricklewood: 041059
17A Derby: 041159

Derby Works: Nil. EHC: Derby: 181259-291259 NC (22532).
St Pancras: 010160 (16.25 St Pancras-Manchester Central) (with D5704)
Derby Works: 110160
14A Cricklewood: 120360/ 130360
66A Polmadie: 170460
Derby: 160560 (07.25 Manchester Central-St Pancras) (with D5718)
Derby Works: Nil. EHC: Derby: 200660-010760 NC (40341). Not listed 030760.
17A Derby: 080760 (turntable incident)/ 070860

Derby Works: 120860 (Diesel Shop)/ 130860/ 150860 (Diesel Shop)/ 270860/ 280860/ 040960 (Diesel Repair Shop)/ 250960. Not listed 231060. EHC: Derby: 170760-201060 LC (40924).
Leicester: 311060 (07.25 Manchester Central St Pancras/ 14.25 St Pancras-Manchester passenger) (with D5711)
14A Cricklewood: 220161
17A Derby: 050261/ 120261/ 260261/ 140561/ 250661/ 130861/ 240961. Not listed 300461/ 070561.
Hauled from Derby to Dukinfield: 201061

Metro-Vick, Dukinfield: 201061 EHC: Dukinfield: 161061-230163 HC (56719).

To 12B: 030262.

12F Workington: 110563
12E Barrow: 150663
Windermere/Lakeside: 060763 (passenger)
12E Barrow: 160863
12C Barrow: 290963
Crewe Works: 090264 (E.Shop)/ 150264 (E.Shop)/ 230264 (E.Shop, for storage)/ 010364/ 250364 (E.Shop)/ 310364/ 010464 (E.Shop)/ 050464
5B Crewe South: 060464
Crewe Works: 070464/ 120464 (Electric Traction Shop Yard)/ 180464 (Yard; in store)/ 250464/ 260464 (Electric Traction Shop Yard)/ 030564 (Outside P.Shop). Not listed 100564. EHC: Crewe: 270164-020564 Unscheduled (-).
Wigan: 070564
Forton: 220864 (10.53 Workington-Euston passenger)
Morecambe South Jct: 290864 (Lancaster-Barrow passenger)
Carnforth: 290864 (Barrow-Morecambe)
Preston: 050964 (09.50 Manchester Victoria-Workington)
XX: xx0365 (cross-London freight trials)
Crewe Works: 060665 (Diesel Test Roads). Not listed 300565.
12D Workington: 200665
12C Barrow: 010865/ 110865/ 150865
Carnforth: 070466 (piloting Stanier 5MT on passenger ex-Barrow)
12D Workington: 100466
XX: 020566 (damaged by fire, location unknown) (FDTL)
12B Carlisle Upperby: 070566
Crewe Works: 050666/ 120666/ 190666/ 260666 (In store)/ 240766 (E.Shop)/ 310766/ 070866 (E.Shop)/ 140866/ 110966 (Test Roads)/ 180966/ 021066. Not listed 290566 and 091066.
10A Carnforth: 071166/ 121166
Crewe Works: 111266 (Test Area)/ 181266 (Works Yard). Not listed 201166.
12D Workington: 090167
Barrow: 08-090267 (assisted 23.10 Preston-Barrow d.m.u. from Ulverston to Barrow)
12D Workington: 260367/ 070567
12B Carlisle Upperby: 200567
10A Carnforth: 110667
Hay Fell (north of Oxenholme): 120667 (hauled by Standard 4MT 75024, with D5715)
12B Carlisle Upperby: 160667
12E Tebay: 170667(morning, gone by late afternoon)
12B Carlisle Upperby: 180667
Crewe Works: 020867/ 060867/ 160867/ 200867 (Works Yard & Test Area)/ 230867/ 270867 (Arr.Sdgs). Not listed 100967.
12B Carlisle Upperby: 081067/ 281067/ 291067. Not listed 071067.
10A Carnforth: 091267/ 101267
12A Carlisle Kingmoor (Diesel): 280168
10A Carnforth: 250268/ 200468/ 240568
Ulverston/Ravenglass: 260568 (SLS 'Ravenglass & Eskdale' Railtour - Ulverston-Ravenglass/Ravenglass-Carnforth F&M Jct., after D316 failed)
12A Carlisle Kingmoor (Diesel): 150668
Bare Lane: 170668 (guards van)
10A Carnforth: 290668
12A Carlisle Kingmoor (Diesel): 270768
10A Carnforth: 140868
Carlisle New Yard (North): 250868

Withdrawn: w/e 070968 (D10).

12A Carlisle Kingmoor (Steam): 060968 (stored)/ 080968/ 300968/ 241068/ 071268/ 311268/ 040169/ 110169
Carlisle Kingmoor Yard: 020469/ 030569/ 120569/ 260569/ 060769/ 050869/ 200869/ 210869/ 230869/ 240869/ 040969
Carlisle Yard to Great Bridge (booked transfer): 170969 (with D5716)
J. Cashmore Ltd, Great Bridge: Nil. Not noted xx1169.

Disposal: J. Cashmore Ltd, Great Bridge - 0969-1169 (D&ELfS). Not proven.

Annual mileages (EHC):

	1958	1959	1960	1961	1962	1963	Total
D5717	-	23602	30409	2708	94	47637	104,450

Notes:
1. See 'Additional Note' No.1 for D5712.
2. 'A visitor to Derby Works on February 5th [1961] . . . Yet more of the Metrovick Type 2 Co-Bos, Nos. D5701/6/15/7, were stored outside Derby depot, making a total of 13 of this class inactive, but Nos. D5700/5/14/8 were observed at work.' (TI0461)
3. First Class 28 shopped at Crewe Works.
4. Dragged Carlisle Kingmoor (steam) depot to Carlisle Marshalling Yard February 1969. (A. Whitaker)

Individual Locomotive Histories • 119

D5718

D5718, 17A Derby, 30 April 1960. *(Colour-Rail)*

D5718, 10A Carnforth, 6 September 1963.
(*Noel A. Machell*)

Bowesfield Works: 100259 (E.Shop: under construction)

New: 070759

Kilnhurst: 070759
St Pancras: 280859 (16.25 St Pancras-Manchester Central) (with D5702)
Derby Works: 171259 (Yard). Not listed 141159 and 140160. EHC: Derby: 171259-181259 NC (19351).
14A Cricklewood: 140260
Derby Works: 130360 (Works Yard)/ 160360 (Klondyke Sidings)/ 270360/ 130460 (Works Yard)/ 240460. EHC: Derby: 160260-280460 LC (23281).
17A Derby: 300460
St Pancras: 090560 (St Pancras-Manchester Central) (with D5710)
St Pancras: 100560 (16.25 St Pancras-Manchester Central) (with D5710)
Derby: 160560 (07.25 Manchester Central-St Pancras) (with D5717)

Derby Works: 030760/ 070860/ 120860 (Diesel Test House)/ 130860/ 150860 (Test House)/ 270860/ 280860/ 040960 (Diesel Repair Shop)/ 250960. Not listed 290560/ 140660 and 231060. EHC: Derby: 170760-171060 LC (33161).
XX: 261060 (piloting steam loco on down 'Palatine')
Leicester: 121260 (07.20 Manchester Central-St Pancras) (with D5701)
17A Derby: 120261/ 260261/ 140561/ 250661/ 130861/ 240961. Not listed 300461/ 070561.
Hauled from Derby to Dukinfield: 201061

Metro-Vick, Dukinfield: 201061. EHC: Dukinfield: 221061-271162 HC (36590).

To 12B: 030262.

9G Gorton: 111162
12E Barrow: 150663
24L Carnforth: 100763/ 060963
Preston: 210264 (09.50 Manchester Victoria-Workington

Crewe Works: 060464. Not listed 010464.
Preston: 070464 (09.50 Manchester Victoria-Workington)
Preston: 100464 (13.03 Workington-Manchester Victoria)
Preston: 240464 (13.03 Workington-Manchester Victoria)
10A Carnforth: 060664
12C Barrow: 050764/ 110764
Preston: 250764 (13.03 Workington-Manchester Victoria)
Brock (Preston): 200864 (passenger)
12C Barrow: 300864/ 010565
Crewe North: 200665. Not listed at Crewe Works on 060665 and 270665.
10A Carnforth: 070865
12D Workington: 110865
10A Carnforth: 171065
12C Barrow: 280266
Arnside: 020466 (Barrow-Carnforth freight)
12D Workington: 100466
Grange-over-Sands: 260666 (freight)
12D Workington: 060766
12C Barrow: 060866/ 280866
Crewe Works: 091066 (E.Shop)/ 161066 (E.Shop)/ 231066/ 301066 (E.Shop)/ 061166 (E.Shop)/ 131166 (E.Shop)/ 201166 (E.Shop)/ 111266 (E.Shop)/ 181266 (Test Roads). Not listed 021066.
10A Carnforth: 070167
12C Barrow: 090167
10A Carnforth: 260367
12B Carlisle Upperby: 070567
12D Workington: 180667
12E Tebay: 270667
12D Workington: 270667

12B Carlisle Upperby: 280667
Arnside: 020767
12D Workington: 060767
Ravenglass: 070767 (Workington-Barrow freight)
10A Carnforth: 050867
12B Carlisle Upperby: 190867
12D Workington: 220867
12C Barrow: 310867
9C Reddish: 220967
12C Barrow: 011067
10A Carnforth: 071067
12B Carlisle Upperby: 081067
10A Carnforth: 261067
12B Carlisle Upperby: 291067
10A Carnforth: 181167/ 091267
12D Workington: 060168
12A Carlisle Kingmoor (Diesel): 280168
10A Carnforth: 140268/ 240268/ 250268/ 170368/ 220468
Scout Green: 020568 (banking D342 on mail vans)

Withdrawn: w/e 040568 (12A).

12A Carlisle Kingmoor (Steam): 110568/ 060668/ 150668/ 200768/ 270768. Not listed 210668.
12A Carlisle Kingmoor (Diesel): 100868/ 250868
12A Carlisle Kingmoor (Steam): 060968/ 080968/ 300968
J. MacWilliam, Shettleston: 061068 (being cut-up, completed by 201068)

Disposal: J. MacWilliam, Shettleston 0968 (D&ELfS).

Annual mileages (EHC):

	1958	1959	1960	1961	1962	1963	Total
D5718	-	20879	15485	226	4968	51188	92,746

Notes:
1. See 'Additional Note' No.1 for D5712.
2. 'A visitor to Derby Works on February 5th [1961] . . . Yet more of the Metrovick Type 2 Co-Bos, Nos. D5701/6/15/7, were stored outside Derby depot, making a total of 13 of this class inactive, but Nos. D5700/5/14/8 were observed at work.' (TI0461)
3. S(u): 10/04/61-28/10/61 (EHC).
4. 'Scout Green – Thursday May 2, 1968. D5718 banked D342 on mail vans.' (*Traction Annual* 2010/11). Previously unknown for Metrovicks to be used on Shap banking duties. Was D5718 actually DIT ('dead-in-tow') from Carnforth to Carlisle and ultimate withdrawal?
5. Movements between Kingmoor Steam and Diesel depots, presumably to facilitate spares recovery for other class members.

122 • THE METROPOLITAN-VICKERS TYPE 2 CO-BO DIESEL-ELECTRIC LOCOMOTIVES

D5719

D5719, 12E Barrow, 8 September 1963. Note the 12E depot code on the buffer beam. The following day the code for Barrow changed from 12E to 12C. *(Stewart Blencowe)*

D5719 (with Standard 2MT 2-6-2T 84021), Crewe Works, 14 June 1964. (*N. Skinner*)

Bowesfield Works: 100259 (E.Shop Yard: bodyshell)
Ripon: xx1059

New: 131059

Derby Works: 151059 (just arrived)
Derby: 211059 (04.20 St Pancras-Manchester Central) (with D5704)
Derby: 031159 (07.25 Manchester Central-St Pancras) (with D5700)
St Pancras: 211159 (14.25 St Pancras-Manchester Central) (with D5705)
Derby Works: Nil. EHC: Derby: 121259-181259 NC (9963).
Derby Works: 110160
14A Cricklewood: 140260/ 120360/ 130360
Kilnhurst: 190460
Chinley: 210460 (16.00 Derby-Manchester Central passenger)
Derby Works: 160560
17A Derby: 290560/ 270860/ 280860. Not listed 070860/ 120261.
9E Trafford Park: 260261/ 260361/ 090461/ 160461

Metro-Vick, Dukinfield: Nil. EHC: Dukinfield: 130561-211261 HC (22757).

To 12B: w/e 301261 & 030262.

Preston: 291261
12E Barrow: 040262
12F Workington: 150762
12E Barrow: 290762
Carnforth: 060862 (light engine)
Carnforth: 200862
Lancaster: 040663 (passenger ex-Workington)
12C Barrow: 080963
9E Trafford Park: 220963
Crewe Works: 290364/ 310364/ 010464 (Outside E.Shop)/ 050464/ 070464/ 120464 (Electric Traction Shop Yard)/ 180464 (Yards, stored)/ 260464 (Electric Traction Shop Yard)/ 030564 (Erecting Shop)/ 100564 (Electric Traction Shop Yard)/ 140664 (Electric Traction Shop Yard)/ 200664/ 210664 (Electric TractionShop Yard, stored)/ 260764 (Electric Traction Shop Yard)/ 120864 (E.Shop)/ 150864/ 300864 (Test Roads)/

010964. Not listed 250364, 160864 and 130964/ 200964.
EHC: Crewe: 070364-040964 Unscheduled (-).
Skew Bridge: 080964
Preston: 210964 (09.50 Manchester Victoria-Workington)
Preston: 260964 (09.50 Manchester Victoria-Workington)
12C Barrow: 111064
10A Carnforth: 061264
12C Barrow: 200265
10A Carnforth: 160465
Preston: 280465 (failed on Heysham-Manchester boat train near Preston; assisted to to Manchester by Stanier 5MT)
Oldham: 280465 (20.50 Oldham-Carnforth parcels)
12C Barrow: 010565
10A Carnforth: 200665
12D Workington: 240865
12C Barrow: 171065
Crewe Works: 260666 (In store). Not listed 190666 and 240766.
12B Carlisle Upperby: 060866/ 070866/ 140866/ 060167/ 070167/ 080167
12D Workington: 110267
XX: 270367 (1T82 Barrow-Preston relief)
10A Carnforth: 150467
Penrith: 150767 (light engine, with D1850)
9C Reddish: 200567
10A Carnforth: 260667
12C Barrow: 270667
12B Carlisle Upperby: 020867/ 030867
12A Carlisle Kingmoor: 040867

12B Carlisle Upperby: 230967/ 021067/ 241067.
Not listed 300967.
9C Reddish: 251167
12B Carlisle Upperby: 101267
12A Carlisle Kingmoor (Diesel): 100268 (D5712/9 towed in by Stanier 8F 48272).
Not listed 250268.
10A Carnforth: 310368
12A Carlisle Kingmoor (Diesel): 120468/ 130468/ 150468/ 180468/ 110568
Crewe Works: 090668 (Arr.Sdgs)/ 230668.
Not listed 190568 and 210768.
12A Carlisle Kingmoor (Diesel): 270768/ 290768/ 100868/ 250868
9C Reddish: 310868

Withdrawn: w/e 070968 (D10).

12A Carlisle Kingmoor (Steam): 300968/ 241068/ 071268/ 311268/ 030169/ 040169/ 110169.
Not listed 060968.
Carlisle Kingmoor Yard: 020469/ 120569/ 260569/ 060769/ 050869/ 200869/ 210869/ 230869/ 240869/ 040969
Carlisle Yard to Great Bridge (booked transfer): 180969 (with D5714)
J. Cashmore Ltd, Great Bridge: xx1169

Disposal: J. Cashmore Ltd, Great Bridge - 0969 (D&ELfS).

Annual mileages (EHC):

	1958	1959	1960	1961	1962	1963	Total
D5719	-	10997	12524	196	41028	38999	103,744

Notes:
1. See 'Additional Note' No.1 for D5712.
2. S(u): 12/12/60 [Crossed out, with note 'See - W.E. 4/2/61 'Awaiting Works''] (EHC).
3. S(u): 20/03/61-15/05/61 (EHC).
4. 'The next day [29/12/61] D5712 passed light through Preston northbound, presumably on the way to its new sphere of work in Furness.' (MR0262). N.B. Presumably D5719 listed incorrectly.
5. Dragged Carlisle Kingmoor (steam) depot to Carlisle Marshalling Yard February 1969. (A.Whitaker)

Chapter 8
EARLY PERFORMANCE

8.1 General.
The March 1959 edition of *Trains Illustrated* carried a short article entitled 'Talking of Trains: The Diesels Disappoint', which made the statement:

'One of the disappointments of the last few months has been the failure of some of the main line diesels coming into service to make their anticipated impact on operation. Past propaganda has always underlined the diesel's great advantage over the steam locomotive of reliability.'

A proportion of this commentary will have undoubtedly been directed at the Metrovicks.

8.2 Crossley Engine Issues – Australian and Irish Experiences.
Early experience with Crossley 1,045hp engines on the Western Australian Government Railways (WAGR) highlighted the very significant issues associated with these engines, notably:

- burning of significant quantities of lubricating oil (and associated smoky exhausts),
- inadequate lubrication of the crankshaft bearings,
- cracked cylinder heads and pistons,
- bent connecting rods,
- piston ring scuffing and failure,
- cracked crankcases,
- high exhaust temperatures,
- fuel injection issues,
- severe vibration due to unbalanced engines (causing whole locomotive body vibration and consequent oil, fuel and water pipe leakages),
- radiator failures.

It is generally accepted that it was only the engineering expertise and perseverance of the WAGR Workshop staff which kept the locomotives operating. Ultimately, around 650 design faults, mainly related to the Crossley engine, were overcome, including the replacement of aluminium pistons and cylinder heads with cast iron, and, replacement of the Crossley fuel injection system with CAV equipment. The WAGR (later Westrail) locomotives retained their Crossley engine through to final withdrawal in 1988.

The low axle-load stipulation of the WAGR contract resulted in detrimental weight-saving initiatives, some of those affecting the Crossley engine itself. The use of hollow crankshafts reduced resilience to the cyclic demands of railway operation and the 'lightened' engine block inevitably resulted in reduced overall structural strength.

Similar problems were experienced in Ireland (CIE) with the uprated 1,200hp engine. Ultimately CIE re-engined the A-class fleet with GM-645-E 1,325hp engines during the period May 1968 to November 1971, with the original electrical equipment retained.

8.3 Crossley Engines - British Railways.
Crossley Bros. was a respected firm producing well-regarded engines for stationary and marine applications over many years. However, the company did not fully appreciate early enough the more demanding nature of rail traction work with its frequent cycling between full power and idling. Crossley, and indeed other manufacturers, suffered the consequences.

After only a very short period in service with British Railways, the Metrovicks started to suffer from the same issues as the Australian and Irish locomotives before them. Crossley carried out numerous modifications, with the assistance of BR engineers, in an attempt to eliminate these problems.

There is no evidence to suggest that the 'lightened' engine deployed in the WAGR fleet was provided in strengthened form for the Irish or BR contracts. Given the nature of the failures experienced, it would appear that the engines were very similar apart from the uprating to 1,200hp; in Colonel H.C.B. Rogers' *Transition from Steam* book, R.C. Bond is quoted as saying that 'It may be that the uprating of the engine was a mistake'. Modest loads over short distances were within the Co-Bo's capabilities at first; it was sustained running which soon tripped them up.

R.M. Tufnell's excellent *The Diesel Impact on British Rail* book provides many interesting insights into the problems experienced with the Crossley engines:

- 'The HST engine had been designed to employ the 'pulse-scavenge' system, whereby the exhaust pulse assists in drawing air into the cylinder connected to that exhaust manifold. This system only works effectively at one particular rate of air or gas flow, and is not really suitable to the variations of rail traction work.'
- 'It was . . . found that the spring adjusting collars on the fuel injectors fractured, resulting in failure to atomise the fuel, and this increased the tendency to smoke. These collars failed after only some twenty minutes on full load, but this was cured by using injectors of Crossley's own design which worked well.'
- 'The crankcases themselves were soon in trouble and that on D5719 failed after only four weeks in service. There were also problems with the cylinder heads, which were originally of aluminium. These fractured on the combustion face, extending eventually into the water space and the gas pressure resulted in water being pumped out via the overflow pipe.'
- 'The other most serious problem was with the pistons; the piston crowns kept coming adrift.'
- 'There was also a terrible tendency to leak oil, water and fuel and the engine room floors were often awash with a mixture of these. As these engines were fitted with two monobloc fuel pumps mounted over the compressor, some of the fuel pipes were excessively long and were difficult to secure against vibration. This reacted on the pipe joints with the inevitable fuel leakage.'
- 'The fuel pumps on these engines were of Crossley's own design and manufacture. The method of control from the governor was by means of a cam actuating what they called a 'pecker', which operated a control valve spindle; this controlled the amount of fuel to the plunger which was operated, via the pump lever, by the fuel cam. This device was very sensitive to the gap between the tappet head and the control valve spindle and this could only be set after some twenty minutes idling for each cylinder. As a result engines often had to be sent out without proper adjustment and with individual cylinders receiving varying amounts of fuel. After some time a gauge was devised for this purpose to which the 'pecker' locknut could be preset with much saving in time.'
- 'As set by the makers these engines always smoked badly, and the LMR suggested that the fuel timing be advanced by 3°. This resulted in a clean exhaust, but the peak pressures went up from 1100 lb/in² to 1400lb/in² and after investigation it was decided that the main bearings, being of white metal, could not take this increased pressure. A compromise was reached with an advance of 1.5° and a less clean exhaust.'
- 'One feature of the pulse-scavenge system was the need for a non-return or 'transfer' valve to prevent exhaust gasses blowing into the inlet manifold. These transfer valves were prone to blockage and fatigue fracture.'
- 'The large flat crankcase doors were difficult to make oil-tight and in attempts to cure leaks the door studs were often overtightened and sheared off. This . . . could no doubt have been solved by adopting a centre fixing door, but there was neither the time or money

for this or other design improvements which could have made this into a good rail traction engine.'

8.4 Electrical.
In marked contrast to the engine, the electrical equipment proved to be very robust and reliable and was rarely the reason for failures in traffic.

8.5 Additional Issues.
8.5.1 Route Availability (RA).
The 'Talking of Trains: The Diesels Disappoint' article referred to earlier also commented:

> 'Another puzzling aspect of the dieselisation to date is the restricted availability of some types compared with their anticipated sphere of activity . . . Recently our eye caught a long list of the S.R. routes . . . from which the Metropolitan-Vickers Type 2 will be barred . . . The wide route availability of diesels has been another reiterated propaganda point in their favour, but these machines seem more restricted than the average steam locomotive of the same power.'

An internal BR memorandum 'Selection of Diesel Locomotive Types' produced by the BTC Central Staff in July 1956, stated that 'route availability depends upon axle weight, total weight and axle spacing, the latter being important not only on the individual locomotive, but also as to distance apart of the adjacent end axles of two locomotives coupled together'. Whilst a locomotive's axle-load on its own is generally considered to be the determinant of route availability, it is clear that the broader considerations impacted on the route availability number allocated to the Metrovicks specifically.

a) Axle Loading.
Comparative route availability details for the Type 2 diesel-electric classes operated by British Railways are listed below:

Locomotive Class	Diagramme No. (1961)	Max Axle Load (Imperial)	RA
BR/Sulzer (D5000-49)	DE/2000/1	19t 19cwt	7
MV (D5700-19)	DE/2003/1	19t 14cwt 2q	8
BRCW (D5300-19)	DE/2001/1	19t 12cwt	7
EE (D5900-09)	DE/2004/1	18t 11cwt	6
BR/Sulzer (D5050-113)	DE/2000/5	18t 8cwt	6
BRCW (D5320-46)	DE/2001/2	18t 8cwt	6
NBL (D6100-37)	DE/2005/1	18t 5cwt	6
Brush (D5500-19)	DE/2002/1	18t 4cwt	6

The D5000-19 locomotives had higher axle-loadings compared with the Metrovicks, yet they were given Route Availability 7 compared with the Metrovick's 8.

b) Number of Axles.
The 'Selection of Diesel Locomotive Types' memorandum also stated that:

> 'It is a merit of diesel traction that the necessary power can be obtained with light axle loads by multiplication of axles to obtain the required total adhesion, either in the form of multi-axled locomotives or by working several locomotives in multiple unit. On the other hand, every additional pair of axles increases the locomotive weight, capital cost and annual charges for a given nominal hp, so that for minimum locomotive costs there will be a preference towards the smallest number of axles to do the work, which in turn leads to preference for the BB [Bo-Bo] wheel arrangement.'

It would appear that Metropolitan-Vickers were attempting find a compromise solution between power and weight and, as a consequence, goes some way towards explaining the unusual Co-Bo wheel arrangement.

c) Range of Axle-Loadings.
Whereas the axle-loading for D5000-19 was a consistent 19t 19c across all four axles, the five Metrovick axles were 18t 17c, 19t 14c, 19t 13c for the Co-bogie and 19t 4c and 19t 14c for the Bo-bogie, a variation of 17cwt or nearly an Imperial ton between the heaviest and lightest. However, a larger variation was to be found on the

Brush Type 2s with significantly lower axle-loadings on the non-powered axles.

d) Combined impact of Wheel Diameter and Axle Loading.
Once again quoting from the 'Selection of Diesel Locomotive Types' memorandum:

'Experience with intensive dieselisation in the U.S.A. and theoretical investigation by the Research Department have also indicated that if wheels smaller than a certain ratio of diameter to weight carried are used, high rail stresses will result, leading to rail fracture in time. Since there is a limit to the size of wheel which can be carried by a bogie type locomotive, so there is a resultant limitation in maximum axle weight due to this cause.'

The Civil Engineers proposed a maximum ratio of axle weight (expressed in tons) divided by the wheel diameter (expressed in feet) of 4.5 to meet this condition. This was a very onerous requirement on locomotive design as the following table indicates:

Locomotive Class	Max Axle Load (Imperial ton)	Wheel Diam. (ft)	Ratio	RA
BR/Sulzer (D5000-49)	19.95	3.75	5.32	7
MV (D5700-19)	19.73	3.29	6.00	8
BRCW D5300-19)	19.60	3.58	5.47	7
EE (D5900-09)	18.55	3.58	5.18	6
BR/Sulzer (D5050-113)	18.40	3.75	4.91	6
BRCW D5320-46)	18.40	3.58	5.14	6
NBL (D6100-37)	18.25	3.58	5.10	6
Brush (D5500-19)	18.20	3.58	5.08	6

All of the Type 2s exceeded the engineer's stipulated threshold ratio of 4.5, although the Metrovicks had the highest ratio by quite some considerable margin.

The 'Selection of Diesel Locomotive Types' memorandum noted:

'Since 4' 0" is about the largest bogie wheel diameter which will satisfactorily clear an underframe carrying a large diesel engine, the maximum axle load for diesel traction becomes 20 tons if some tolerance can be obtained on the proposed P/D value of 4.5. Since only isolated and unimportant routes require axle loads as low as 13 tons, the effective range of axle loads for future locomotive design is 16-20 tons inclusive.'

Ultimately the Civil Engineering standards were relaxed, through permanent way upgrading, and it was only the 100mph WCML ac electric fleet which was built with 4ft diameter wheels.

e) Axle Spacing.
Comparative data for the Type 2 classes:

Locomotive Class	Axle Spacing (Imperial)
BR/Sulzer (D5000-49 and D5050-D5113)	8ft 6in
MV (D5700-19)	Co-Bogie – 5ft 11in + 6ft 2½in, Bo-bogie – 8ft 6in
BRCW (D5300-19 and D5320-D5346)	10ft 0in
EE (D5900-09)	8ft 6in
NBL (D6100-37)	8ft 6in
Brush (D5500-19)	A1A-bogies – 7ft 0in + 7ft 0in

Anecdotal comments seem to suggest that it was specifically the Bo-bogie which was the cause of problems on the Metrovick locomotives. An article in *Trains Illustrated* (January 1960) covering G. Freeman-Allen's footplate experience on the 'Condor' freight service from Carlisle to Hendon commented:

'The Metrovick locomotive rode like a carriage, but the decided stress in the rhythm when one pair of wheels on the two-axle bogie struck a rail-joint seemed some confirmation of rumours alleging that the weight of them restricts the Co-Bo's route availability quite seriously.'

The 'Selection of Diesel Locomotive Types' memorandum also refers to riding quality and lateral flange forces, stating that '6-wheeled bogies already exist in considerable variety of design, which will give good riding at 90mph but no 4-wheel bogies design so far exists in this country which has proved its good riding qualities at this speed'. Whilst specifically referencing 90mph, riding characteristics below this speed were also inferior in comparison with three-wheeled bogies.

It is believed that there was a miscalculation in the weight distribution on the Metrovicks and the Bo end had more weight on the *inner* axle than the outer. There are certainly accounts that, when riding jointed track, the Bo bogie went 'Thump-THUMP' through the joints suggesting one axle was more highly loaded than the other!

8.5.2 Traction Characteristics.
With 3ft 3in driving wheels, compared to the 3ft 7in or 3ft 9in of their rivals, the Metrovicks proved to be very competent at starting heavy trains. Comparative Type 2 tractive effort statistics are given below:

Locomotive Class	Maximum Tractive Effort (Imperial)	Continuous Tractive Effort (Imperial)
BR/Sulzer (D5000-49)	40,000 lb, 22.3% adhesion	21,300 lb, 14.8mph
MV (D5700-19)	50,000 lb, 23% adhesion	25,000 lb, 13.5mph
BRCW (D5300-19)	42,000 lb, 23% adhesion	30,000 lb, 11.25mph
EE (D5900-09)	47,000 lb, 29.1% adhesion	30,600 lb, 9.4mph
BR/Sulzer (D5050-113)	40,000 lb, 24.5% adhesion	21,300 lb, 14.8mph
BRCW (D5320-46)	42,000 lb, 23% adhesion	30,000 lb, 11.25mph
NBL (D6100-37)	45,000 lb, 28% adhesion	30,000 lb, 10.2mph
Brush (D5500-19)	42,000 lb, 26% adhesion	22,400 lb, 16.5mph

8.5.3 Braking Characteristics.
The Metrovicks were considered to have good braking characteristics being particularly effective on unfitted trains. See also Section 12.3.

8.5.4 Train Heating Boilers.
The Spanner Mk 1 train heating boilers had some interesting characteristics as the following two anecdotes describe:

- 1959/60: 'the stories told in the [Trafford Park] mess-room of . . . train heating boilers blowing out when passing under bridges and then relighting themselves with a bang and flash of flame that lit up the surrounding area, made me glad I was just a . . . Passed Cleaner, and had not been trained on the Spanner Mk 1 train heating boiler.' ('Oranges and Lemons', December 2003, *Traction*).

The ventilation characteristics of the Metrovicks were such that the problem of 'blowing out' only occurred in one direction of travel.

- Mid-1960s: 'On another occasion . . . the London to Barrow and Workington train had sent news ahead that the train heating system had broken down. The fitter and electrician duly went to Barrow station to meet the train and investigate. Often, the electrodes that ignited the fuel in the boiler . . . were a problem and it was thought that this was the cause of the trouble. After removing and cleaning and resetting them the button was pressed and the boiler fired up and started. There were shouts of alarm from passengers and staff on the station platform, agog at the spout of flame that had shot out of the top of the loco when the reservoir of fuel had ignited'. ('Metro-Vicks at the Edge: Barrow's Unsung Co-Bos', March 2012, *British Railways Illustrated*)

8.5.5 General Build Quality.
The build quality of the locomotives was generally recognised as being excellent. The phrase 'built like tanks' was regularly used and may explain why the as-built working weight was 97tons 3cwt, compared with the 91tons 5cwt quoted on the Engine History Cards and 91tons on the internal builder's plates.

8.6 Mileages Operated and Availability Statistics (1959-61).
During 1960, the first year when the full fleet of Metrovicks was in traffic, the gross mileage was 487,699. The average annual mileage per locomotive was 24,385 (with D5712 the lowest at 3456 and D5705 the highest at 52,507). Three locomotives achieved less than 10,000 miles (D5707/12/3). See Section 7 for individual locomotive mileages.

The BR 'Locomotives - Annual Mileage and Analysis of Weekdays' reports for the period 1959 to 1961, containing comparisons with the BR/Sulzer Type 2s, make for interesting reading:

Average per Locomotive - Year 1959 (based on locomotives in stock [whole year]):

	Metrovick
Operating Stock at 31.12.59	20
Annual Mileage	37,184
Repairs (No. of weekdays):	
Classified Shop & Shed	12
Running Repairs & Exams	137
Total Repairs	149
Available but not required (No. of weekdays)	3
Total Out of Service (No. of Weekdays)	152
In Service (No. of Weekdays)	163
Percentage of Total Possible	52%

Average per Locomotive - Year 1960 (based on locomotives in stock [whole year]):

	Metrovick	BR/Sulzer Type 2
Operating Stock at 31.12.60	20	49
Annual Mileage	24,385	38,969
Repairs (No. of weekdays):		
Classified Shop & Shed	105	21
Running Repairs & Exams	101	53
Total Repairs	206	77
Available but not required (No. of weekdays)	3	7
Total Out of Service (No. of Weekdays)	209	81
In Service (No. of Weekdays)	100	228
Percentage of Total Possible	32%	74%

Early Performance • 131

Average per Locomotive - Year 1961 (based on locomotives in stock [whole year]):

	Metrovick	BR/Sulzer Type 2
Operating Stock at 31.12.61	20	55
Annual Mileage	3,647	37,067
Repairs (No. of weekdays):		
Classified Shop & Shed	139	41
Running Repairs & Exams	69	38
Total Repairs	208	79
Available but not required (No. of weekdays)	4	5
Total Out of Service (No. of Weekdays)	212	84
In Service (No. of Weekdays)	97	225
Percentage of Total Possible	31%	73%

The Engine History Cards provide details of weekdays (Mondays-Saturdays) out of service for 1960, as follows:

	Classified Repairs				Running Repairs	Total	Mileage Achieved
	Waiting Repair Decision	Waiting Works	On Works	Total			
D5700	7	17	42	66	102	168	39357
D5701	10	12	53	75	127	202	24036
D5702	-	1	55	56	119	175	37428
D5703	-	-	-	-	258	258	11732
D5704	2	14	48	64	112	176	29114
D5705	-	1	50	51	97	148	52507
D5706	-	-	-	-	147	147	28697
D5707	4	-	206	210	60	270	7964
D5708	1	5	182	188	66	254	14416
D5709	4	167	-	171	79	250	16872
D5710	36	7	90	133	71	204	29506
D5711	16	31	69	116	85	201	28129
D5712	5	177	-	182	103	285	3456
D5713	-	196	33	229	25	254	6266
D5714	-	-	-	-	134	134	40539
D5715	-	-	-	-	155	155	25995
D5716	-	-	-	-	211	211	33267
D5717	3	13	75	91	100	191	30409
D5718	10	19	110	139	72	211	15485
D5719	-	187	-	187	49	236	12525

The EHC figures suggest an overall fleet availability of circa 33%. Is it any wonder that both British Railways, and indeed Metropolitan-Vickers, felt that urgent remedial action was required to address their extreme unreliability?

The Appendix 'A' reports attached to the BTC Motive Power Committee monthly meeting minutes provided statistical information covering Metrovick availability and weekday (Monday-Saturday) mileages. Full details covering the period from July 1959 to October 1961 (the point where all twenty Metrovicks were out of action awaiting or undergoing rehabilitation) are listed below:

Week ending	Operating Stock	% Available Whole 24hrs	Miles Per Loco Per Weekday Locos in use	Miles Per Loco Per Weekday Op. Stock	Comments
18/07/59	19	54.2	266.7	145	
25/07/59	19	56.8	237.4	137	
01/08/59	19	54.2	253.3	138	
08/08/59	19	47.4	249.9	119	
15/08/59	19	50.0	226.9	114.0	
22/08/59	19	51.1	205.0	104.9	
29/08/59	19	52.6	245.0	128.8	
05/09/59	19	51.5	239.0	122.3	
12/09/59	19	49.5	258.0	115.4	
19/09/59	19	48.4	250.2	114.5	
26/09/59	19	51.6	254.5	127.2	
03/10/59	19	56.8	290.4	117.7	
10/10/59	19	52.6	357.9	169.5	
17/10/59	20	54.0	233.5	128.4	
24/10/59	20	50.0	283.0	141.5	
31/10/59	20	48.5	317.4	149.2	
07/11/59	20	57.5	286.9	162.1	
14/11/59	20	58.5	271.7	154.9	
21/11/59	20	70.0	279.2	191.3	
28/11/59	20	64.0	235.9	145.1	
05/12/59	20	57.5	255.6	138.1	
12/12/59	20	63.0	246.5	149.2	
19/12/59	20	52.5	293.3	136.4	
26/12/59	20	48.5	265.7	115.6	
09/01/60	20	66.0	240.2	108.1	
16/01/60	20	52.0	170.6	74.2	
23/01/60	20	55.0	187.6	84.4	
30/01/60	20	56.5	188.5	99.0	
06/02/60	20	51.5	239.6	117.4	
13/02/60	20	46.0	224.5	95.4	

Early Performance • 133

Week ending	Operating Stock	% Available Whole 24hrs	Miles Per Loco Per Weekday Locos in use	Miles Per Loco Per Weekday Op. Stock	Comments
20/02/60	20	37.5	284.1	102.3	
27/02/60	20	37.0	216.2	75.7	
05/03/60	20	28.5	260.5	70.3	
12/03/60	20	26.5	251.6	66.7	
19/03/60	20	29.5	185.6	52.9	
26/03/60	20	27.5	213.3	56.5	
02/04/60	20	33.5	189.9	60.8	
09/04/60	20	36.5	243.6	82.8	
16/04/60	20	41.0	97.0	54.3	
23/04/60	20	36.0	165.7	64.6	
30/04/60	20	40.0	243.1	97.2	
07/05/60	20	30.0	318.3	95.5	
14/05/60	20	33.5	230.1	77.1	
21/05/60	20	40.0	283.3	113.3	
28/05/60	20	22.0	234.4	77.4	
04/06/60	20	32.5	237.0	73.5	
11/06/60	20	34.5	299.4	91.3	
18/06/60	20	27.5	386.9	83.2	
25/06/60	20	43.5	230.9	100.5	
02/07/60	20	40.0	264.7	103.2	
09/07/60	20	37.5	275.5	100.6	
16/07/60	20	21.0	265.7	55.8	
23/07/60	20	30.0	213.1	56.5	
30/07/60	20	28.5	289.0	82.4	
06/08/60	20	26.0	193.6	45.5	
13/08/60	20	23.5	303.4	71.3	
20/08/60	20	22.5	318.8	63.8	
27/08/60	20	31.0	230.2	67.9	
03/09/60	20	28.5	314.2	86.4	
10/09/60	20	20.0	316.0	36.2	
17/09/60	20	21.0	373.2	72.8	
24/09/60	20	28.5	272.1	77.6	
01/10/60	20	32.5	308.7	100.3	
08/10/60	20	27.5	254.7	70.0	
15/10/60	20	15.0	235.3	35.3	
22/10/60	20	26.0	227.9	59.3	

Week ending	Operating Stock	% Available Whole 24hrs	Miles Per Loco Per Weekday Locos in use	Miles Per Loco Per Weekday Op. Stock	Comments
29/10/60	20	26.5	232.7	61.7	
05/11/60	20	22.5	208.4	44.8	
12/11/60	20	20.0	191.6	38.3	
19/11/60	20	24.0	175.6	42.1	
26/11/60	20	23.5	221.7	52.1	
03/12/60	20	37.5	232.5	83.7	
10/12/60	20	28.5	298.2	85.0	
17/12/60	20	24.0	200.6	41.1	
24/12/60	20	25.0	148.5	31.9	
31/12/60	20	21.0	168.9	35.5	
07/01/61	20	23.3	150.8	33.2	
14/01/61	20	10.5	298.8	26.9	
21/01/61	20	6.0	192.6	6.7	
28/01/61	20	12.5	NIL	NIL	
04/02/61	20	19.5	15.5	0.5	
11/02/61	20	15.5	196.9	27.0	
18/02/61	20	11.5	175.4	20.2	
25/02/61	20	19.0	301.3	42.2	
04/03/61	20	15.0	164.4	22.2	
11/03/61	20	21.5	196.3	32.4	
18/03/61	20	15.0	202.4	22.3	
25/03/61	12	12.5	109.2	13.7	8 locos S(u).
01/04/61	10	20.0	199.0	35.8	
08/04/61	10	7.0	NIL	NIL	
15/04/61	9	22.2	280.6	56.1	
22/04/61	9	13.3	355.7	47.4	11 locos S(u).
29/04/61	9	28.9	299.3	76.5	
06/05/61	9	38.9	262.5	93.3	
13/05/61	9	35.6	194.9	69.3	
20/05/61	8	33.8	196.2	61.3	12 locos S(u).
27/05/61	8	25.0	250.0	53.1	
03/06/61	8	27.5	245.8	67.6	
10/06/61	10	28.0	216.7	49.9	
17/06/61	9	20.0	204.4	36.3	9 locos S(u), 2 locos Rehab.

Early Performance • 135

Week ending	Operating Stock	% Available Whole 24hrs	Miles Per Loco Per Weekday – Locos in use	Miles Per Loco Per Weekday – Op. Stock	Comments
24/06/61	10	15	197.2	29.6	
01/07/61	10	3	83.9	2.5	
08/07/61	10	3	333.9	10.0	
15/07/61	9	NIL	NIL	NIL	6 locos S(u), 5 locos Rehab.
22/07/61	11 (5)	NIL	NIL	NIL	Reporting policy change; see Note 2.
29/07/61	11 (5)	NIL	NIL	NIL	
05/08/61	11 (5)	NIL	NIL	NIL	
12/08/61	11 (5)	NIL	NIL	NIL	9 locos S(u), 6 locos Rehab.
19/08/61	11	NIL	NIL	NIL	
26/08/61	11	NIL	NIL	NIL	
02/09/61	11	NIL	NIL	NIL	
09/09/61	11 (5)	NIL	NIL	NIL	9 locos S(u), 6 locos Rehab.
16/09/61	No data published.				
23/09/61	No data published.				
30/09/61	No data published.				
07/10/61	14 (5)	NIL	NIL	NIL	No data published; commentary only. 6 locos S(u), 9 locos Rehab.
14/10/61	14 (5)	NIL	NIL	NIL	
21/10/61	17 (5)	NIL	NIL	NIL	
28/10/61	20 (0)	NIL	NIL	NIL	
04/11/61	20 (0)	NIL	NIL	NIL	20 locos Rehab.

Notes:
1. Bold dates signify four-week 'Period-ending' dates.
2. The statistics indicate that there was a change in reporting policy with respect to locomotives undergoing rehabilitation and whether or not they were included in the Operating Stock figure. Up to and including P/E 15/07/61 the locomotives undergoing rehabilitation were excluded from Operating Stock; however, from P/E 12/08/61 the locomotives undergoing rehabilitation were included in Operating Stock.

   The bracketed Operating Stock figures for Periods Ending 12/08/61, 09/09/61, 07/10/61 and 04/11/61 represent the true Operating Stock figures.
3. No tabulated data was published for the four week Period Ending 07/10/61, thus the Operating Stock figure for w/e 07/10/61 represents my calculation based on the commentary provided in Appendix 'A' of the MPC Minutes.
4. Selected and/or edited period-ending (PE) commentary from the Appendix 'A' statistics is provided below.
5. The statistics indicate that all of the Metrovicks were out of service by w/e 15/07/61, although five were still showing up as on 'Operating Stock' until October 1961. These were, in all probability, D5700/2/15/7 and D5716 which appear to have been taken out of service in April/May 1961 and January 1961 respectively (see Section 9.2), but were never formally recorded as stored on the Engine History Cards.

P/E 08/08/59 to P/E 16/07/60 (inclusive).
These reports highlighted the issues being experienced with the Metrovicks including:

- engine mountings, defective engine balance weights, fractured crank cases (four locomotives in P/E 08/08/59, six in P/E 05/09/59), seizure of pistons necessitating piston renewal on affected engines.
- defective fuel pumps, fractured lubricating oil pipes, water seepage into the fuel tanks.
- burnt out exhaust silencers, exhaust flexible pipes.
- flat batteries.
- difficulty obtaining cab windows.

P/E 13/08/60 to P/E 04/11/61 (inclusive).
During this period the emphasis changed to highlighting the numbers of locomotives 'on works' or 'awaiting works' attention, and, later on, locomotives stored awaiting or undergoing refurbishment at Dukinfield, as follows:.

P/E 13/08/60: Nearly 50% of the fleet 'on' or 'awaiting works' attention during the last two weeks of the period.
P/E 10/09/60: Thirteen locos 'on' or 'awaiting works' or receiving attention by Crossley to fractured crank cases.
P/E 08/10/60: Eight locos 'on' or 'awaiting works' attention.
P/E 31/12/60: By the end of the period ten locomotives 'on' or 'awaiting works' attention.
P/E 28/01/61: Ten locos 'on' or 'awaiting works' attention.

P/E 25/02/61: Nine locomotives waiting works attention during the whole period.
P/E 25/03/61: Eight locomotives stored unserviceable during w/e 25/03/61 having been standing waiting works attention during the first three weeks of the period.
P/E 22/04/61: Eleven locomotives stored unserviceable.
P/E 17/06/61: Two locomotives being refurbished at Dukinfield Works. Nine stored unserviceable.
P/E 15/07/61: Six locomotives being refurbished at Dukinfield Works. Five stored unserviceable.
P/E 12/08/61: Six locomotives being refurbished at Dukinfield Works. Nine stored unserviceable.
P/E 09/09/61: Six locomotives being refurbished at Dukinfield Works. Nine stored unserviceable.
P/E 07/10/61: Nine locomotives being refurbished at Dukinfield Works. Six stored unserviceable.
P/E 04/11/61: At the beginning of the period six locomotives were stored unserviceable but by the end of the period all twenty locomotives were stopped for refurbishing.

8.7 Casualty Statistics.

A BR 'Diesel Main Line Locomotives – Mechanical/Electrical Casualties' report for four weeks ended 03/12/60 provides an insight into the issues suffered by the Metrovicks (with a comparison to those experienced by the BR/Sulzer Type 2s):

Type (Operating Stock) Mechanical/Electrical Casualty	No. of Casualties	Miles per Mechanical/Electrical Casualty
Metrovick Type 2 (20)		1,526
Brake, Whistle, Sanding	1	
Steam Heating Equipment	3	
Pipes	1	
Power Units and Super-Chargers	4	
Fuel System (excl. Pipes)	1	
Traction Machines and Transmission	2	
Control Equipment	4	
Cables	<u>1</u>	
	<u>17</u>	
BR/Sulzer Type 2 (47)		6,705
Brake, Whistle, Sanding	1	
Steam Heating Equipment	2	
Pipes	5	
Power Units and Super-Chargers	3	
Traction Machines and Transmission	1	
Control Equipment	<u>1</u>	
	<u>13</u>	

8.8 Driver's Environment.

G. Freeman-Allen, describing the previously mentioned footplate ride on the 'Condor' from Carlisle to Hendon noted that he was 'at once impressed by the very efficient soundproofing of a Metrovick Co-Bo's cab, which is unsurpassed on any BR diesel I have so far ridden. Little more than a background noise of travel penetrated to the engine crew, even when the controller was on full power'.

8.9 Passengers' Opinions.

To passengers, the Metrovicks were 'intrusive on account of excessive noise and exhaust fumes.', with the noise within the confines of stations having 'to be experienced to be believed.' (*British Railways Fleet Survey*, B. Haresnape, 1981). It is understood that the BTC received a number of complaints from customers regarding fumes in passenger compartments

8.10 Maintenance Facilities.

Whilst the early history of the Metrovicks was undoubtedly difficult enough, the problems were not helped by poor maintenance facilities at Derby shed where the general steam-age infrastructure continued to prevail.

Chapter 9
PRE-DUKINFIELD STORAGE

9.1 Storage.
Train Illustrated (March 1959) reported: 'on January 18th (*1959*) all of the class delivered by that date were congregated at Derby depot and there was a rumour that they had been temporarily withdrawn from service'. Only eighteen to twenty months later, from mid-1960, the serious technical problems with the Metrovick fleet saw the progressive storage of the class; the July 1960 edition of the *Railway Observer* reported that: 'During the week ended 4th June [1960] no fewer than seventeen of the twenty 1,200 hp diesel locomotives of the D5700 series were stopped at Cricklewood and Derby sheds'. Most of these locomotives returned to service but this was very much a precursor for the 'permanent' removal of the fleet from traffic over the next twelve to fifteen months prior to repairs at Dukinfield.

The November 1960 edition of *Train Illustrated* commented that 'No fewer than eight of the Metro-Vick Type 2 diesels were congregated at Derby Works in mid-September (1960); it is believed that some modification of the Crossley engines . . . is under consideration'.

Trains Illustrated (February 1961) carried a report indicating that two locomotives from D5703/7/8/9/12/3/9 (presumably D5707/8) had been stored unserviceable at Derby since April 1960, with the remainder since May or June. When D5707/13 entered Dukinfield works in June 1961, the August 1961 edition of *Trains Illustrated* commented that 'all but two of the class were out of service'.

Some 1960/61 storage details are included on the Engine History Cards (EHC) and are included in the table below. For comparison, some published information is also included in the table; this information appeared to first see the light of day in 'Supplement 3&4' (December 1983) of D. Strickland's *Locomotive Directory* and has been repeated several times by C .Marsden up to at least August/September 2017 (*Modern Locomotives Illustrated* No.226).

	EHC	**Locomotive Directory/MLI 226**
D5700	Nothing recorded.	S(s): 01/61, R/I: 02/62
D5701	S(u): 19/06/61-w/e 21/10/61	S(s): 02/61, R/I: 02/62
D5702	Nothing recorded.	S(s): 02/61, R/I: 02/62
D5703	S(u): 12/12/60 (*Crossed out, with note* 'See - W.E. 4/2/61 'Awaiting Works') S(u): 20/03/61-18/09/61	S(s): 02/61, R/I: 02/62
D5704	S(u): 12/12/60 (*Crossed out, with note* 'See - W.E. 4/2/61 'Awaiting Works')* S(u): 20/03/61-18/09/61	S(s): 02/61, R/I: 02/62
D5705	S(u): 12/07/61-w/e 21/10/61	S(s): 02/61, R/I: 02/62
D5706	S(u): 12/06/61-w/e 21/10/61	S(s): 02/61, R/I: 02/62

	EHC	Locomotive Directory/MLI 226
D5707	S(u): 12/12/60 (*Crossed out, with note 'See - W.E. 4/2/61 Awaiting Works'*) S(u): 20/03/61-19/06/61	S(s): 02/61, R/I: 02/62
D5708	S(u): 12/12/60 (*Crossed out, with note 'See - W.E. 4/2/61 Awaiting Works'*) S(u): 20/03/61-17/07/61	S(s): 02/61, R/I: 02/62
D5709	S(u): 12/12/60 (*Crossed out, with note 'See - W.E. 4/2/61 Awaiting Works'*) S(u): 20/03/61-15/05/61	S(s): 01/61, R/I: 02/62
D5710	S(u): 27/03/61-18/09/61	S(s): 02/61, R/I: 02/62
D5711	S(u): 27/03/61-28/10/61	S(s): 02/61, R/I: 02/62
D5712	S(u): 12/12/60 (*Crossed out, with note 'See - W.E. 4/2/61 Awaiting Works'*) S(u): 20/03/61-17/07/61	S(s): 02/61, R/I: 02/62
D5713	S(u): 12/12/60 (*Crossed out, with note 'See - W.E. 4/2/61 Awaiting Works'*) S(u): 20/03/61-19/06/61	S(s): 01/61, R/I: 02/62
D5714	S(u): 19/05/61-28/10/61	S(s): 02/61, R/I: 02/62
D5715	Nothing recorded.	S(s): 02/61, R/I: 02/62
D5716	Nothing recorded.	S(s): 02/61, R/I: 02/62
D5717	Nothing recorded.	S(s): 02/61, R/I: 02/62
D5718	S(u): 10/04/61-28/10/61	S(s): 02/61, R/I: 02/62
D5719	S(u): 12/12/60 (*Crossed out, with note 'See - W.E. 4/2/61 Awaiting Works'*) S(u): 20/03/61-15/05/61	S(s): 02/61, R/I: 12/61

Notes:
1. EHC: Seven Metrovicks are shown as being placed in store en bloc with effect from w/e 12/12/60 i.e. D5703/7-9/12/3/9. Locomotives were almost certainly in store before this date. All were subsequently shown as 'Awaiting Works' from w/e 04/02/61. An eighth locomotive, D5704, may also have been recorded as stored unserviceable from w/e 12/12/60, given that the entry on the EHC appears to have been erased and overwritten (*).
2. EHC: Storage details for D5701/3-5/10/1/4/8 appear to be individually specific entries.
3. EHC: End-storage dates relate to dates of entry to Dukinfield for rehabilitation.
4. EHC: No storage details are given for D5700/2/15-7 which either suggests that they were in traffic up to the point of their movement to Dukinfield (unlikely - see Section 8.6 (page135)), or, that the locomotives were never formally recorded as being stored. The Sighting Information in Section 9.2 would suggest that D5700/2/15/7 and D5716 were store in April/May 1961 and January 1961 respectively.
5. On the basis of the above, the last Metrovick taken out of use was D5705 during w/e 12/07/61.
6. Locomotive Directory/MLI No.226: Information shows absolutely no resemblance with the EHC data. The storage periods quoted include part of the time in Dukinfield Works undergoing rehabilitation work. The re-instatement (R/I) details actually show the date when locomotives were reallocated to 12E Barrow, rather than their actual return to traffic. In addition, all locomotives are listed as stored serviceable as opposed to the more realistic unserviceable on the EHCs.

9.2 Summary of Sightings immediately pre-Dukinfield.

Sightings of Metrovicks immediately prior to their rehabilitation at Dukinfield provide an insight into the storage periods for each locomotive before the commencement of repair work; details are tabulated below:

D5700	**17A Derby:** 300461/ 070561/ 140561/ 250661/ 240961. Not listed 260261/ 130861.
	Hauled Derby to Dukinfield: 191061
D5701	**Derby Works:** 130461
	17A Derby: 250661/ 130861/ 240961
	Hauled Derby to Dukinfield: 191061
D5702	**17A Derby:** 140561/ 040661/ 130861/ 240961. Not listed 070561 and 250661.
	Hauled Derby to Dukinfield: 181061
D5703	**17A Derby:** 270860/ 280860. Not listed 070860.
	9B Stockport Edgeley: 041260 (with D5713)
	9E Trafford Park: 260261/ 260361/ 090461/160461/ 180661/ 250661/ 130861/ 200861. Not listed 170961.
D5704	**9E Trafford Park:** 260261/ 260361/ 090461/ 180661/ 250661/ 130861/ 200861. Not listed 160461 and 170961.
D5705	**17A Derby:** 130861/ 240961. Not listed 250661.
	Hauled from Derby to Dukinfield: 191061
D5706	**17A Derby:** 250661/ 130861/ 240961. Not listed 140561.
	Hauled Derby to Dukinfield: 191061 (RO)
D5707	**Derby Works:** 160560/ 290560/ 140660/ 030760/ 070860/ 280860/ 040960/ 250960/ 231060/ 061160/ 131160/ 271160. Not listed 270360/ 240460, 080760/ 130860/ 270860 and 091260/ 120261.
	9E Trafford Park: 260261/ 260361/ 160461. Not listed 090461 and 180661.
D5708	**Derby Works:** 030760/ 080760/ 070860/ 270860/ 280860/ 040960/ 250960/ 231060/ 061160/ 131160/ 271160. Not listed 140660, 130860/ 150860 and 091260/ 120261.
	9E Trafford Park: 260261/ 260361/ 090461/ 160461/ 180661/ 250661
D5709	**17A Derby:** 270860/ 280860. Not listed 070860 and 120261.
	9E Trafford Park: 260261/ 260361/ 090461/ 160461
D5710	**17A Derby:** Nil. Not listed 170261.
	9E Trafford Park: 260261/ 260361/ 030461/ 090461/ 160461/ 180661/ 250661/ 130861. Not listed 200861/ 170961.
D5711	**17A Derby:** 260261/ 140561/ 040661/ 250661/ 130861/ 240961
	Hauled Derby to Dukinfield: 201061
D5712	**17A Derby:** 270860/ 280860. Not listed 070860 and 120261.
	9E Trafford Park: 260261/ 260361/090461/ 160461/ 180661/ 250661
D5713	**17A Derby:** 270860/ 280860. Not listed 070860 and 120261.
	9B Stockport Edgeley: 041260 (with D5703)
	9E Trafford Park: 260261/ 260361/ 090461/ 160461. Not listed 180661.

D5714	17A Derby:	250661/ 130861/ 240961. Not listed 140561.
	Hauled Derby to Dukinfield:	201061
D5715	17A Derby:	140561/ 250661/ 130861/ 240961. Not listed 070561.
	Hauled Derby to Dukinfield:	191061
D5716	Derby Works:	220161/ 120261/ 260261/ 260361
	17A Derby:	140561/ 250661/ 130861/ 240961. Not listed 300461/ 070561.
	Hauled Derby to Dukinfield:	201061
D5717	17A Derby:	140561/ 250661/ 130861/ 240961. Not listed 300461/ 070561.
	Hauled Derby to Dukinfield:	201061
D5718	17A Derby:	140561/ 250661/ 130861/ 240961. Not listed 300461/ 070561.
	Hauled Derby to Dukinfield:	201061
D5719	17A Derby:	270860/ 280860. Not listed 070860 and 120261.
	9E Trafford Park:	260261/ 260361/ 090461/ 160461

Notes:
1. The high incidence of D5707 and D5708 shown as being "Not listed" is probably due to these locomotives being sheeted over preventing ready identification.
2. Note the sightings of D5700/2/15-7, the five locomotives never officially recorded as stored prior to Dukinfield rehabilitation.

Chapter 10

PRE-DUKINFIELD STORAGE LOCATIONS

10.1 Cricklewood (1960/1).

As mentioned in Section 9.1, seventeen Metrovicks were reported stopped at Derby and Cricklewood depot during early June 1960. During the second half of 1960, the Metrovicks commenced periods of long-term storage prior to major repair work; whether any of these were stored at Cricklewood is not known, although available sighting information would suggest probably not, or, for limited periods only prior to transfer to Derby.

10.2 Derby (1960/1).

Trains Illustrated (November 1960) reported: 'No fewer than eight of the Metro-Vick Type "2" diesels were congregated at Derby works in mid-September'. This was followed in the April 1961 edition with: 'A visitor to Derby Works on February 5th . . . Yet more of the Metrovick Type 2 Co-Bos, Nos. D5701/6/15/7, were stored outside Derby depot, making a total of 13 of this class inactive, but Nos. D5700/5/14/8 were observed at work.'

Based on the table in Section 9.2, the eight at Derby in mid-September 1960 were D5703/7-9/12/3/9, plus D5704 in Derby Works. The identities of the additional five "making a total of 13" in February 1961 is unclear (although probably included D5710/1/6), and will certainly not have been the four listed; the reference to D5701/6/15/7 being in store is clearly an error as evidenced by the EHC information (see Section 9.1).

Based on sightings, D5700/2/15/7 appear to have been stored during April/May 1961, although never officially recorded as such.

The outstanding five locomotives (D5701/5/6/14/8) were progressively stored during 1961, with D5705 operating up to mid-July 1961.

The November 1961 edition of the *Railway Observer* reported that: 'D5702 was hauled from Derby [to Dukinfield] on 18th October, D5700/1/5/6/15 on 19th October and D5711/4/6/7/8 on 20th October.'

D5707, Derby Works, 13 November 1960. D5707 with, it is believed, D5708 behind. Both these locomotives were recorded as having sheeted cabs on a visit to Derby Works on 4 September 1960. These two were possibly the first two locomotives of the Metrovick fleet to be stored pending major repairs. Tarpaulins were used to protect the cabs and prevent water ingress into the radiator compartment. (*N. Skinner*)

10.3 Trafford Park (1960/1).

Trafford Park (9E) shed was the temporary dump for nine of the class (D5703/4/7-10/2/3/9). D5703/13 may have been the first arrivals being noted at 9B Stockport Edgeley depot on 4 December 1960.

'The Allocation History of BR Diesels & Electrics (Part 5)' quotes D5708/13 as arriving at Trafford Park by about 01/61 and D5703/4/7/9/10/2/9 by 02/61, which broadly fits with the Engine History Card remarks for D5703/4/7-9/12/3/9 showing 'W.E. 4/2/61 Awaiting Works'.

From May 1961 the number of Metrovicks at Trafford Park started to diminish as locomotives were dragged to Dukinfield for commencement of repairs.

Trafford Park sighting summary:

26/02/61	D5703/4/7-10/2/3/9	
26/03/61	D5703/4/7-10/2/3/9	
09/04/61	D5703/4/8-10/2/3/9	D5707 not listed.
16/04/61	D5703/7-10/2/3/9	D5704 not listed.
End-05/61	Seven 'noted out of use'	One not listed, plus D5719 to Dukinfield 13/05/61
18/06/61	D5703/4/8/10/2	D5707/9/13 to Dukinfield (D5709 (05/06/61), D5707/13 (19/06/61)
25/06/61	D5703/4/8/10/2	
13/08/61	D5703/4/10	D5708/12 to Dukinfield (10/07/61)
20/08/61	D5703/4	D5710 not listed.
17/09/61	Nil	D5703/4/10 to Dukinfield (18/09/61)

D5710, 9E Trafford Park, 1961. D5710 awaiting the very short journey to Dukinfield. Modified windows. (*Rail-Online*)

D5710, 9E Trafford Park, 1961. Given the modified windows, the second loco is likely to be D5704. *(Rail-Online)*

D5711, 9E Trafford Park, 1961. The other Metrovick at Trafford Park with modified windows. No.1 end: no 25kV sign; No.2 end 25kV sign (see photograph on page xxx). *(Rail-Online)*

Chapter 11
DUKINFIELD REHABILITATION

11.1 Rehabilitation.

After extended periods in store, agreement was finally reached for the rehabilitation of the Metrovick fleet by Metropolitan-Vickers at the former Great Central Railway Dukinfield C&W Works in Manchester.

The Engine History Cards indicates that D5719 was the first of the class to enter Dukinfield for 'Heavy Casual' repairs in May 1961, closely followed by D5709. However, according to the August 1961 edition of *Trains Illustrated*, D5707/13 were the first to enter the works in June 1961, a 'fact' erroneously repeated many times over the coming years!

It might have been expected that the rehabilitation work would have been undertaken at Bowesfield Works, Stockton, where the locomotives were initially constructed. However, these Works had been closed in February 1961. The following statement had been made by Metropolitan-Vickers-Beyer, Peacock Limited on December 5 1960:

'The directors of M-V-Beyer, Peacock Co. have come to the conclusion that it is now no longer able to maintain their locomotive facility at Stockton-on-Tees, County Durham, in continuous or profitable operation.

'As... there is no immediate prospect of further orders for locomotives, the factory will cease to operate as a manufacturing unit, in February 1961, upon completing the locomotive work now in hand.'

Work on the Metrovick locomotives at Dukinfield involved the repair, refurbishment and modification of numerous components including:

- complete renovation of the power units, undertaken off-site at the Crossley facility in Openshaw,
- fitting of new design crankcases to address the cracking issue, 'with strengthened corners in the 'A' bank drive end, with longer retention studs to put this corner under compression' (R.M. Tufnell, *The Diesel Impact on British Rail*),
- new cast iron cylinder heads, replacing the previous aluminium heads,
- new design of pistons,
- new fuel injectors,
- compressor modifications,
- attention to the persistent oil, fuel and water leakage problems,
- attention to the Spanner Mk 1 train heating boiler, and,
- completion of cab windscreen modifications to those members of the class not already modified.

Based on EHC data, each of the twenty locomotives resided at Dukinfield for an average of over 10 months.

After completion, each locomotive was moved to Gorton depot for static testing, followed by loaded trials on the Midland Main Line. On return to traffic, the Metrovick were transferred to 12E Barrow-in-Furness depot for operation in the Furness and West Cumberland areas.

11.2 Transition from Inactivity to Rehabilitation.

Combining information from the monthly BTC Motive Power Committee Appendix 'A' reports with information on the individual Engine History Cards gives an insight into the transition from progressive inactivity during 1961 to the commencement of rehabilitation.

Week ending	Operating Stock (MPC Appendix A)	Comments (Black text - from MPC Appendix A, Blue text - from EHCs, Red text - additional information or extrapolations)
11/03/61	20	
18/03/61	20	
25/03/61	12	8 Stored (unserviceable) D5703/4/7-9/12/3/9 stored 20/03/61.
01/04/61	10	10 Stored (unserviceable) (D5703/4/7-13/9). D5710/1 stored 27/03/61.
08/04/61	10	10 Stored (unserviceable)
15/04/61	9	11 Stored (unserviceable) (D5703/4/7-13/8/9). D5718 stored 10/04/61.
22/04/61	9	11 Stored (unserviceable)
29/04/61	9	11 Stored (unserviceable)
06/05/61	9	11 Stored (unserviceable)
13/05/61	9	11 Stored (unserviceable)
20/05/61	8	12 Stored (unserviceable) (D5703/4/7-14/8/9). D5714 stored 19/05/61.
27/05/61	8	12 Stored (unserviceable)
03/06/61	8	12 Stored (unserviceable)
10/06/61	10	10 Stored (unserviceable) (D5703/4/7/8/10-4/8). 2 undergoing refurbishment (D5709/19) (included in Op Stock).
17/06/61	9	11 Stored (unserviceable) (D5703/4/6-8/10-4/8). D5706 stored 12/06/61. 2 undergoing refurbishment (D5709/19) (included in Op Stock).
24/06/61	10	10 Stored (unserviceable) (D5701/3/4/6/8/10-2/4/8). D5701 stored 19/06/61. 4 undergoing refurbishment (D5707/9/13/9) (included in Op Stock).
01/07/61	10	10 Stored (unserviceable), 4 undergoing refurbishment.
08/07/61	10	10 Stored (unserviceable), 4 undergoing refurbishment.
15/07/61	9	9 Stored (unserviceable) (D5701/3-6/10/1/4/8). D5705 stored 12/07/61. 6 undergoing refurbishment (D5707-9/12/3/9).
	Adjusted 11 (5)	N.B. See Note 1 below.
22/07/61	11 (5)	9 Stored (unserviceable), 6 undergoing refurbishment.
29/07/61	11 (5)	9 Stored (unserviceable), 6 undergoing refurbishment.
05/08/61	11 (5)	9 Stored (unserviceable), 6 undergoing refurbishment.
12/08/61	11 (5)	9 Stored (unserviceable) (D5701/3-6/10/1/4/8). 6 undergoing refurbishment (D5707-9/12/3/9). 5 'in traffic' (D5700/2/15-7).
19/08/61	11 (5)	9 Stored (unserviceable), 6 undergoing refurbishment.
26/08/61	11 (5)	9 Stored (unserviceable), 6 undergoing refurbishment.

Week ending	Operating Stock (MPC Appendix A)	Comments (Black text - from MPC Appendix A, Blue text - from EHCs, Red text - additional information or extrapolations)
02/09/61	11 (5)	9 Stored (unserviceable), 6 undergoing refurbishment.
09/09/61	11 (5)	9 Stored (unserviceable) (D5701/3-6/10/1/4/8).
		6 undergoing refurbishment (D5707-9/12/3/9).
		5 'in traffic' (D5700/2/15-7).
16/09/61	No data.	9 Stored (unserviceable), 6 undergoing refurbishment.
23/09/61	No data.	6 Stored (unserviceable) (D5701/5/6/11/4/8).
		9 undergoing refurbishment (D5703/4/7-10/2/3/9)
30/09/61	No data.	6 Stored (unserviceable), 9 undergoing refurbishment.
07/10/61	14 (5)	6 Stored (unserviceable) (D5701/5/6/11/4/8).
		9 undergoing refurbishment (D5703/4/7-10/2/3/9).
		5 'in traffic' (D5700/2/15-7).
14/10/61	14 (5)	9 undergoing refurbishment (D5703/4/7-10/2/3/9).
21/10/61	17 (0)	17 undergoing refurbishment (D5700-10/2/3/5-7/9).
28/10/61	20 (0)	20 undergoing refurbishment (D5700-19).
04/11/61	20 (0)	20 undergoing refurbishment.

Notes:

1. The Motive Power Committee Appendix A statistics indicate that there was a change in reporting policy with respect to locomotives undergoing refurbishment i.e. whether or not they were included in the Operating Stock figure.
   Up to and including P/E 15/07/61 the locomotives undergoing refurbishment were excluded from Operating Stock; however, from P/E 12/08/61 the locomotives undergoing refurbishment were included in Operating Stock figures.
   The bracketed Operating Stock figures for Periods Ending 12/08/61, 09/09/61, 07/10/61 and 04/11/61 represent the true Operating Stock figures.
2. No tabulated data was published for P/E 07/10/61, thus the Operating Stock figure for w/e 07/10/61 represents my calculation based on the commentary provided in Appendix 'A' of the MPC Minutes.
3. The reference to only two Metrovicks undergoing rehabilitation by the end of P/E 17/06/61 appears understated, given that 6 are listed on their respective Engine History Cards as having arrived at Dukinfield. Perhaps the two represents where work had physically started.
4. Comparison of the above 'official' information with the Sighting information in Section 9.2 does show up a number of discrepancies, notably:

   D5703/4/7-9/12/3/9 being stored en bloc during w/e 20/03/61 even though actual storage took place much earlier,
   D5710/1 being stored en bloc during w/e 27/03/61 even though actual storage took place at least one month earlier, and,
   Storage of D5700/2/15/7 (circa April/May 1961) and D5716 (circa January 1961) never being officially recorded. Allowance for these discrepancies would obviously result in a substantially modified table compared to the one presented above.

11.3 Repairs at Dukinfield.
11.3.1 Numerical Order.
All information from Engine History Cards.

	Rehabilitation Period	Mileage pre-Dukinfield	Mileage post-Dukinfield to end-1963	Notes
D5700	19/10/61-30/08/62	99251	65012	
D5701	19/10/61-17/08/62	86299	59771	See Note (6)
D5702	16/10/61-19/12/62	86214	45740	See Note (4)
D5703	18/09/61-23/05/62	42914	77628	
D5704	18/09/61-08/06/62	83737	71507	
	06/08/62-14/08/62 (Rect)			
D5705	16/10/61-27/06/62	107484	62346	
D5706	19/10/61-30/07/62	81209	60698	See Note (6)
D5707	19/06/61-29/03/62	42956	89354	See Note (5)
D5708	10/07/61-19/04/62	62557	62570	See Note (5)
D5709	05/06/61-23/02/62	63171	89570	See Note (6)
D5710	18/09/61-08/06/62	88561	77916	
D5711	23/10/61-07/12/62	68141	55311	See Note (4)
D5712	10/07/61-18/05/62	38364	76531	See Note (5)
D5713	19/06/61-15/03/62	41005	73457	
D5714	22/10/61-08/11/62	88852	55518	
D5715	16/10/61-28/03/63	73259	42587	See Notes (1) and (3)
D5716	18/10/62-05/10/62	63647	60039	See Notes (1) and (2)
D5717	16/10/61-23/01/63	56719	47731	See Note (3)
D5718	28/10/61-27/11/62	36590	56156	See Note (7)
D5719	13/05/61-21/12/61	23521	80223	See Notes (1 and 5)

Notes:
(1) EHC: D5715/6 Gorton entries presumably in error for Dukinfield. EHC for D5719 shows Gorton entry crossed out and Dukinfield inserted in its place.
(2) EHC: D5716 repair period incorrect; based on mileages the entry should presumably read 18/10/61.
(3) EHC: Unclear as to how D5715 and D5717 achieved 78 and 94 miles respectively in 1962; both were in Dukinfield throughout 1962.
(4) EHC: Mileages for D5702/11 on arrival at Dukinfield not recorded; mileages calculated from 'Annual Statistics'.
(5) EHC (Pre-Dukinfield mileage):   D5707 Card shows 42887 but excludes 69 miles in 1961.
    D5708 Card shows 62508 but excludes 49 miles in 1961.
    D5712 Card shows 38347 but excludes 17 miles in 1961.
    D5719 Card shows 22757 but excludes 196 miles in 1961.
(6) D5709 was noted in Gortons Works on 22/02/62 and D5701/6 were noted in the Paint Shop on 29/07/62. However, there were no Metrovick observations at Gorton Works on 01/10/61, 08/10/61, 15/10/61, 17/12/61, 06/01/62, 18/03/62, 14/04/62, 13/05/62, 24/06/62, 01/09/62, 02/09/62, 14/10/62, 18/11/62, 15/12/62, 06/01/63.
(7) D5708 and D5718 was noted at 9G Gorton depot on 14/04/62 and 11/11/62 respectively, presumably en route to or from Gorton Works for re-acceptance testing.

11.3.2 Arrival Order.

	Rehabilitation Period	Notes
D5719	13/05/61-21/12/61	Ex-Trafford Park
D5709	05/06/61-23/02/62	Ex-Trafford Park
D5707	19/06/61-29/03/62	Ex-Trafford Park
D5713	19/06/61-15/03/62	Ex-Trafford Park
D5708	10/07/61-19/04/62	Ex-Trafford Park
D5712	10/07/61-18/05/62	Ex-Trafford Park
D5703	18/09/61-23/05/62	Ex-Trafford Park
D5704	18/09/61-08/06/62	Ex-Trafford Park
D5710	18/09/61-08/06/62	Ex-Trafford Park
D5702	16/10/61-19/12/62	Ex-Derby 18/10/61
D5705	16/10/61-27/06/62	Ex-Derby 19/10/61
D5715	16/10/61-28/03/63	Ex-Derby 19/10/61
D5717	16/10/61-23/01/63	Ex-Derby 20/10/61
D5716	18/10/61-05/10/62	Ex-Derby 20/10/61
D5700	19/10/61-30/08/62	Ex-Derby 19/10/61
D5701	19/10/61-17/08/62	Ex-Derby 19/10/61
D5706	19/10/61-30/07/62	Ex-Derby 19/10/61
D5714	22/10/61-08/11/62	Ex-Derby 20/10/61
D5718	22/10/61-27/11/62	Ex-Derby 20/10/61
D5711	23/10/61-07/12/62	Ex-Derby 20/10/61

Notes:
Some minor date discrepancies exist for locomotives originally stored at Derby.

11.3.3 Release Order.

	Rehabilitation Period
D5719	13/05/61-21/12/61
D5709	05/06/61-23/02/62
D5713	19/06/61-15/03/62
D5707	19/06/61-29/03/62
D5708	10/07/61-19/04/62
D5712	10/07/61-18/05/62
D5703	18/09/61-23/05/62
D5710	18/09/61-08/06/62
D5705	16/10/61-27/06/62
D5706	19/10/61-30/07/62
D5704	18/09/61-08/06/62, 06/08/62-14/08/62 (Rectification)

150 • THE METROPOLITAN-VICKERS TYPE 2 CO-BO DIESEL-ELECTRIC LOCOMOTIVES

	Rehabilitation Period
D5701	19/10/61-17/08/62
D5700	19/10/61-30/08/62
D5716	18/10/61-05/10/62
D5714	22/10/61-08/11/62
D5718	22/10/61-27/11/62
D5711	23/10/61-07/12/62
D5702	16/10/61-19/12/62
D5717	16/10/61-23/01/63
D5715	16/10/61-28/03/63

D5709, Gorton Works, 22 February 1962. According to the *Engine History Card*, this was one day prior to release from Dukinfield Works after rehabilitation; D5709 was presumably present at Gorton for acceptance testing purposes. Modified windows fitted, plus 25kV warning sign. No yellow warning panel. *(Paul Claxton)*

11.4 Cumbria Arrival Reports.

Metrovick arrivals in Cumbria were variously reported as follows:

- 'The next day [29/12/61] Metrovick Type 2 diesel No.D5712 [sic D5719] passed light through Preston northbound, presumably on the way to its new sphere of work in Furness.' *Modern Railways* (February 1962)
- 'The first locos. reported out-shopped after modification were D5712 (*sic*) and D5719 during December (*1961*).' SLS *Journal* (March 1962)
- 'By the end of February (*1962*), only one Metrovick Type 2 Co-Bo diesel, No. D5719, was yet at work in Furness, based on Barrow.' *Modern Railways* (April 1962)
- 'According to correspondent's reports only three of the units, Nos.D5709/13/9, had reached the area by late March.' *Modern Railways* (May 1962)
- 'By the end of April only one of the five Metro-Vick Co-Bo diesels then received by Barrow depot, Nos.D5707-9/13/9, was working a public service diagram.' *Modern Railways* (June 1962)
- 'Only five of the 20 Metro-Vic diesels, D5707/8/9/13/9, are working from Barrow shed at present.' *Railway Observer* (July 1962):
- 'By the end of April, only five Metro-Vick . . . locos. D5707-9, D5713 and D5719 had arrived at Barrow (12E) following modifications at their maker's works in Dukinfield.' SLS *Journal* (July 1962)
- 'By the beginning of June, Barrow's complement of Metro-Vick Type 2 Co-Bo diesels had grown to seven, D5703/7/8/9/12/3/9.' *Modern Railways* (August 1962)
- 'By the beginning of September, Barrow's stud of Metrovick Type 2 diesels had grown to 14 [sic 13] units [D5700/1/3-10/2/3/9].' *Modern Railways* (November 1962)
- 'The entire class of Metrovick Type 2 Co-Bo diesels [sic 19] had reached Barrow depot.' *Modern Railways* (March 1963)
- 'All the Metro-Vic diesels have now been seen in Barrow; the last was D5702 [sic D5715] at the beginning of April.' *Railway Observer* (August 1963)

Chapter 12
POST-DUKINFIELD PERFORMANCE

12.1 Post-'Rehabilitation' Performance.

From late-1961/early-1962, the Metrovicks returned to traffic working from their new base at Barrow-in-Furness. The final locomotive was released from Dukinfield in March 1963.

As P.C. Johnstone describes ('Metro-Vick Memories', *Cumbrian Railways* magazine No.124):

'The decision in the early sixties to transfer the entire class of twenty Metropolitan-Vickers Crossley diesel-electric locos to Barrow . . . came as something of a surprise to the loco men there. Always an out of the way part of the rail network, Barrow was usually kept supplied with ancient and worn-out cast-offs from other depots with which to work the mainly heavy traffic of the Furness line. So it came as quite a shock to be thrust into the twentieth century with relatively new diesel-electric locomotives. Of course it soon dawned on us that the reason we got them was the fact that no one else wanted them! *Plus ça change?*

'Crew training was carried out at Barrow, Carnforth and Workington and consisted of two training trains with empty coaches. One ran between Barrow and Workington for Barrow and Workington men and one between Carnforth and Barrow for Carnforth men, with the drivers training on the traction and the firemen training on the Spanner train heating boilers.'

Initially the fleet performed slightly better than when originally delivered. T. Hartley penned an article in *The Iron House* (Journal of the Lakeside Railway Society') which was subsequently reproduced in *British Railways Illustrated* (March 2012); he described his experiences at Barrow depot and with the newly-arrived Metrovicks:

'The Metrovick-Crossley Co-Bo locomotives arrived in Barrow in the early-1960s after being stored at Dukinfield and refurbished . . . with a two-year guarantee period from AEI (the owners of Metro-Vick) and Crossley . . . The Contractor's team was located in what would now be called portacabins outside the shed and were responsible for the maintenance and upkeep during this period. The shed staff in Barrow saw to the day to day duties of fuelling and watering as well as being trained by the contractors for the time when the guarantee expired, when they would become fully responsible for all the running [maintenance].'

The article continued by describing some of the first problems encountered (with some solutions):

- Crankcase failures,
- Main crankshaft bearing issues,
- Cylinder head gasket failures (alternative gasket material),
- Cylinder air induction valve issues (necessitating frequent removal and cleaning),
- Cylinder liners incorrectly 'chromed' allowing water from the cooling jacket to get into the sump, leading to overheating (liner renewal),
- Fuel supply issues causing engine shutdown

(partially resolved by fitting a new type of filter),
- Engine timing difficulties to minimise smoke emissions,
- Heavy oil consumption,
- Broken pipes and hoses due to engine vibration,
- Air supply from the compressors (solved by AEI by making the compressors work continuously, with the unloader valve opening when pressure was reached),
- Steam heating boiler ignition issues (and flaring issues on re-ignition).

Modern Railways (June 1962) reported: 'Local railwaymen say the diesels are good performers but erratic, being particularly prone to blocked fuel filters and broken fuel pipes'.

However, Hartley maintains that 'when the Co-Bos worked properly they were one of the strongest locomotives around'. As with Derby before, much of the work done at Barrow was carried out 'under the most unpromising conditions with very basic facilities and equipment. The genius for improvisation came into its own'. Furthermore, 'in those days such difficulties were resolved through the ingenuity of the fitting staff, improvising with the simple tools and equipment that were available. There were no modern facilities . . . but many problems were nevertheless overcome'. P.C. Johnstone comments, 'when any of the locos required the cylinder heads to be lifted off or any other heavy engine parts had to be removed, Barrow's steam breakdown crane was used for the lifting which of course was done outside the shed.'

The list of issues looks to be remarkably similar to those experienced pre-Dukinfield, although the general 'feel' is that the frequency of problems were reduced and that the perseverance of the Barrow foremen and fitters may have been greater than those at Derby (maybe driven by necessity, with Barrow having a significantly smaller fleet of diesels to call upon).

An Appendix to the 1965 National Traction Plan included a graph illustrating the weekly availability percentage statistics of the Metrovick fleet for the April to December 1964 period. The high point was four consecutive weeks above 80 per cent in late-May/early-June (highest 84.5 per cent) and a low-point of 49.5 per cent in w/e 25 November. The average was about 70 per cent.

The Crossley crankcase issue remained the key problem and as R.M. Tufnell (*The Diesel Impact on British Rail*) describes, 'The crankcases were a considerable improvement, but the same trouble showed up on the "B" bank over a longer period'. As early as January 1965, the BR CME Department was reporting that 'further extensive cracking has been experienced, and one of the twenty locomotives [thought to be D5709] has been laid up for this reason'

A Technical Report to the BRB from the Chief Engineer (Traction & Rolling Stock) dated 16 October 1967 contained an Addendum entitled 'Diesel Locomotive Performance & Efficiency'. Information included in this document covering the Metrovick locomotives is provided below:

1. Availability: Range 50-70%.
2. Reliability (Miles per Casualty): Average 5000.
3. Principle Technical Problems:

Item:	Action Required or Taken:
Engines.	Engines.
Aluminium cylinder heads fracturing.	Replaced by cast iron cylinder heads.
Crankshaft difficulties due to main bearings.	Main bearings being replaced.
Crankcase fractures.	Replacement crankcases fitted as necessary.
Fuel pump springs incorrectly made.	Corrected by manufacturer.
Unbalanced engine due to faulty calibration of fuel pumps.	Corrected by manufacturer.
Fuel pipe defects.	Better clipping and maintenance.

No electrical issues were flagged up, once again reflecting the robustness of the Metropolitan-Vickers equipment.

12.2 Availability and Utilisation.

Appendix 'A' of the BTC Motive Power Committee Meeting Minutes provided availability and utilisation reports pre- and post-rehabilitation statistics covering the Metrovicks. Statistics for the period December 1961 to early October 1962 as the locomotives were being reintroduced to traffic are provided below:

Availability and Weekday (Monday-Saturday) mileage statistics:

Week ending	Operating Stock	% Available Whole 24hrs	Miles Per Loco Per Weekday — Locos in use	Miles Per Loco Per Weekday — Op. Stock	Comments
09/12/61	20	NIL	NIL	NIL	20 undergoing rehabilitation.
16/12/61	20	NIL	NIL	NIL	20 undergoing rehabilitation.
23/12/61	20	2.5	NIL	NIL	19 undergoing rehabilitation.
30/12/61	20	5.0	46.0	1.2	19 undergoing rehabilitation.
27/01/62	20	5.0	150	6	19 undergoing rehabilitation.
24/02/62	20	6.5	131	7	18 undergoing rehabilitation.
24/03/62	20	11.5	252	13	18 undergoing rehabilitation.
21/04/62	20	16.0	271	28	15 undergoing rehabilitation.
19/05/62	20	18.5	233	31	14 undergoing rehabilitation.
16/06/62	20	35.0	168	46	12 undergoing rehabilitation.
14/07/62	20	44.0	194	85	10 undergoing rehabilitation.
11/08/62	20	43.5	173.1	75.3	9 undergoing rehabilitation.
08/09/62	20	60.0	184.4	108.8	7 undergoing rehabilitation.
06/10/62	20	57.0	181.1	101.4	6 undergoing rehabilitation.

By the beginning of 1963, only D5715 and D5717 remained out of traffic at Dukinfield. Unfortunately, after 1963, the mileage data for the Metrovicks ceased to be recorded on the Engine History Cards. However, by 'adjusting' the 1963 figures for D5715 and D5717 to the full year equivalent, an indicative picture of the average mileages achieved by the Metrovicks can be ascertained.

The total Metrovick recorded fleet mileage for 1963 was 907,848. With the annual figure adjusted to 920,738 to allow for the part-year operations of D5715/7, the calculated average annual mileage for 1963 was 46037, virtually double that achieved in 1960 (see Section 8.6), with a range from 31506 (D5708) to 56819 (D5707).

Alternatively, the average annual mileage for the 18 locomotive in traffic throughout 1963 (i.e. excluding D5715/7) was 45428.

The 1963 BR 'Miles of Traction Units' (BR1712/438) reports give an interesting comparison between the Metrovicks and the BR/Sulzer Type 2s in the 'Western, Midland and North Western Lines' area.

		Net Op Stock	Average Number used per Day	Total Miles Worked (Weekdays)	Miles per Weekday per Unit — In Stock	Miles per Weekday per Unit — In Use
we 23/02/63	Crossley/MV	20	15.1	15,359	128.0	169.5
	BR/Sulzer	71	39.0	33,897	79.6	144.9
we 23/03/63	Crossley/MV	20	15.7	17,074	142.3	181.3
	BR/Sulzer	71	47.5	40,103	94.1	140.7

Post-Dukinfield Performance • 155

		Net Op Stock	Average Number used per Day	Total Miles Worked (Weekdays)	Miles per Weekday per Unit In Stock	Miles per Weekday per Unit In Use
we 06/04/63	Crossley/MV	20	16.2	17,820	148.5	183.3
	BR/Sulzer	71	50.3	43,306	101.7	143.5
we 18/05/63	Crossley/MV	20	16.8	17,037	142.0	169.0
	BR/Sulzer	71	46.8	49,390	115.9	175.9
we 15/06/63	Crossley/MV	20	18.4	18,013	150.1	163.2
	BR/Sulzer	71	44.4	38,290	89.9	143.7
we 13/07/63	Crossley/MV	20	16.7	18,536	154.5	185.0
	BR/Sulzer	71	51.6	45,268	106.3	146.2
we 03/08/63	Crossley/MV	20	17.0	20,726	172.7	203.2
	BR/Sulzer	71	50.5	44,026	103.3	145.3
we 07/09/63	Crossley/MV	20	16.3	18,902	157.5	193.3
	BR/Sulzer	71	48.3	43,365	101.8	149.6
we 05/10/63	Crossley/MV	20	16.3	16,589	138.2	169.6
	BR/Sulzer	71	45.6	36,649	86.0	134.0
we 02/11/63	Crossley/MV	20	15.5	17,163	143.0	184.5
	BR/Sulzer	71	49.7	44,902	105.4	150.6
we 30/11/63	Crossley/MV	20	14.3	15,186	126.6	177.0
	BR/Sulzer	71	47.9	47,555	111.6	165.5
we 21/12/63	Crossley/MV	20	14.5	14,875	124.0	171.0
	BR/Sulzer	71	53.0	46,245	108.6	145.4

Somewhat surprisingly perhaps, the Metrovick performance was consistently ahead of the BR/Sulzer Type 2's during this period.

The BR (LMR) 'Availability by Classes of Locomotives and Power Cars' (BR.1712/437) reports for 1963 yield the following information:

Metropolitan-Vickers Type 2 - Average Weekday Position (1963).

Number and Percentage of Net Operating Stock

	Net Op Stock	Available No. (%)	Not Available Works No. (%)	Not Available Depots No. (%)	Not Available Awaiting Materials No. (%)
we 26/01/63	20	11.3 (56.5)	1.3 (6.5)	7.2 (36.0)	0.2 (1.0)
we 23/02/63	20	15.1 (75.5)	1.0 (5.0)	2.2 (11.0)	1.7 (8.5)
we 23/03/63	20	15.7 (78.5)	2.0 (10.0)	1.3 (6.5)	1.0 (5.0)
we 06/04/63	20	16.2 (81.0)	1.0 (5.0)	1.0 (5.0)	1.8 (9.0)
we 18/05/63	20	16.8 (84.0)	1.0 (5.0)	2.2 (11.0)	0.0 (0.0)
we 15/06/63	20	18.4 (92.0)	0.0 (0.0)	0.4 (2.0)	1.2 (6.0)

THE METROPOLITAN-VICKERS TYPE 2 CO-BO DIESEL-ELECTRIC LOCOMOTIVES

	Net Op Stock	Available No. (%)	Not Available Works No. (%)	Not Available Depots No. (%)	Awaiting Materials No. (%)
we 13/07/63	20	16.7 (83.5)	0.0 (0.0)	3.3 (16.5)	0.0 (0.0)
we 03/08/63	20	17.0 (85.0)	0.2 (1.0)	2.8 (14.0)	0.0 (0.0)
we 07/09/63	20	16.8 (84.0)	1.0 (5.0)	2.2 (11.0)	0.0 (0.0)
we 05/10/63	20	17.0 (85.0)	1.0 (5.0)	1.4 (7.0)	0.6 (3.0)
we 02/11/63	20	15.5 (77.5)	1.0 (5.0)	2.7 (13.5)	0.8 (4.0)
we 30/11/63	20	14.3 (71.5)	1.0 (5.0)	4.0 (20.0)	0.7 (3.5)
we 21/12/63	20	14.5 (72.5)	0.0 (0.0)	3.5 (17.5)	2.0 (10.0)

Net Op. Stock: Net Operating Stock
Not Available Works: In Works & Awaiting Works
Not Available Depots: Under/Awaiting Repairs and Under/Awaiting Exams

The National Traction Plan 'Progress Report and Assessment of Position as at 18th April 1966' provided comparative information for the BR Type 2 fleet:

Selected Type 2 Availability (w/e 13 April 1966):

Locomotive Description	Net Operating Stock	Availability (%) Actual	N.T.P.	Difference	Equivalent No. of Locos
BR/Sulzer 1160hp	151	75%	87%	-12%	-18
BR/Sulzer 1250hp	285	84%	87%	-3%	-8
MV/Crossley 1200hp	16	50%	87%	-37%	-6

D5709, Skew Bridge, September 1964. Negatively impacting the availability statistics, D5709 is returned to base (presumably Barrow) by Fowler 4F 0-6-0 steam locomotive 44200. (*Author's Collection*)

12.3 Driver's Views.

In a letter from Driver Philip C. Johnstone of Ulverston to myself in February 2004, he described his impressions of the Metrovicks:

'The Crossleys gave us a good grounding in diesel traction, most of us carried a tool kit of some description and the fact that at first they were maintained by AEI and Metro-Vic staff meant that we could ask the men who knew if we had any problems. After various modifications, the Crossleys performed OK especially on loose-coupled freights, their 97 tons made them good braking engines. They were often troublesome on passenger trains especially when operating Spanner train heat boilers. Things got so bad that they were banned south of Carnforth on passenger trains. Another job they were fine on were the Lindal bank engine turns, the notched controller, good DSD pedal and quick acting direct air brake made them easy and safe to work with.

'When we worked the Millom coke trains, we would change crews at Workington and you could bet that if we had a Crossley on the empties and the Carlisle men had a Sulzer, that the driver would say he "didn't know Crossleys"! So we would take the Crossley back to Millom with the coke. Actually the Crossley was probably the better loco for the job. Most Barrow men had a soft spot for them.'

Another railway man, Arnie Furness, concurs:

'I used to work with an ex Barrow driver who said that he really liked these locos, despite their unreliability, and that they were the best "ride" of any diesel he drove!'

Modern Railways (March 1963) reported:

'A local driver told one of our correspondents that they were showing as good a reliability as any other brand of main line diesel on the L.M.R. and proffered his opinion that they were improperly handled when on the Midland Lines.'

P.C. Johnstone also described some of his personal operating experiences in the *Cumbrian Railways* magazine (see Section 12.1):

'Broken fuel pipes . . . continued to be a problem and this compounded another nuisance. The cab window demisters used air drawn from the traction motor blowers, which were mounted at No.1 end in the engine compartment and in No.2 end adjacent to the Spanner boiler. As there always seemed to be a fine mist of diesel fuel in the engine compartment, this was drawn into the traction motor blowers and blown out in the cab, which after a while became very unpleasant for the crew. At No.2 end the trouble was the train heat boiler which at times filled the boiler compartment with smoke which, of course was drawn into the traction motor blowers and consequently would end up in No.2 cab. Many's the time I've lost sight of my mate in No.2 cab when it filled with smoke! These demisters were soon plugged with newspaper to block off this nuisance!'

'AMTK484' commented on the *End of the Line* web forum:

'I grew up in Barrow and talked to a lot of the older drivers. Superb ride on the boiler end – the Co – so they used to try to get them boiler end leading whenever they could. The Bo end was a bit bouncy [N.B. The boiler was actually at the Bo end, but the point is taken].

'Very fast loading – straight to 9 which, if you know the Furness Line, is very useful.

'Good slow speed control as well. Better on nudging up than [the BR/Sulzer] 25's.

'The only problem was fuel guzzling. Barrow-Lancaster and back was OK, Barrow-Preston and back was scary, but there were some better than others and they'd diagram accordingly.'

A. Whitaker, in a letter to *British Railways Illustrated* (December 2010) entitled 'In Defence of the Co-Bos', wrote about the later Carlisle days:

'I met and interviewed a Carlisle Traction Inspector who had long experience of the class. Among other subjects, I asked him about his memories of the Metro-Vicks and his view was that they were 'decent locos' towards the end of their careers and would have been worth keeping . . . He said that, during 1968, the Kingmoor fitters had finally got to grips with the recurring faults which had plagued the Co-Bos for years and, as long as they were kept well oiled, they were as reliable as any Class 25, and far more reliable than the Clayton Type 1s which were also based at the depot at that time.

'The directive to eliminate the Co-Bos apparently caused frustration among some depot staff who had worked long and hard to improve their reliability to an acceptable level and now they were being told to "get rid".'

The re-allocation of the Metrovicks to the new Carlisle Kingmoor depot in January 1968 represented the first time in their career that they were maintained in purpose-built diesel traction facilities, 9½ years into their ten year career!

12.4 Visits to Reddish (Manchester).

From 1963, the Metrovicks frequently visited 9C Reddish depot for specialist attention by Crossley staff, this continuing right up their withdrawal in 1968. Tyre re-profiling work was also undertaken at Reddish.

Reported sightings of visits to 9C Reddish are listed below:

D5701	Undated photographic evidence (post-November 1967).
D5702	090467, 020268/150268/170268
D5705	xx0568
D5706	150467/ 200567, 010867, 140668/220668/210768/040868
D5707	110965/171065, 040868/310868
D5708	211063/ xx1163, 090565/220565, 190367, 140668
D5711	010964, 220967, 151067
D5712	250667, Late-1267, 280468/030568/050568/120568/260568/300568/020668
	N.B. D5712 was also noted at 9A Longsight on 310766/070866.
D5714	190367, 020268/150268, 040868
D5715	160767/ 010867, xx0568
D5716	031167/251167, 150268
D5717	xx0568, xx0868
D5718	220967
D5719	200567, 251167, 310868

D5715 and D5706, 9C Reddish, 1 August 1967.
(John Grey Turner)

D5712, 9C Reddish, 12 May 1968.
(*Author's Collection*)

12.5 Further Crossley Engine Developments.

As already discussed, during the Dukinfield rehabilitation process the Metrovicks received new crankcases with strengthened corners in the 'A' bank drive end, new cast iron cylinder heads and a new piston design. However, over time, the same problem showed up on the 'B' bank.

When it became obvious that the rehabilitated locomotives were going to suffer in the same way as the original design, they were, between 1966 and 1968, progressively withdrawn from service. However, Crossley, in ongoing attempts to address the problems, once again redesigned the crankcase assembly.

A demonstration completely-redesigned crankcase was supplied by Crossley to British Railways and fitted to D5705 shortly before the Metrovick fleet was authorised for complete withdrawal. A paragraph in the December 1968 edition of *The Railway Magazine* reads:

'D5705, fitted with an experimental crankcase, is at present under examination at Carlisle depot and will shortly be transferred to the Derby Research Unit, where it will undergo final strain tests before scrapping. The crankcase being developed is intended for other types of locomotive and will not affect the fate of the Co-Bos which have merely been the test-bed.'

It is unlikely that D5705 really got a satisfactory trial, given the Derby Research Unit workload, although various sources suggest that the engine was completely satisfactory.

D5705, Crewe Works, 16 August 1967. D5705 midway through its extended stay at Crewe Works (April-November 1967) during which time it received a demonstration engine with a completely redesigned crankcase. (*John Grey Turner*)

Chapter 13
THE RE-ENGINING PROPOSAL AND OTHER DEVELOPMENTS

13.1 Introduction.

The proposal to re-engine the Metrovick fleet with an established English Electric engine is well known. Perusal of available archive material provides some background to the proposal, as well as a very interesting insight into some of the trials and tribulations associated with project. The National Traction Plans of February 1965 and November 1967 were the drivers behind both the re-engining process and its ultimate cancellation and relevant extracts are provided below.

Archive information is inevitably incomplete. The following is heavily based on BRB, Works & Equipment Committee and Supplies Committee meeting minutes and supporting memoranda, together with fairly extensive correspondence between the Chief Engineer, the Chief Operating Officer and the Supplies Manager. So, not the total story by any means, but a very interesting and useful insight nonetheless.

13.2 Re-Engining - An Archive Perspective.

13.2.1 National Traction Plan - February 1965.

The BR Re-shaping Plan (published 27 March 1963) specified extensive route rationalisation and withdrawal of passenger services across the whole of British Railways as well as new initiatives such as 'merry-go-round' operations for coal traffic and the significant development of liner-train container services. It was recognised that this Plan, plus Freight and Coal Concentration Schemes and the Freight Sundries Plan would have a significant impact on forward motive-power requirements.

As a consequence, the need for a detailed plan to fully understand forward locomotive requirements was identified. T.C. Boynton-Hughes was made responsible for the production of such a plan and the first BR National Traction Plan (NTP) was published in February 1965. This involved the total re-appraisal of locomotive and multiple-unit requirements on a national scale based on revised future passenger and freight traffic requirements and acceptable standards of locomotive availability and utilisation. In locomotive terms, the Plan defined the numbers of units required by type for each operating Region, identifying any surpluses or shortfalls, and the support maintenance and servicing infrastructure required to achieve the required levels of locomotive availability and utilisation.

At the end of 1964, the NTP identified the total stock of main-line diesels as 2,463 locomotives (including electro-diesels), increasing to 3,101 once all outstanding orders had been completed and delivered. This compared with an assessment of locomotives required made at the end of 1963 of 3,731.

Future requirements were determined based around forecast train mileages, train speed improvements (15 per cent increase assumed), freight train payload increases, locomotive utilisation improvements (to 12 hours hauling trains per day), motive power availability improvements (87 per cent assumed for Type 2 locomotives) and various contingency factors. The re-assessment of traffic requirements and identified improvements resulted in a re-defined locomotive requirement of 3,101 locomotives, albeit with identified surpluses in the Type 2 and Type 3 categories (28 and 77 respectively) and deficiencies in the Type 1 and Type 4 categories (57 and 48 respectively). Judicious national deployment of locomotives was seen as the solution to this issue.

Being cynical, one wonders whether the efficiency improvements deployed in the plan were deliberately set to achieve the neutral result between locomotives delivered and on order (3,101) and those needed to cover future requirements (3,101)! The result, however, was the avoidance of £55 million capital investment (at 1965 prices) i.e. 630 less diesel locomotives.

The NTP identified the need for 975 Type 2 locomotives (of the 3,101 total), based on 87 per cent availability. The Plan included an assessment of the impact of worse than Plan availability levels, thus at 80% availability the requirement for Type 2s increased to 1,070, and at 75 per cent availability it was 1,132. The Plan indicated that the availability rate for Type 2s averaged 82.1 per cent during the period April-December 1964, although the Metrovicks were substantially lower at 'between 50% and 70%'. Subsequent problems in achieving the required 87 per cent level certainly impacted on the timing of the elimination of steam, actually August 1968 instead of the end-1967 point proposed in the NTP.

The NTP specifically included the twenty Metrovicks in the make-up of the 1,003 Type 2 fleet (i.e. 975 required, plus 28 surplus). However, whilst the NTP explicitly referenced the re-engining of the Scottish Region NBL Type 2s with Paxman engines and the Eastern Region Brush Type 2s with English Electric engines, no such mention to upgrading the Metrovicks was made at this point.

13.2.2 Re-engining - From Proposal to Authorisation.

A Memorandum to the BRB Works & Equipment Committee (W&EC) dated 2 April 1965 (produced by the Chief Operating Officer, Chief Engineer (Traction & Rolling Stock) and Financial Controller) included a section on the 'Re-engining of Type 2 Diesel-Electric Locomotives' in which the following statement was made:

'The conclusions drawn in the National Traction Plan that the total number of locomotives already authorised will in due course meet the total requirement, are based on the continued use of all Type 2 locomotives already in service.

'Authority has already been given for the re-engining of 58 Type 2 N.B. locomotives allocated to the Scottish Region, but has only been implemented in respect of 20.

'It is further proposed that 20 Crossley-Met.Vic. Type 2 locomotives should be re-engined at a cost of £360,000.'

This recommendation to the W&EC for the upgrade of twenty Metrovick locomotives appears to be the first time that the re-engining of the MetroVicks has surfaced in available archive documentation and presumably reflects the desire to ensure that the Metrovick locomotives represented an effective component of the Type 2 fleet with availability levels at the prescribed 87+ per cent level.

Appendix B to the Memorandum provided additional detail:

20 Met.Vic./Crossley Type 2 Locomotives.

'20 of these locomotives were included in the initial orders placed for diesel locomotives and were delivered in 1958/59. They incorporate the Crossley two-stroke engine which has been costly to maintain and has given repeated trouble with fractured crankcases and cylinder heads and excessive wear of the cylinder liners. The engine manufacturers have endeavoured to overcome these problems but difficulties are still being experienced and two locomotives have now been withdrawn from traffic as unserviceable. The mechanical and electrical parts of these locomotives have given good service and it is proposed that they should be re-engined with the English Electric 8SVT engine which is identical to that fitted to English Electric Type 1 locomotives where it has proved to be one of the most reliable of engines in service. For application to the Type 2 locomotives the engine should be rated at 1,200 hp and would thus give comparable performance to the existing engine. Provision of the engines and installation costs, etc. is estimated to cost £18,000 per locomotive and authorisation is therefore sought to an expenditure of £360,000 for the re-engining of the 20 locomotives. The programme for which could be completed during the second half of 1966.'

Note that this report is already referencing the withdrawal from traffic of two locomotives (presumably D5704/13).

Minute No.2664 of the BRB W&EC dated 6 April 1965 reveals discussion of the re-engining of the Metrovicks:

'Mr Cox explained that the estimates quoted were based on figures given by the English Electric Company but that detail design work had not yet been done. Mr Shirley suggested that the English Electric Company should be approached with a view to their doing the design and re-engining, the incentive being conversion of all the locomotives following successful tests of an initial conversion. The Committee asked the Supplies Manager and Chief Engineer (Traction and Rolling Stock) to collaborate in putting this proposition to the Company and to report back to the Committee at their next meeting.'

'*Modern Railways*' reported the following in its October 1965 edition:

'Metrovick Co-Bos to be rebuilt?'
'Rebuilding of the 20 1,200 hp Metrovick Type 2 diesel-electric Co-Bos, Nos. D5700-19, is contemplated by BR . . . It is understood that the proposal is to replace the Crossley engines and certain other mechanical components with English Electric products, but to retain the existing AEI electrical equipment.'

Eight months after the action of 6 April 1965, on 23 December, a further Memorandum was submitted to the W&EC (produced by the Chief Operating Officer, Chief Engineer (Traction & Rolling Stock) and Supplies Manager); this included a review of further progress and their recommendation:

'The position has been discussed with the English Electric Company who have stated that they "note the proposal that we should re-engine the initial locomotive at our expense, the incentive being that the remaining 19 locomotives would be converted when the prototype has been proved satisfactory. This proposal has been given very careful consideration and while we have confidence in our ability to produce a satisfactory prototype, we feel that adequate safeguards are provided by the guarantee provisions contained in your standard Contract Conditions BTC.10, provisions which we have always interpreted in a generous manner as we feel sure you will agree. The request that we should finance the prototype would appear to be an extension of normal guarantee conditions and as such we regret that we could not accept an order in the terms suggested."

'General design work on this project has continued in BR drawing offices and detailed drawings can now be made available for the re-engining.

'Quotations have accordingly been sought for the complete re-engining of these locomotives from both the English Electric Company and Workshops which, including the estimated cost of the associated modifications to the electrical components, are as follows:

		Delivery of completed locomotives
English Electric Co.	£24,460	May 1967 - Dec 1968
BR Workshops	£19,300	May 1967 - May 1968

'It is proposed therefore that the Workshops should undertake the re-engining of these locomotives and that an order should be placed on the English Electric Company for the supply of the engine and mounting feet.

'Authority is therefore sought for the estimated expenditure of £386,000 for the re-engining of the 20 Met/Vic Crossley Type 2 locomotives with English Electric 8CSVT engines.

'Subject to authority being given, the Supply Committee are requested to approve the placing of an order with the English Electric Company for the supply of the engine and mounting feet at the quoted price of £14,996 and for the work of installation to be undertaken by the Workshops.'

The approach adopted by BR in asking English Electric to finance a prototype conversion was presumably the cause of the apparent delay between the W&EC action in April 1965 and the recommendation finally proposed in December 1965. Ultimately, the relative difference in the price of the conversion work resulted in the work being allocated to the BR Workshops.

Minute 2755(5) of the W&EC dated 18 January 1966 recorded the recommendation to the Board for approval of the re-engining of the 20 Metrovick locomotives at an estimated cost of £386,000. In turn, Minute 66/14(b) of the BRB Meeting held on 27 January 1966 recorded final authorisation for re-engining. As a consequence, Minute 409(vi) of the BRB Supply Committee which took place on 10 February 1966 confirmed the approval of the following Contract:

'English Electric for the supply of the engine and mounting feet required for the re-engining of 20 MET/VIC Crossley Type 2 locomotives with English Electric 8CSVT engines at the quoted price of £14,996 each, the work of installation to be undertaken by BR Workshops at a cost of £4,304 each.'

13.2.3 Technical - English Electric Engine Selection.

During February 1966, correspondence between H.R. Gomersall (BRB) and C.P. Scott-Malden (Ministry of Transport) took place with Scott-Malden questioning the deployment of the English Electric 8CSVT engine:

'could you let us know why the Board have decided to use uprated English Electric 8CSVT engines for this particular type of locomotive rather than the 12SVT version by the same manufacturer which has already been successfully tested in the Brush Type 2s?'

Gomersall replied:

'These Crossley locomotives are of a shorter length than the Brush Type 2s and the reason why the 12SVT engine cannot be used in the Crosselys is simply that it is too long to fit into the available space, and only a major alteration to the locomotive would enable the larger engine to be fitted.

'The 8CSVT to be fitted in the Met/Vic Crosselys is a slightly uprated version of the 1,000hp English Electric engine which is the most reliable unit we have on British Railways.'

13.2.4 Technical Issues or Procrastination?

At some point during the first few months of 1966, technical issues started to surface, requiring a major re-think. These issues are believed to have included English Electric engine cooling issues when utilising existing equipment already installed in the Metrovicks, and engine/generator compatibility difficulties. The following memo from R.B. Hoff/R.C. Brown (Supplies) to J.F. Harrison (Chief Engineer [T&RS]) dated 22 March 1966 highlights the situation:

'Referring to our letter of 8th March, it would appear necessary from the minutes of the meeting held on 3rd March that when all the technical features for the re-engining have been resolved, English Electric and Workshops will have to submit revised quotations for this work.

'If you agree, we shall be glad to have details of the revised specification in order that up-to-date quotations may be obtained, including a delivery programme of work.'

This was followed up by another memo from R.B. Hoff/R.C. Brown to J.F. Harrison dated 20 June 1966 as follows:

'We shall be glad to know how matters are progressing in regard to this project but you will, of course, be aware that present requirements differ from that authorised, having regard to the technical discussions which have taken place, and, in our view, before we can place any orders, revised authority will be necessary. The authorised expenditure stands at £386,000, whereas the revised expenditure, after allowing for price variation, could be £495,000. A comparison of authorised with probable expenditure is as follows:

	Price per locomotive		
	Authorised expenditure £		Probable expenditure £
English Electric	14,996	say	16,000
A.E.I.	700		4,045
Workshops	3,600		3,600
	19,296		23,645
Add price variation	-		1,100
	19,926		24,745
or say	386,000	say	£495,000

'Under the heading "Probable expenditure", the 6 sets of brake equipment is excluded, and there is no allowance for any adjustment of Workshops price as a result of the change in specification. In this latter respect you have still not said whether revised specifications have been issued to Workshops to enable a new quotation to be submitted, and we shall be glad to know whether Workshops are now in a position to quote. Because of this we have no way of knowing when it is expected the work will be completed, and our assessment of price variation covers possible increases up to December 1967.'

A further memo from R.B. Hoff/C.E. Reynold (Supplies) to J.F. Harrison dated 21 July 1966 repeated the need for clarification. A pencil annotation on this memo (source unknown) reads 'This has doubtful future now.' Certainly from this point onwards there is no specific mention in available literature of English Electric being the replacement engine supplier.

13.2.5 Investment Contraints and Back to the Drawing Board.

Slow technical progress was further exacerbated by the removal of the Metrovick re-engining project from the 1967 Investment Programme. This was highlighted in a memo from G.R. Evans (for Chief Officer [New Works]) to J.F. Harrison (with copies to the Supplies Manager and Chief Operating Officer) dated 15 August 1966:

'You will be aware that this project was removed from the 1967 Investment Programme in the course of the recent cuts in Capital Investment.

'Assuming that it is considered necessary to proceed with the re-engining of these locomotives, you may consider it prudent to deal with one locomotive in 1967 as a 'prototype' for trial purposes before proceeding with the remaining 19 in 1968.'

J.F. Harrison (Chief Engineer T&RS) replied on 25 August 1966 (with copies to the Chief Operating Officer and Supplies Manager):

'With reference to your letter of 15th August I note that this project has been removed from the 1967 Investment Programme.

'Under the circumstances I see no reason therefore, in proceeding with one locomotive as a prototype in 1967, and I think the whole matter should now be left in abeyance until November 1967 when we can then re-assess the motive power position and whether or not the programme should be abandoned.

'Under the circumstances I am notifying the firms concerned that no orders will be placed in the near future and that they must consider the whole programme held in abeyance for at least another 12 months.'

This maybe deliberately provocative reply elicited a flurry of responses:

Memo from Chief Officer (New Works) to Chief Engineer (T&RS) (copies to Supplies Manager and Chief Operating Officer), 26 August 1966:
   'Thank you for your letter of 25th August. I wonder, however, if it is wise to delay the conversion of a prototype. I would have thought that the deferment in the investment programme would have provided valuable time thoroughly to test the prototype and enable an immediate start to be made on the full conversion programme once the need has been confirmed and money is again available.
   'This seems to be the right course unless the Chief Operating Officer confirms now that the conversion will be unnecessary.'

Memo from Chief Operating Officer to Chief Engineer (T&RS), 31 August 1966:
   'Thank you for your letter of 25th August; you will recall that in my letter to you of 21st October 1965, it was pointed out that the 20 Metrovic Crossley Type 2 locomotives were included in the ultimate requirements set out in the National Traction Plan for the London Midland Region. This requirement still stands.
   'It would appear, therefore, that there is good reason for proceeding with the re-engining of one of these locomotives as a prototype and thus enable operating experience to be gained with it so that any desirable modifications, the need for which may become apparent, may be incorporated when the full conversion programme applicable to the remaining 19 locomotives is commenced.'

Memo from Supplies Manager to Chief Engineer (T&RS) (copy to Chief Officer (New Works) and Chief Operating Officer), 31 August 1966:
   'If it is now proposed not to re-engine the 20 Metrovic locomotives, surely consideration should be given to disposing of them. I believe they have not been available for service for some time.'

Memo from Chief Engineer (T&RS) to Chief Operating Officer (copy to Chief Officer (New Works) and Supplies Manager), 31 August 1966:
   'You are in receipt of a letter dated 26th August from the Chief Officer (New Works). I do not feel disposed to divert manpower on to the prototype in view of all other commitments as it is far from clear that this project will ever materialise.
   'I am advising the C.M. & E.E. of the Midland Region to proceed to cannibalise locomotives that have been withdrawn from service to keep the remainder of the fleet going as long as possible even though this has the effect of virtually reducing the locomotives one by one to scrap.

'In this way a number of the locomotives will be available for four or five years when it may be more prudent to allocate other standard locomotives in their place.'

Memo from Chief Operating Officer to Chief Engineer (T&RS) (copy to Chief Officer (New Works) and Supplies Manager), 2 September 1966:
   'Your letter of the 31st August has apparently crossed mine of the same date. I have, however, noted the contents of your latest letter but still hold the views expressed in my letter of 31st August to the effect that the re-engining of one of these locomotives should go ahead since all 20 of the type will be required under the National Traction Plan.
   'I shall be glad to hear that you are arranging this.'

Memo from Chief Engineer (T&RS) to Chief Operating Officer, 12 September 1966:
   'I thank you for your letters of the 31st August and 2nd September and note that you think that we ought to proceed with a prototype conversion, so eventually these locomotives can be re-built and take their full part with the fleet.
   'It would appear to me that the opportunity should be taken to develop a new prototype of locomotives rather than how to make the present one rated at 1,250 hp work with a new engine. I therefore propose to look into the possibility of re-equipping one of these

locomotives with a higher powered engine as a prototype for future locomotives.

'This may mean of course, that the actual conversion and re-engining may be put back a bit, but the effect will be well worthwhile and I should be glad of your confirmation that I have your support in proceeding accordingly.'

The next archive correspondence surfaced in March 1967 with the following memo from R.B. Hoff/R.C. Brown to Chief Officer (New Works) (copy to J.F. Harrison) dated 3 March 1967:

'We shall be interested to know the present position regarding these 20 locomotives and whether it will be the ultimate intention to re-engine them.'

There were two replies:

Memo from Chief Officer (New Works) to Supplies Manager (copy to Chief Engineer (T&RS) and Chief Operating Officer), 9 March 1967:

'In reply to your letter of 3rd March asking about the present position on the project to re-engine these locomotives, the Chief Operating Officer maintains that these 20 locomotives are still required as part of the National Traction Plan.

'In the meantime, it has been agreed that the Chief Engineer (T&RS) should develop an entirely new power equipment for installation in one of these locomotives as a prototype and he will be giving you further information on this project. If the prototype is successful it will then be the intention to re-equip all 20 locomotives.

'In the latest revision of the Investment Budget provision has been made for 10 locomotives to be dealt with in 1968 and 10 in 1969.'

Memo from Chief Engineer (T&RS) to Supplies Manager (copies to Chief Officer (New Works) and BRB Director of Design), 13 March 1967:

'With reference to your memo of the 3rd March; the present position on these locomotives as agreed with the Chief Operating Officer is that the rehabilitation work previously authorised is suspended and the Director of Design is working out proposals to make a new locomotive with completely modern power equipment.

'The proposal is to develop one prototype on this basis and if successful to then modify the others which would then possibly become another new standard locomotive for BR'

13.2.6 Metrovicks with Sulzer engines.

Reference to the re-engining of the Metrovicks in all of the documentation held at the National Archives relates to English Electric providing the replacement power units; no other engine type is specifically mentioned. However, Rob Mason (Chairman of the Class 15 Preservation Society) has provided evidence via Facebook and flickr that the use of the Sulzer 8LDA28 engine was considered at least to the extent of full engineering drawings being produced. This may be related to the Chief Engineer (T&RS)'s memo to the Chief Operating Officer dated 12 September 1966 regarding a 'new high powered prototype' (see Section 13.2.5 above).

The Sulzer 8LDA28 engines, as deployed in the BRCW Type 3s (Class 33), were rated at 1550hp. The Sulzer option compared with the envisaged 1250hp from the up-rated English Electric 8CSVT previously deployed in their Type 1s (Class 20).

The above-mentioned engineering drawing (No. DV/268) was produced by the BR London Midland Region, Locomotive Development Office at Derby, and was entitled 'Proposed scheme showing 1200hp Crossley HST Vee8 engine replaced by 1550hp Sulzer 8LDA28 engine'. The date on the drawing is unclear (possibly 8/11/66). Side, end and top elevation drawings show the original Metrovick body (with wrap-around windows!) at a scale of ½ inch to 1 foot.

It is abundantly clear from the diagrams that the deployment of the 6LDA28 engine would have been a very tight fit. Various annotations were included on the drawings to highlight the main issues; these include:

- 'Clearance between turbo-chargers and roof requires checking.'
- 'Underframe centre longitudinal and cross-

stretchers require modifications to clear engine sump and generator.'
- 'Sump drain will require positioning to clear centre member of underframe.'
- 'Capacity of radiators may require increasing for the higher hp engine (original engine 1200hp, new engine 1550hp).'
- 'Motor driven compressor required as existing compressor is integral with the replaced engine & generator.'
- 'Generator blower assembly and bulkhead may not be required if Sulzer engine is fitted.'
- 'Gangway required on opposite side of locomotive to facilitate maintenance of diesel engine.'
- 'Change door to opposite hand to prevent fouling of gangway.'

No archive reference is made to any electrical alterations to cope with either the English Electric or the higher output Sulzer engine, although it is widely believed that the Metropolitan-Vickers equipment could have been suitably modified to cope with the new engine speeds.

13.2.7 Cancellation.

After March 1967, available archives go very quiet once again. However, a Technical Report to BRB from the Chief Engineer (Traction & Rolling Stock) dated 16 October 1967 contained an Addendum entitled 'Diesel Locomotive Performance & Efficiency' which provided final clarification on the future of the Metrovicks.

The 'Diesel Locomotive Performance and Efficiency' addendum covered a number of diesel types, including the Metrovicks, indicating that fourteen of these locomotives were in service on 30 June 1967. The review noted that since the preparation of the various locomotive 'reviews' (up to end-June 1967), the long-term Revenue Forecasts had indicated the need for a substantial reduction in the locomotive fleet by 1974. The review then stated:

'Clearly any such reduction would need to be planned to eliminate known troublesome locomotives and minority types. It is, therefore, of considerable importance that an agreed run-down of the fleet over the next seven years be formulated at the earliest possible date to ensure that no undue expenditure is incurred on heavy locomotive repairs, provision of spares or technical modifications for locomotives expected to be withdrawn in the foreseeable future.'

All steam classes and also certain diesel locomotives, notably the Scottish Region NBL Type 2s (Class 21) and the Metrovicks were squarely in the immediate firing line. The review then made a very explicit statement, as follows:

'. . . due to the consideration being given to the early withdrawal from traffic of the 38 Type 2 N.B.L./M.A.N. and 20 Type 2 Met-Vic./Crossley diesel-electric locomotives, all modifications have been suspended on these locomotives and no expenditure is therefore included.'

Quite clearly decisions were made regarding the Metrovicks between March and October 1967. In the summary paragraph specifically relating to the Metrovicks, the review states:

'The persistent inferior performance of the Crossley engines fitted to these locomotives, even after refurbishing by the makers, led to proposals for re-engining the locomotives with English Electric engines, and the Board authorised this work. Capital investment considerations led to this work being deferred and this factor, coupled with the expected reduced requirements for this type of locomotive, have now made it clear that the project should be abandoned. Six locomotives are now in store 'unserviceable' and all current modifications have been cancelled.'

An updated National Traction Plan was published in November 1967 taking into account the latest traffic and financial projections. As regards the Type 2 fleet, the new NTP forecast the following requirements:

Region	Stock at 31.7.67	Year Ending (Locomotive Requirement)				
		1967	1968	1969	1970	1971
London Midland	385	407	426	412	402	392
Total	1002	972	947	918	891	864
MV/Crossley Nos.D5700-19		20	10	-	-	-

Supporting commentary:

'Due to reduced requirements the proposed re-engining of the 20 Met/Vic. locomotives has now been abandoned. Six locomotives are unserviceable and the remainder have only short life expectancy. A submission is being prepared for their condemnation.'

It can be seen, therefore, that the lead-up work prior to the publication of the November 1967 NTP had already been sufficient to effectively sanction not only the abandonment of the re-engining proposal but also the condemnation of the whole fleet. Section 18 deals with the decisions and documentation surrounding the actual condemnation of the Metrovicks.

The transfer of D5704/9/10/3, long-term residents at Crewe Works, to 12B Carlisle Upperby in late-February/early-March 1967 might well suggest that the decision to abandon the re-engining of the Metrovicks took place as early as this time.

13.3 Re-engining - Summary Timeline.

02/04/65	Initial re-engining proposal.
	Engine selection (EE approached) but no design work, preliminary costings (work presumably started during late-1964/early-1965).
	Anticipated completion second half of 1966.
23/12/65	Developed re-engining proposal.
	General design work completed, quotations obtained from EE and BR Workshops.
18/01/66	W&EC approval.
27/01/66	BRB Authorisation.
15/08/66	Project deferral (exclusion from 1967 Investment Programme).
25/08/66	Memo from Chief Engineer (T&RS); project effectively put into abeyance until at least November 1967 (in anticipation of 1968/69 Investment Programmes).
12/09/66	Chief Engineer (T&RS) suggestion to develop the Metrovicks with a higher-power engine.
Circa-11/66	Investigations into the deployment of Sulzer 8LDA28B engines instead of EE engines.
Late-02/67, early-0367	D5704/9/10/3 (long-term Crewe Works residents) transferred to Carlisle for storage; indicative of decision taken to cancel redevelopment of the Metrovicks at this time?
End-0667	*Diesel Locomotive Performance and Efficiency* reports indicate all Metrovick locomotive modifications already suspended.
11/67	National Traction Plan published. Metrovick re-engining formally abandoned and early fleet withdrawal envisaged based on forecast traffic requirements.

13.4 Locomotive Selection.
13.4.1 Locomotive Evaluation and Potential Initial Recipients.

It has been variously suggested that one or both of D5716 (Crewe Works, August to November 1964) and D5719 (Crewe Works, March to September 1964) were the subject of initial evaluations for re-engining. Similarly, D5709, which became ensconced in the Crewe Works Paint Shop from June 1965, and/or D5715 (Crewe Works from May to September 1965) may also have been the subject of more detailed design assessments during 1965.

No official archive evidence has been found to corroborate these suggestions.

Several Metrovicks were stored at Crewe Works for extended periods from mid-1965 to early-1967 in anticipation of replacement engines; suggested initial recipients were:

	Crewe Works	**Ultimate outcome**
D5709	06/65-02/67	To Carlisle Upperby; further storage, condemned.
D5715	01/66-05/66, 12/66-02/67	Released to traffic with repaired Crossley engine on both occasions.
D5704	03/66-02/67	To Carlisle Upperby; further storage, condemned.
D5710	04/66-02/67	To Carlisle Upperby; further storage, condemned.
D5717	06/66-10/66	Released to traffic with repaired Crossley engine.
D5713	01/67-02/67	To Carlisle Upperby; further storage, condemned.
D5703	04/67-09/67	To Carlisle Upperby; further storage, condemned.
D5705	04/67-11/67	Released to traffic with re-engineered Crossley engine.

13.4.2 Post-August 1966 Deferral Decision.

With the decision to effectively put the Metrovick re-engining into abeyance in August 1966, locomotives shopped at Crewe continued to be released with repaired Crossley engines. D5701/2/5-8/11/4/5/7/8 were put through Crewe during late-1966 and 1967, these including D5705/15/7 from the above list with D5705 receiving the strengthened Crossley engine.

Chapter 14
ACCIDENT AND FIRE DAMAGE

14.1 Accident/Derailment Damage.

D5717, 17A Derby, 8 July 1960. After this little incident, a three month visit to Derby Works was required to effect the necessary repairs. *(Mick Mobley)*

D57xx, Lancaster Castle, Undated. Derailment immediately to the north-west of Lancaster Castle station where the line to Glasson (closed 1964) and Lancaster Quay (closed 1969) diverged from the West Coast main line. The position of the No.1 cab front-end 25kV sign suggests that the locomotive is one of either D5703, D5707, D5708, or D5713, with D5703 or D5713 being the most likely contenders. The picture quality precludes accurate identification of the bodyside 25kV sign position. *(Stuart Martin)*

Above, below and below left: **D5713, Workington Yard, Undated.** This incident may explain the damage sustained by D5713 on its 2-1 side, its subsequent long-term storage and ultimate withdrawal. See also photographs on pages 236/8/40/3. *(Ray Winthrop)*

14.2 Fire Damage.
14.2.1 *Fires on Diesel Train Locomotives* Reports 1961-68.
The British Railways 'Fires on Diesel Train Locomotives' reports, produced by the Locomotive Performance & Efficiency Development Unit at Derby and covering the period 1961-68, yield the following information with respect to the Metrovicks:

Loco No.	Date of fire	Source of ignition	Material involved	Degree of damage	Additional notes
D5710	21/01/64	E	2	NS	
D5701	23/01/64	E	2	NS	
D5701	26/02/64	E	2	NS	
D5704	19/05/64	F	1	NS	
D5714	26/07/64	C	1	NS	
D5704	13/11/64	B	3	NS	
D5712	05/01/65				Preston
D5702	21/01/65	F	2	S	
D5712	29/01/65				Silverdale
D5712	12/02/65	F	2	NS	
D5707	05/07/65	B	2	NS	
D5710	08/09/65	C	1/3	S	
D5717	02/05/66	A	1	NS	
D5711	20/07/66	A	3	S	
D5715	20/09/66	A	1	NS	
D5715	28/10/66	A	1	NS	
D5716	11/08/67	C	3	NS	

Source of ignition:
A Brake block sparks.
B Hot engine parts, including exhaust blows.
C Electrical overloads or arcs.
E Train Heating Boiler Burners.
F Unknown.

Material involved:
1 Oil impregnated dirt or waste.
2 Fuel/lubricating oil sprays or leaks.
3 Electrical insulation.

Degree of damage:
S Severe (requiring works attention).
NS Not severe.

Notes:
1. Full reports seen for 1961-67.
2. No information seen for January-March 1968.
3. Summary reports only seen for April-September 1968; no Metrovick casualties reported.

14.2.2 Fire at Barrow Depot.

On 31 May 1966, a fire at Barrow depot destroyed much of the roof above the designated diesel roads (Nos.7-10).

Philip C. Johnstone recalls:

'I can remember driving to work from Ulverston . . . and on turning down the shed yard I said to my mate who was going to work with me "What's different about the shed?" We found out on arrival that half the roof had gone! The cause of the fire was D5714 which had been giving the usual Crossley problem of the Spanner boiler not working. The fitter had started the boiler up and left D5714 running to test the boiler. Unfortunately the boiler set fire to the wooden roof which was of course soaked in oil from other diesels. No locos were written off, three or four other Crossleys suffered damage to their paintwork, but the staff on afternoons had managed to shift most of the locomotives outside. D5714 had most of its paint burned off but I went with it to Crewe Works under its own power shortly afterwards. It certainly looked a sight but it returned sometime later repainted and continued to work until it was withdrawn some years later.'

The damaged shed roof was never replaced, although the tracks continued to be used for diesel stabling and minor repairs.

As might be expected, the local paper, the *North Western Evening Mail* on Wednesday, June 1, 1966, carried a significantly more dramatic report:

'One Diesel is Destroyed and Two Others Badly Damaged.'

'Fire swept through the Barrow motive power depot of British Railways last night, destroying a diesel locomotive and severely damaging others.

'Engine drivers who braved flames, flying glass and falling debris to save nine diesel and steam locomotives from destruction, were unable to save three of the diesels, one of which was damaged beyond repair. Two others were severely damaged.

'The fire broke out at the depot in Salthouse while a diesel locomotive was being tested in the shed. The engine suddenly caught fire and the flames quickly set fire to the roof.

'A fitter working in the cab scrambled to safety as the flames spread. More than 25 firemen, working from five appliances from Barrow, Ulverston and Dalton, fought the blaze and had it under control in just over an hour.'

The newspaper report was perhaps somewhat exaggerated. D5714, the cause of the fire, lived to fight another day with the locomotive being seen at 12B Carlisle Upperby (where it was allocated by this time) during July 1966 presumably awaiting inspection and decision, and then at Crewe Works during the period July to September 1966 when it received a full repaint.

The Philip Johnstone and *North Western Evening Mail* reports indicate that other Metrovicks were affected. D5700/3/10 have been variously suggested as the other locomotives involved, presumably because they were early withdrawals, but observations suggest otherwise (see Section 7). D5700 and D5710 were already stored at this time, at 12B Carlisle Upperby and Crewe Works respectively.

D5703, however, represents a *possibility*, being noted at Barrow during successive visits during the August 1966 to January 1967 period prior to movement to Crewe Works by April 1967. The only photograph of D5703 seen with a date post-31 May 1966 is illustrated on page 242; from the visible side at least, the external condition of D5703 does not look too bad.

As far as any other Metrovick were concerned, only D5719 was *admitted* to Crewe Works in the two-month period after 31 May 1966 (excepting D5711 and D5717 which suffered fire damage in separate incidents on 20 July 1966 and 2 May 1966 respectively).

D5706, 12C Barrow, Undated (post-May 1966). . D5706 beneath the fire-damaged roof at Barrow depot. (*Transport Topics*)

Chapter 15
OPERATIONS: A HIGH-LEVEL SUMMARY

15.1 Midland Lines.

The Metrovicks first saw service on the Midland Division of the London Midland Region (LMR).

Early plans envisaged fourteen of the fleet based at Derby for passengers duties with the remaining six allocated to Cricklewood to cover long-distance freight duties between London and Glasgow, commencing early 1959. In the event, all of the Metrovicks were initially allocated to Derby, although the workload rostering remained as originally planned with locomotives frequently operated in multiple.

Passenger work involved the express services between St Pancras and Manchester Central, via the Chinley and Peak Forest route, from October 1958, usually as pairs, and 'local turns' between Derby and Manchester Central, usually singly.

The express services included the 0725 and 1025 from Manchester Central to St Pancras and the 0420, 1425 and 1625 services from St Pancras to Manchester Central.

Two regular 'local' passenger diagrams in early-1959 were: the 0710 Derby-Manchester Central and 1225 return, followed by the 1910 Derby-Manchester Central and, after light running from Manchester, the 2355 Marple-Derby parcels (originating at Bolton at 2035); and the 0202 Derby-Manchester parcels (1940 ex-St Pancras), the 0730 passenger back to Derby, followed by the 1600 Derby-Manchester Central and 1945 return.

The failure rates suffered by the Metrovicks and the introduction of other new diesel classes (BR/Sulzer Type 2s and 4s) inevitably resulted in reduced rostering of the class during 1960.

In terms of freight, the Metrovicks were famously associated with the 'Condor' high-speed freight service from London to Glasgow from the outset, but were also used on coal traffic (e.g. Loughborough-Brent) and other local freight work.

D5713, St Pancras, 1959. *(Rail-Online)*

176 • THE METROPOLITAN-VICKERS TYPE 2 CO-BO DIESEL-ELECTRIC LOCOMOTIVES

D5705 and D5706, St Pancras, September 1960. (*Alan F. Coottrell [Transport Treasury]*)

D5706, Millers Dale, 26 September 1960. Local service to Manchester. (*Alan H. Roscoe [Transport Treasury]*)

Operations: A High-Level Summary • 177

D5714 and an unidentified sister locomotive, Chinley, Date unknown .
St.Pancras-Manchester Central passenger service.
(A.H. Bryant [Rail-Photoprints])

D5702, Disley, Date unknown . Manchester Central-Derby local passenger service.
(A.H. Bryant [Rail-Photoprints])

178 • THE METROPOLITAN-VICKERS TYPE 2 CO-BO DIESEL-ELECTRIC LOCOMOTIVES

D5704 and D5708, Spondon Junction (Down St Pancras–Manchester Central express), **25 May 1959.** (*Transport Treasury*)

D5716 and D5710, Midland Main Line, 26 April 1960. Midland Main Line freight trials with 16T mineral wagons. Marked by the seller as 26 April 1960, but may be 16 October 1960 (RO1160): 'Midland Division . . . a D5700 was noted on a coal train with a dynamometer car on Sunday, 16th October.'(*J. McCann [OTP]*)

15.2 City Widened Lines.

The March 1960 *Trains Illustrated* magazine noted that:

'Because of the Southern Region's reluctance to return any of the BR/Sulzer Type '2' diesel locomotives it has on loan, Metro-Vick Type 2 units . . . have been allocated to Cricklewood mainly for the Moorgate services; when the BR type is returned by the S.R., they will replace the Metro-Vick units on the Moorgate duties. It will be recalled that the S.R. was loaned part of the L.M.R.'s allocation of the BR/Sulzer type pending delivery of its own Birmingham/Sulzer Type 3 units, the appearance of which was imminent at the end of January, though considerably behind schedule....'

Later that year, *Railway Locomotives* (September 1960) reported that 'Class 2 Sulzer diesels D5088-93 have now taken over all the Moorgate passengers absolutely revolutionising the service and the Metro-Vicks are setting sail for Derby'. D5712-9 were progressively returned to 17A Derby between July and October 1960.

15.3 Cross-London Transfer Freights (1960).

The May 1960 *Trains Illustrated* magazine reported that:

'In March Metro-Vick Type 2 Co-Bo diesels were scheduled to make three trial trips between the Midland Lines and the S.R. on London transfer freight workings. However, on the second of these excursions, on March 23, No. D5700 suffered a derailment, reportedly because its braking power was insufficient and it over-ran signals, with the result that the third trial was cancelled. No. D5700 was considerably damaged internally in this incident'.

It appears further trials were undertaken in April 1960 with a photo caption in *D for Diesels 11* mentioning that 'D5714 worked onto the Southern Region during the month and went to Norwood shed to work test trains over a two-day period (6th and 7th) past the track testing station at Balcombe tunnel'.

15.4 'Condor'.
15.4.1 Introduction.

The duty for which the Metrovicks will always be associated was the 'Condor' (CONtainer DOor-to-dooR) freight service, which the class operated daily between Hendon (London) and Gushetfaulds (Glasgow), often carrying a distinctive blue-and-red headboard.

15.4.2 Trials.

Prior to the introduction of the 'Condor' service a series of special test trains were organised consisting of 'Platefit' wagons each loaded with two containers, a brake van, and a dynamometer car hauled by D5700 and D5701. Results were published in the report 'Two 1200hp Crossley/Met.Vick. D.E. Locos. Hauling Special Container Train Hendon-Gushetfaulds October 1958' (CM&EE Department, Derby, August 1959).

Calculated timings were initially provided by the Locomotive Testing Section of the CM&EE Deptartment. Details of the first two trains (24 wagons) are as follows:

Run No.	Date	Route	Purpose of Test
572	1.10.58	Hendon-Gushetfaulds	To check the calculated timings/speeds, obtain locomotive performance data (drawbar tractive effort, main generator output, field weakening changes, etc), establish train resistance values, test wagon stability at up to 75mph.
573	2.10.58	Gushetfaulds-Hendon	

The train ran with Cricklewood enginemen and a St Pancras guard. A Sheffield conductor was provided to Carlisle, where Polmadie men took over. The special returned by the same route on 2 October. Although the 'Condor' service was envisaged to run with up to twenty-seven wagons, the test trains were booked to operate with twenty-five wagons to allow for the weight of the dynamometer car, although, in the event, the above trains actually operated with twenty-four due to the removal of a defective wagon).

During the trials, both locomotives illustrated deficiencies relative to the designed equivalent drawbar tractive effort curve and field weakening characteristics, particularly above 48mph. Offsetting the locomotive shortfalls, however, the train resistance characteristics were better than anticipated probably due to the combined effect of:

(a) the containers being closer together than was anticipated giving a smaller air and wind resistance.
(b) significantly lower than anticipated resistance in the previously untested 50 to 75mph range, and,
(c) only light winds being encountered during the test.

A summary of results is given below:

1. Pre-Test Point-to-Point Aggregated Running Times (based on estimated train resistance, Rail Tractive Effort derated by 10% and 'perfect' operating conditions).

	Hendon-Gushetfaulds	Gushetfaulds-Hendon
Calculated (min)	484	483
Recommended (min)	537	537

2. Post-Test Point-to-Point Aggregated Running Times (based on test train resistance results, Rail Tractive Effort derated by 10% and 'perfect' operating conditions) (23 minute improvement).

	Hendon-Gushetfaulds	Gushetfaulds-Hendon
Calculated (min)	463	458
Recommended (min)	514	514

3. Post-Test Point-to-Point Aggregated Running Times (based on test train resistance results, full Rail Tractive Effort and 'perfect' operating conditions) (further 18 minute improvement).

	Hendon-Gushetfaulds	Gushetfaulds-Hendon
Calculated (min)	444	441
Recommended (min)	496	494

4. Actual Test Point-to-Point Timings (including booked stops, signal checks, speed restrictions, etc) (adverse 40 minute impact compared with [2]).

	Hendon-Gushetfaulds	Gushetfaulds-Hendon
Booked (min)	557	563
Actual (min)	555	554

Subsequent to these initial trials, D5700 and D5701, again working with twenty-four wagons, a brake-van and a dynamometer car, operated from Hendon to Derby on 5 October, as follows:

Run No.	Date	Route	Purpose of Test & Results
574	5.10.58	Hendon-Chaddesden	To obtain stopping distance data. Stopping distance outside 'S' curve and therefore not satisfactory.

After these initial tests, it was stated by the C&W Dept. that the load per vehicle was too high. The loads were reduced and further test trains (now with twenty-five wagons and brake-van) were organised:

Run No.	Date	Route	Purpose of Test & Results
575	26.10.58	Chaddesden-Bedford	To obtain stopping distances with the reduced load. Slight
576	26.10.58	Bedford-Chaddesden	improvement in stopping distances but still not satisfactory.

Westinghouse Quick Service Application (Q.S.A.) valves were fitted to the wagons and further tests (with twenty-five wagons) were made:

Run No.	Date	Route	Purpose of Test & Results
	9.11.58	Chaddesden-Bedford	To obtain stopping distances with Q.S.A. valves fitted.
	9.11.58	Bedford-Chaddesden	Stopping distances within 'S' curve and satisfactory.

The end-to-end operational timings used from March 1959, were 592 and 590 minutes northbound and southbound respectively giving substantial recovery times to secure high on-time arrival results for this prestige service.

15.4.3 The 'Condor' Service.

Key features of the Condor service (based on information contained within *Trains Illustrated* magazines during 1959 and 1960):

- Start Date: Monday, 16th March (*1959*).
- Haulage: Two Metrovicks.
- Route: Glasgow (Gushetfaulds) to London (Hendon) via Motherwell, Carlisle, Settle, Leeds, Sheffield and Leicester.
- Schedule: Glasgow (Gushetfaulds) departure 1935hrs (Su) and 1950hrs (M-Th) arriving Hendon 0540hrs. Hendon departure 1923hrs (M-F) arriving Gushetfaulds 0515hrs.
- Trains crewed by Cricklewood, Carlisle Kingmoor and Glasgow Polmadie men.
- Consist: Up to 27 'Platefit' wagons weighing circa 550 tons, plus brake van.
- Speed: Average of over 40mph, covering 402¼ miles in 10 hours; maximum speed 75 mph.
- Wagons: Long-wheelbase, roller-bearing, vacuum-brake fitted flat wagons, with a load capacity of 12 tons. Each wagon capable of carrying one large (700 cu.ft.) and one small container (300 cu.ft.); both container types able to carry 4 tons payload. Wagons fitted with screw couplings, semi-permanently coupled.
- Traffic: High-speed freight service, transporting containers collected in the afternoon and delivered the following morning.
- Service offering: Fast service delivery, halving average times taken by door-to-door road vehicles between London and Glasgow.
- Cost: Door-to-door cost £16 for small or £18 for large containers (irrespective of type of goods carried and point of despatch or delivery within Greater London area and a 10-mile radius from Glasgow's city centre).

The inaugural 'Condor' freights ran on the night of 16/17 March (*1959*) in each direction. *Trains Illustrated* (May 1959) reported:

'The first journey was not free of incident, as one of the two Metrovick Co-Bos suffered a blown vacuum exhauster fuse near Skipton, and the "Condor" was 20 min. late into Carlisle, where the trouble was rectified; there was evidently some lively running thereafter, as Glasgow was reached 1 min. early'.

During the summer of 1959 the locomotive working arrangements for the Condor were revised. The 'Down' Glasgow 'Condor' was no longer worked by the same pair of Co-Bos that arrived with the 'Up' train in the morning. Instead, it was operated by the pair which worked the 10.25 Manchester-St Pancras, another pair being allocated to the 16.25 St Pancras-Manchester return.

Demand was such that trains were reduced, initially to nineteen wagons and then thirteen wagons by August/September 1959, with the consequent payload requiring only a single locomotive. During the Summer months of 1960, bogie vans were attached to the consist for the movement of perishable goods, with the 'Platefit' component ranging between thirteen to twenty wagons.

It was believed that the 'Condor' schedule had at least 45 minutes 'spare', relative to the potential of the motive power, but this did allow some margin for delays or failures en route and ensure that reliability, a critical part of the service offering, was achieved. During September 1960, the down train services showed that only one train arrived at the destination over 30 minutes late. In the up direction, all services bar three were within eight minutes of booked time, all due to diesel locomotive failures.

15.4.4 Locomotive Substitutions. Specific rules for substitute motive power were applied in the event of diesel failures en route. A failed diesel had to be replaced by a Class 5MT 4-6-0, to be inserted between the remaining diesel and the train. If a diesel failed before the journey commenced, two Class 5MT 4-6-0s were stipulated to be substituted for both diesels. These rules were applied to ensure reliability on this highly time-critical traffic.

Some very interesting commentary is provided by P. Brock in his book entitled *Calling Carlisle Control*, (Ian Allan, 1990) indicating that alternative arrangements applied in reality:

'One evening the 'Condor' failed to appear at the scheduled time. Then, at 10p.m., there was the familiar sight of Upperby "Black Five" No. 44930 . . . now complete with 'Condor' headboard. Harry Fisher was at the regulator, the shovel being in the hands of Senior Fireman Willie Walters, then 35 years of age. He faced a 310-mile trip on this crack service with a steam engine.'

'On another occasion, the "green light" had come on south of Trent on Driver 'Marrow' Hogarth's Metrovick. This indicated high water temperature on the diesel and the only cure was a fresh engine. That night '9F' 2-10-0 No.92001 had the honour of bringing the down "Condor" non-stop over the remaining 200 miles to Carlisle.'

'Among the strange combinations that I witnessed at the head of both the up and down "Condor" included a single Metrovick assisting '5' 4-6-0 No. 44960 (and choking the steam crew half to death with exhaust fumes), twin BR "5" 4-6-0s, a '9F' 2-10-0 and, not least, "Britannia" No. 70054.'

'All too often, these crews were being pushed to the limit of their endurance working steam engines on the "Condor" on occasions when the temperamental Metrovicks had been failed with minor ailments.'

Railway Locomotives (September 1959) reported: 'There have been at least three failures on the up "Condor", resulting in steam workings – 45380+44683 (24/7), 92123 (31/7) and 45592+44803 (5/8).'

15.4.5 'Condor' Fill-In Services. Day-time and weekend fill-in turns were actively pursued for the Metrovicks in an attempt to improve their utilisation:

- 'It was understood that crews from Ladyburn shed, Greenock, had been trained to use each of the pair singly on trips to Gourock, but although one worked the 8.23 a.m. Glasgow-Gourock and 10.35 a.m. back on March 13, before the "Condor" service began, this idea seems to have been abandoned for reasons unknown. On Saturdays one of the units was reported to have a diagram including trips on the 8.18 a.m. and 1.30 p.m. Cathcart Outer Circle and the 3.15 p.m. Glasgow-Wemyss Bay and 6.18 p.m. back, as well as the 9.45 a.m. Glasgow-Gourock and 11.40 a.m. back.' (*Trains Illustrated*, May 1959)
- 'At weekends the pair of Metrovick Type "2" Co-Bo diesels "lodging" in Scotland after Friday night's down "Condor" freight working are employed on Anglo-Scottish night trains between Glasgow and Carlisle.' (*Trains Illustrated*, June 1959) i.e. Glasgow-Euston (to Carlisle) and Euston-Glasgow (from Carlisle) return.

- 'At weekends – there is no Friday or Saturday (*evening*) CONDOR train - overnight work saw them running together on the 10.20p.m. Friday sleeper to Carlisle and the 7.15a.m. return; also on Saturdays the 5.30p.m. St.Enoch to Carlisle . . . Soon after the introduction of the CONDOR, the Co-Bos laying over in Glasgow did not work any services on the Gourock line and instead one of the pair acted as spare on the 9.15a.m. Bridgeton-Stirling freight and a return coal train from Plean to Shieldhall.' (*D for Diesels 11*)
- 'Metrovick Co-Bo diesel No. D5701 was noted at Stirling on empty stock, heading south, on July 18 (*1959*); the previous day one of these units was noted on an Isle of Man boat train heading for Ardrossan.'
- 'A Metrovick Co-Bo Type "2" diesel worked through to Oakley yard, between Dunfermline and Alloa, with mineral wagons from the Glasgow area on August 26 and 29 (*1960*).' (*Trains Illustrated*, October 1960)

15.4.6 Metrovick Successors.

BR/Sulzer Type 2 locomotives were allocated to Cricklewood from mid-1960 (D5088-91), followed by D5084-7 in December 1960/January 1961. The March 1961, *Railway Observer* reported, 'the long awaited take-over of this working ('*Condor*') by BR/Sulzer Class 2's seemed to have been effected by the end of January.' Steam power usually provided any required assistance up to this point.

However, it seems that the Metrovicks were still used well into 1961 despite the influx of the BR/Sulzers. The maximum loading of the 'Condor' with a single BR/Sulzer Type 2 was progressively increased to 18 and then 24 'Platefits'; it is believed that the service ran with 25 wagons with a single locomotive on occasions. BR/Sulzer Type 4 ('Peak') locomotives are also known to have operated the service.

D5704 and D5701, Hendon, 7 July 1959.
(*Rail-Online [K.L. Cook, Rail Archive Stephenson]*)

184 • THE METROPOLITAN-VICKERS TYPE 2 CO-BO DIESEL-ELECTRIC LOCOMOTIVES

D57xx (x2), Ampthill, 1961, . 'Condor' service. Modified windows and 25kV sign on the leading locomotive, possibly D5700. Compare with the photograph on page 60. (*Transport Treasury*)

D5710 and D5708 (sic D5709?), Elvanfoot, Sunday 19 April 1959. The Saturday night/Sunday morning Euston-Glasgow sleeper service deployed Metrovick motive power from Carlisle Citadel to Glasgow Central as a 'fill-in' between 'Condor' duties. The *Railway Observer* records the previous evening's 17.30 Glasgow St Enoch-Carlisle passenger service as being hauled by D5710 and D5709. (*D. Anderson [Rail-Photoprints]*)

Operations: A High-Level Summary • 185

D5706 and D5708, Kilmarnock, Saturday 25 July 1959. Carlisle-Glasgow 'fill-in' service. *(Bill Hamilton)*

186 • THE METROPOLITAN-VICKERS TYPE 2 CO-BO DIESEL-ELECTRIC LOCOMOTIVES

D5713, Stirling, Undated. (*Transport Treasury*)

D5709 and D5706, Auldgirth (Nith Valley route), 13 June 1959. 1730hrs Glasgow St Enoch-Carlisle stopping service. (*Transport Treasury*)

15.5 Furness & West Cumberland.

Following rehabilitation at Dukinfield, the Metrovicks returned to service in the Furness and West Cumberland area, based operationally at Barrow and Workington depots, with official allocation to 12E Barrow. The first locomotive was released from Dukinfield in December 1961, the last in March 1963.

Early reported workings for the Metrovicks were:

'By the end of April (*1962*) only one of the five Metrovick Co-Bo diesels then received by Barrow depot, Nos. D5707-9/13/9, was working a public service diagram; this covered the 5.42 a.m. London mail from Barrow to Workington, 9.53 (10.3 MO) a.m. Whitehaven-Carnforth, 3.40 p.m. Carnforth-Barrow, 5.40 p.m. Barrow (3.12 ex-Workington)-Liverpool Exchange as far as Preston and the 10.28 p.m. thence back to Barrow'. (*Modern Railways* (June 1962) (N.B. The other locomotives continued to be used on crew-training runs to Carnforth and Workington.)

'From July 16 (*1962*) Metrovick Type 2 Co-Bo diesels adopted a duty covering the 6.10 a.m. Heysham-Manchester Victoria 'Belfast Boat Express' and the 9.50 a.m. Manchester-Workington and Barrow, previously tasks for a Carnforth Class 5 4-6-0.' (*Modern Railways* (September 1962)

'By the beginning of September (*1962*), Barrow's stud of Metrovick Type 2 diesels had grown to 14 units and in the winter schedules they were allocated a series of regular diagrams for the first time.' *Modern Railways* (November 1962)

15.5.1 Passenger Duties.

Summary of duties:

- Workington/Barrow to Lancaster/Preston/Manchester Victoria.
- Workington/Whitehaven/Barrow to Euston (as far as Preston).
- Millom to Liverpool.
- Barrow to Lakeside.
- Heysham to Manchester Victoria.
- Excursion visits to Morecambe, Blackpool, Southport, Windermere.

Locomotive hauled passenger trains north of Barrow ceased with the May 1966 timetable.

Two Metrovicks were involved on Royal Train duties; P.C. Johnstone (*Cumbrian Railways*) recalls:

'For all their faults, two Crossleys were actually entrusted with the Royal Train. It was the empty stock but never-the-less it was the Royal Train. The locos had been kept coupled together for at least the previous week working the same job, the early mail train to Whitehaven. They completed their Royal Train duty without any trouble but I guess quite a number of railway officials had several sleepless nights! It was the only time I can remember the gangway doors opened to allow passage from one loco to the other.'

D57xx, Scorton (between Preston and Lancaster), 17 July 1962. 09.50 Manchester-Workington passenger. (*Arnold W. Battson [Transport Treasury]*)

188 • THE METROPOLITAN-VICKERS TYPE 2 CO-BO DIESEL-ELECTRIC LOCOMOTIVES

D5700 (sic), Scorton, July 1962. Barrow-Liverpool passenger. D5700 was not released from Dukinfield until August 1962. In addition the large radius corners to the yellow panels are not consistent with the panels carried by D5700. (*Arnold W. Battson [Transport Treasury]*)

D57xx, Lancaster, 1962. The positioning of the front-end and bodyside 25kV signs suggests D5703. (*Colour-Rail*)

Operations: A High-Level Summary • 189

D5712 (sic), Whitehaven, 1 August 1963. Northbound passenger service. The large top corner radius of the yellow warning panel and the extremely low position of the No.2-end 25kv sign indicates that this locomotive is D5713. *(J.N. Smith [Transport Treasury])*

D5717 (right) and D5704, Lakeside 6 July 1963. *(Colour-Rail)*

190 • THE METROPOLITAN-VICKERS TYPE 2 CO-BO DIESEL-ELECTRIC LOCOMOTIVES

D5701 (sic), Parton/Bransty (0825 Carnforth-Workington), 8 August 1964. The front-end 25kV sign is incorrectly positioned for this to be D5701. (*Transport Treasury*)

D5711, Seascale (0637 Lancaster-Workington), 8 August 1964. (*Transport Treasury*)

Operations: A High-Level Summary • 191

D5702, Parton (1053 Workington-London), 8 August 1964.
(*Transport Treasury*)

D57xx, Seascale (Carnforth-Workington), Undated.
(*Transport Treasury*)

192 • THE METROPOLITAN-VICKERS TYPE 2 CO-BO DIESEL-ELECTRIC LOCOMOTIVES

D57xx, North of Bransty, 8 August 1964. Probably D5711.
(*Transport Treasury*)

D57xx, Near Seascale (1053 Workington-Euston), 1963 (sic?). Believed to be D5706, and probably 1965/66.
(*Transport Treasury*)

Operations: A High-Level Summary • 193

D5702, Seascale South (0825 Lancaster-Workington) 18 April 1964. (*Transport Treasury*)

D5707, Carnforth, Undated. (*Transport Treasury*)

D57xx, Seascale, Undated. (*Transport Treasury*)

15.5.2 Parcels.
Preston/Lancaster/Carnforth to Barrow/Whitehaven/Workington.

15.5.3 Freight.
The Furness Line and Cumbian Coast route in the 1960s was heavily industrialised and generated considerable volumes of freight traffic with which the Metrovicks were heavily associated, notably:

- iron/steel works traffic to and from the Workington and Millom Works (raw materials (coke/limestone/iron-ore) and finished products).
- coal traffic from numerous collieries (including Cleator Moor, Egremont, Haig, The William, Harrington).
- Sellafield nuclear waste.
- Fina fuel oil from Heysham to Corkickle.
- soda ash utilising 'Cov-Hop' wagons from Northwich to Corkickle.
- various export traffics via the ports of Barrow, Whitehaven, Workington and Maryport.
- sand from Sandside (Arnside branch).
- general pick-up goods traffic (Carnforth-Barrow, Millom-Carnforth, Barrow-Workington)

15.5.4 Other Cumbrian Duties.

Other notable duties performed by the Metrovicks were:

- Askam to Lindal and Plumpton Junction to Lindal banking duties.
- Coniston Branch (Foxfield-Coniston) demolition duties following closure in 1962.

15.6 Peak District I.C.I. Limestone trains (1963/64).

Modern Railways (July 1963) reported:

'The trials of English Electric Type 4 diesels on the I.C.I. limestone bogie-hopper workings between Tunstead, in the Peak District, and Northwich ... do not appear to have been successful. From reports we have received, it would seem that braking the heavy trailing load taxed the single unit severely, with damaging effects on the wheel tyres and brake linings. There was, therefore, a fresh development on

D5701, Farington Curve Junction, 3 October 1964. Southbound rake of 16t mineral wagons. (*Author's Collection*)

May 21-23 when two of the Metrovick Type 2 Co-Bos from Barrow, Nos.D5711/4, were tested in multiple-unit on the out-and-home workings. On the third day of the tests, the Type 2s tackled a 19-hopper train, whereas it had not been considered prudent to attempt such a trial with the Type 4s, which had handled only the normal 16-hopper trains and had their projected 19-hopper train cancelled. A driver told a correspondent that the Type 2s coped quite well with their new task, although there was still some difficulty with braking. Another correspondent has learned that if these later tests are considered successful, eight of the Type 2s at Barrow will be transferred to Trafford Park for this work.'

The August issue commented that:

'At the end of June, tests of diesels on the I.C.I. Tunstead-Northwich limestone hopper trains were continuing. Metrovick Type 2 Co-Bo No.D5700 was despatched from Barrow to Trafford Park on June 10 and for the next four days handled a 19-hopper train unaided.'

The November edition then speculated:

'It would appear that, following the tests of Type 2 and Type 4 diesels on the I.C.I. limestone bogie-hopper workings between Peak Forest and Northwich reported earlier in the year, the Metro-Vick Co-Bo diesels may be used on this job; a correspondent writes that No.D5719 has recently been at Trafford Park shed for the purpose of training Northwich crews'.

A photograph in the August 1964 edition of *Modern Railways* illustrated D5713 passing Chinley South Junction with empty ICI limestone hoppers from Tunstead to Peak Forest on 4 January 1964 and reports in the '*Railway Observer*' indicated Metrovick operations in January/February 1964. The September 1964 *Railway Observer* reported:

'After trials of Type 2 Co-Bo diesels from May 1963 to February 1964 on the ICI limestone trains from Tunstead (Peak Forest) to Winnington, both singly and in pairs, this class has now disappeared from these workings . . . [and has reverted to] . . . a period of steam haulage by Cl.8F 2-8-0's.'

The ultimate diesel successors for the Metrovicks were the BR/Sulzers. *Modern Railways* (May 1964) reports:

'One of the newly built BR/Sulzer Type 2 diesels, No.D5255, has been undergoing trials on the Northwich-Peak Forest ICI hopper trains, together with Metro-Vick Co-Bo No.D5703, which made a return appearance of the class at the same time.

D5714 (sic), Northenden Junction, May 1963. Test train of empty ICI hoppers to Tunstead. The position of the front-end 25kV sign suggests that this Metrovick id D5717. (*Rail-Photoprints*)

On March 18, 19 and 20 (*1964*), No.D5255 was on a roster covering the 8.45 empties to Wallenscote sidings, Northwich to Tunstead, Peak Forest and the 14.06 loaded hoppers back. On March 18 the load was the normal 16 hoppers and a brake van, but on March 19 No. D5255 tackled unaided a load of 19 hoppers and a brake van – the same as that worked by Nos.D5711/4 in multiple last May. No.D5703 put in an appearance on March 19 when it travelled light coupled to No.D5255 from Trafford Park to Northwich and then preceded No.D5255 with a separate load of empties to Peak Forest. No.D5703 did not, however, make the return journey.'

BR/Sulzers D5274/5/6 had all appeared by June 1964 and full diesel haulage of the ICI limestone trains from Peak Forest (Tunstead) to Northwich commenced on 4 August, using D5274-9. B. Nicholls in an article 'Oranges and Lemons' (*Traction*, December 2003) sheds more light on the subject:

'By the mid-1960s the Tunstead-Wallenscote limestone hopper trains manned by Northwich men, were being trialled with various types of diesel locomotives. A problem had arisen with the braking of these trains down the long gradient from Peak Forest to Cheadle Heath. By the time one of these loaded trains had got down the hill it was found that the loco tyres had heated to the extent that the tyre had turned on the wheel. The particular bogie hoppers used on these trains were vacuum-fitted throughout but had only one brake block per wheel. So the brake power was not as good as a normally fully-fitted train.

'When steam-operated, the vacuum could be dropped to about 14 inches, and while the train brakes held the train, the loco brakes would be just rubbing and no harm done. With a diesel, the loco air brake came on as soon as the vacuum dropped, hence the overheating of the wheels.

'Type 4s were tried, but it was deemed that Type 2 locos were more suitable as only empty hoppers were taken up the hill, and the loads brought down. Type 4s would be a bit of a waste. So it was that 'Crossleys' once more appeared on the Midland Main Line. They were based a Trafford Park because at this time Northwich depot had no fuelling facilities and no fitters trained on the type.

'Each morning a loco would run light engine from Trafford Park to Northwich . . . carry on to Wallenscote and pick the empty hoppers up . . . return to the station (*Northwich*) . . . and . . . carry on to Tunstead.

'A couple of weeks later it was decided that Sulzer Type 2s would be used on the hoppers after triple valves were modified to keep the loco brake off until the vacuum had been reduced to below 14 inches. And so the Crossleys returned to Barrow. Weeks of light engine running and driver training time were wasted.'

15.7 Calder Valley (1963).
One other item of interest was the appearance of a Metrovick in the Calder Valley area during November 1963 on crew-training runs around Todmorden. No further details have come to light but may have been related to banking duties.

15.8 Cross-London Transfer Freights (1965).
In 1965, *Modern Railways* reported further cross-London trials as follows:

'D5708 is reported to have worked into Feltham on March 5 (*1965*) with a block load of cement wagon empties.' (May edition)

'A correspondent provides details of the working which brought . . . D5708 to Feltham (May issue). The train concerned is the 10.45 Purfleet to Feltham, a conditional working conveying loaded cement wagons bound for Southampton. The return working is the 13.47 Q Feltham to Ripple Lane.' (July)

'Another correspondent has amplified the details of the working which led to the appearance of . . . D5708 at Feltham (May and July SR notes). Two locomotives of this type, Nos.D5708/17 were sent to the London area for trials during March on cross-London freight duties. It is expected that Brush Type 4 diesels will ultimately be employed on block freights, presumably from Willesden to Feltham or Eastleigh, but No.D5708 actually carried out tests between Willesden,

Feltham and Nine Elms. Both Type 2s have since returned to their home depot.' (August)

15.9 The Final Years (1966-68).

D5700-3/14-6 were transferred to 12B Carlisle Upperby during the period 4w/e 6 November 1965, followed by D5704-13/7-9 during 2w/e 17 December 1966. These transfers facilitated the more frequent use of the Metrovicks on the Carlisle to Preston route via Shap (local passenger services, together with limestone traffic from Shap Quarry).

Fourteen Metrovicks were transferred to the new 12A Carlisle Kingmoor Diesel Depot at the beginning of January 1968 (D5701/2/5-8/11/2/4-9) following the closure of 12B Carlisle Upperby, the other six having been withdrawn from traffic the previous week.

The Metrovicks became progressively more rare on passenger trains and it was therefore a notable event when D5707 worked several round trips on the Windermere branch on 27 June 1968, substituting for a failed DMU.

D5712, Shap Station (closed). 1 April 1967.
(George Woods)

Operations: A High-Level Summary • 199

D5707 and 'Britannia' 70041, Carlisle Rome Street Junction, 12 August 1966. View looking north-west. *(Colour-Rail)*

D5701, Carlisle, Bog Junction, 8 July 1966. View looking east towards Currock Road bridge. *(Colour-Rail)*

200 • THE METROPOLITAN-VICKERS TYPE 2 CO-BO DIESEL-ELECTRIC LOCOMOTIVES

D5706 and 12083, Carlisle Bog Junction, 15 July 1966. (*Colour-Rail*)

D5708 and D5702, Carlisle Kingmoor, 23 March 1967. 8P73 12.30 Carlisle-Preston via Barrow. Carlisle Diesel Depot, under construction, visible in the background. (*Colour-Rail*)

Chapter 16
DETAIL DIFFERENCES

16.1 Cab Windows Modifications.

The curved wrap-around cab front windows on the Metrovicks had a propensity to crack or fall out, due the flexing of the cab structure and the 'whole body' vibration problem which afflicted the class.

It is a commonly held belief that the Metrovicks all had their cab windows modified as part of the Dunkinfield rehabilitation process. However, the Metrovick Engine History Cards and photographic evidence indicate that at least eight of the Metrovicks were fitted with modified cab windows prior to their visits to Dukinfield, as follows:

	EHC Accounting Entry Date	Works Repair Period
D5700	18/06/60	Derby: 24/03/60-10/06/60 LC
D5701	03/12/60	Derby: 22/08/60-12/11/60 LC
D5704	08/10/60	Derby: 08/07/60-21/09/60 LC
D5705	P/E 28/01/61	Derby: 10/11/60-24/01/61 LC
D5710	28/01/61	Derby: 18/10/60-02/01/61 LC
D5711	25/02/61	Derby: 11/11/60-03/02/61 LC
D5717	06/11/60	Derby: 17/07/60-20/10/60 LC
D5718	03/12/60	Derby: 17/07/60-17/10/60 LC

The modification involved the fitting of new flat-glass screens in rubber-mountings installed in a steel 'sub-frame' fitted into the old window orifices. The cost of the modification was £174 per locomotive.

Whilst it is possible that there were more Metrovicks modified prior to the Dukinfield rehabilitation work, it is thought unlikely.

D5716, Derby Works - Yard, Undated (possibly February/March 1960)
. Driver's window missing. *(Rail-Online)*

202 • THE METROPOLITAN-VICKERS TYPE 2 CO-BO DIESEL-ELECTRIC LOCOMOTIVES

Left: D5704, 17A Derby, 9 May 1959. (*Colour-Rail*)

Right: D5716, Crewe Works, 1 November 1964. Comparison of wind screens before and after. (*Arnold W. Battson [Transport Treasury]*)

D5711, 12B Carlisle Upperby, 5 March 1967. Modified windows; note the flat glass panes rubber-mounted onto new sub-frames. All three windows were reduced in size as a consequence. (*Rail-Online*)

16.2 Trip-Cock Equipment (City Widened Lines).

Because of a reluctance by the Southern Region to return the BR/Sulzer Type 2 locomotives loaned from the London Midland Region, due to delays with the deliveries of the BRCW Type 3 locomotives, eight Metrovicks (D5712-9) were allocated to Cricklewood in January 1960 to work from Bedford/ Luton/ Harpenden to St Pancras and Moorgate via the Widened Lines.

It is generally thought that these eight locomotives were fitted with the requisite trip-cock equipment for use on the Moorgate services, although no photograph evidence of these locomotives exhibiting the trip-cock equipment has been unearthed. The trip-cock equipment will have been removed on their transfer back to Derby later in 1960.

16.3 Gangway Doors.

It has been suggested that the Metrovicks had their gangway doors sealed-up internally during the early-1960s, possibly as part of the Dukinfield rehabilitation process. This may or may not be true, but there is certainly no external evidence of the gangway doors having been welded up.

Chapter 17
LIVERIES

17.1 General.
There is a fairly significant quantity of archive material held at Kew covering the subject of how the Metrovick livery was developed during the design stage. The main players in the debate were:

Roland C. Bond	BTC, Chief Mechanical Engineer, London.
Christian Barman, George Williams Misha Black	BTC, Design Panel, London. Design Research Unit.
Jack Howe	Consultant, Chartered Architect & Industrial Designer.

The following correspondence commencing in early 1956 sheds a considerable amount of light on the subject; it should be noted, however, that once again there are obvious gaps in the correspondence, presumably reflecting 'lost' letters and/or subject matter discussed face-to-face or via telephone.

Letter: J. Howe to C. Barman, 27 March 1956:

'I am . . . enclosing a quick perspective sketch of the locomotive which gives some idea of the front view and its relationship with the train. I appreciate that colours have not yet been decided upon and the red shown is simply my preference.'

Letter: J. Howe to C. Barman, 23 April 1956:

'I saw in Friday's *Manchester Guardian* that it had been decided to adopt maroon colour for all rolling stock except the Southern Region and that diesel locomotives and multiple-units would be green. Is this a very recent decision or is it still possible to change the locomotive colour so that it matches the rolling stock as we discussed? I sincerely hope that it may still be possible to do this because I think it is a very important aspect of the external appearance.'

Letter: J. Howe to C. Barman, 3 August 1956:

'I think you know my views about banding and such methods of 'decorating' locomotives and as I might be more opposed than others I will be grateful if my design could be used to illustrate the fact that this practice is not necessary.'

Letter: J. Howe to C. Barman, 5 November 1956:

'I have studied the colour drawing of the above locomotive in order to try and devise a form of decorative banding which would be appropriate, but so far without success. It seems to me that there are two possibilities. In the first place a band could be incorporated immediately below the filter louvres, but this, of course, would cut across the radiator grille and the doors, and in addition would tend to cut the body in half horizontally. I have, therefore, ruled this out. The other possibility is a band of a different tone or colour at the bottom of the body which would carry round at the two ends to emphasise the buffer beams. Unfortunately this would be contrary to my original idea which was to incorporate the buffer beam with the body work at the ends of the locomotive, and avoid the appearance of detachment which is very evident in all of Metropolitan-Vickers designs. The latest modification is going to lift the body even higher from the bogies than on the colour drawing and it will therefore be a mistake in my opinion to emphasise this fact.

'I think, in the circumstances, it would be better to leave the decision at this point until the design is more settled.

'I am not opposed to decoration of machines of this kind in principle, but I think it must follow a very complete technical grasp of the whole design and as far as diesel-electric locos are concerned I do not think we are nearly at that stage yet. When this design mastery has been achieved, decoration will find its way naturally, and will be appropriate to the form on which it appears.

'I think the fashion of painting horizontal lines on locomotives is not that kind of decoration; it is artificial and in the majority of cases quite unrelated to the design as a whole.'

Letter: J. Howe to C. Barman, 18 April 1957:

'I was with the Traction Department of Metropolitan Vickers yesterday and there are one or two points which they would like settled as soon as possible. These are:

'Has the size and style of the locomotive number been settled yet? If so, I would like to have details and would you also let me know whether Misha is going to position them or whether that will be left to me. This also applies to the symbol.

'I am a little undecided about the roof colour and its junction with the body colour owing to the many changes that have occurred in connection with this project. I have had made a rough working model on which some experiments have been carried out and I am getting MV to send it down soon after the holiday. I would like then to bring it along to show you and ask your advice on this particular point.'

Letter: J. Howe to C. Barman, 5 July 1957:

'I still have the model of the Metrovick locomotive in the office waiting for exterior details to be added, both for your approval and the guidance of the manufacturer, but I have not yet had a reply to my letter of 18th April although I am aware that some of the points have since been cleared.'

Letter: G. Williams to J. Howe, 10 July 1957:

'Christian Barman has passed to me your letter of 5th July in which you refer to your earlier letter of the 18th April discussing the livery of the 1,200hp diesel-electric locomotive.

'I enclose a copy of a typical pro-forma which other designers have been asked to complete for the manufacturer's information. This information must, incidentally, be given to the builders through Mr Bond's office here, so I shall be glad if you will complete it and return it to me as soon as possible.

'You will see that the basic colours are as follows:

Main body	Standard Loco green, BR Spec.30.
Roof	Mid-grey B.S.S. 2660: 9-101
Lining	Light grey B.S.S. 2660: 7-078
Buffer casing and beams	Red B.S.S. 2660: 0-005

'We now await your proposals for the division of these colours and the position of the lining, the numerals and prefix, and the crest, together with any other miscellaneous suggestions, such as the treatment of the window frames, etc.

'In addition to completing the pro-forma I should be glad if you would either complete the model in your proposed scheme, or prepare a side elevation colour sketch which can be sent on to the manufacturers through Mr Bond's office with the pro-forma. We would naturally wish to see your proposals and approve them before we pass them on.

'The number to be used for this particular locomotive is D5700, and should be based on Misha Black's recommendations which have now been accepted . . . The actual number for your locomotive will be drawn up by Misha's office, and we will pass it on to Mr Bond with your final scheme. The symbol to be used is the standard British Railways' design. These are as follows:

Small size	Diameter of roundel	14½in
	Overall length (over the side wings)	2ft 6in
Large Size	Diameter of roundel	1ft 9½in
	Overall length (over the side wings)	3ft 8¼in

'We leave it to you to suggest which you recommend for this locomotive, and where it should be placed.'

Letter: J. Howe to G. Williams, 10 July 1957:

'Thank you for your letter of the 10th July with information about the surface treatment of the above locomotives.

Letter: G. Williams to J. Howe, 2 August 1957:

'Referring to your letter of 10th July; I should be grateful if you could let me have the information regarding the surface treatment of these locomotives as soon as possible.'

Letter: J. Howe to G. Williams, 6 August 1957:

'Thanks for your letter of the 2nd August in connection with the above. You will remember that I said I was holding up the exterior decoration of the locomotive in the hope that something would have been settled about the train identification box but during my visit to Trafford Park last week MV Engineers informed me that they were going ahead with markers and that any modification would have to be dealt with later. I will therefore go ahead and produce the drawing you require irrespective of the possible change regarding train identification.'

Letter: J. Howe to G. Williams, 3 September 1957:

'With reference to your letter dated the 10th July I found it necessary to produce a new coloured drawing of the above locomotive as there have been a number of changes since the last drawing was produced and this is enclosed together with a print showing the colour treatment which, if it meets with Mr Bond's approval, can be sent to Metropolitan Vickers with his instructions.

'In regard to the application of a horizontal band I have never been in favour of this but as it has been insisted upon it is shown on the drawing.

'I would like to explain that originally I aimed at a regular pattern of filter grilles which would be the main horizontal feature of the exterior and it was intended that these should be coloured grey as against the green general background. Also the radiators were then intended to be removed when necessary from the inside and I have specified a simple opening in the body side with the grille immediately behind. MV have now found that it is impossible to remove the radiators internally and the treatment of the grille must be the same as for the filters. Formerly I had aimed at 'losing' the radiator grille by painting it in body colour but now that the treatment is similar to the filters it seems reasonable to paint them the same and this I have done.'

'P.S. I am not enclosing the print mentioned in the first paragraph but will do so when the colour drawing is approved.'

Letter: G. Williams to J. Howe, 12 September 1957:

'Here is the colour sample [painting, numbering, etc] for which you have asked. I should like to have it back when you have finished with it.'

Letter: J. Howe to G. Williams, 16 September 1957:

'I am enclosing three copies of drawing number 125/1E with colours indicated. I understand that Mr Bond will send them on to Metropolitan-Vickers.'

Letter: G. Williams to R.C. Bond, 20 September 1957:

'Attached are three copies of the general instructions for the painting of the above locomotives, and three copies of the drawing prepared by Mr Jack Howe showing the colour arrangement.'

British Transport Commission - General Instructions for Painting Main Line Diesel Locomotives.

Type and Make of Locomotive: 1200hp 'B' Type Metropolitan Vickers.

Item	Colour and Reference
1. Body, except ventilator grilles	Standard Loco Green, BR Spec. 30.
Ventilator grilles	Light grey B.S.S. 2660 7-078
2. Roof, except removable portion	Standard Loco Green, BR Spec. 30.
Removable portion and hub of radiator fan	Mid-Grey B.S.S. 2660 9-101
3. Bogies	
Frames	Light grey B.S.S. 2660 7-078
Equaliser beams	Black
4. Undergear details	
Except battery box	Black
Battery box	Mid-Grey B.S.S. 2660 9-101
5. Buffer casings and beams	Red B.S.S. 2660 0-005
6. Drawhook guide, etc	Black
7. Lining, looking forward towards No.1 end	
Left-hand side	6in wide line to extend between driving cab doors to within 10in of each door.
Right-hand side	6in wide line to extend between driving cab door and second grille from front to within 10in of door and grille. Bottom of each line to be in line with bottom of driving cab doors.
8. Numerals/Prefix, looking forwards to No.1 end	
Left-hand side	Centrally below second window in front end driving cab with top of numbers 10in below bottom of window.
Right-hand side	Centrally below second window in rear end driving cab; top of numbers 10in below bottom of window.
9. Window Frames	Black rubber surrounds where indicated on drawings. Other windows have no frames.
10. Top of outside footplating	-
11. Builders' plate, size, position and colour	Centrally below single window of driver's cab at each end, lined up with colour lining - opposite ends from locomotive numbers.
12. Crest, looking towards No.1 end	
Left-hand side	Centrally below last radiator grille, centre line of badge 1ft 3in below bottom line of grille framing.
Right-hand side	Centrally between locomotive number and rearmost cab door, centre line of crest in line with centre line of locomotive number.

D5715, Great Howard Street Yard, Liverpool, 1959. Trade exhibition. Note the light grey bogie frames; subsequent bogie re-painting in BR workshops was in the more practical black.
(Colour-Rail)

Letter: J. Howe to G. Williams, 4 December 1958:

'You asked me to let you have my further views on the above locomotive as a result of seeing the finished product recently at Marylebone station.

'My remarks contained in the Report which I sent to Metropolitan-Vickers, of which you had a copy, are still valid in all respects and the following are therefore additional to those.'

'The grey horizontal band had been detailed on my drawing to line with the bottom of the radiator grille and it was dimensioned 6in from the lower line of the bodyside. It was, in fact, painted 8in up.'

Several articles produced over the years covering the history of the Metrovicks make reference to the colour 'duck-egg blue' with regards to the bodyside stripe and grilles. It will be noted that in all of the archive correspondence seen at Kew there was absolutely no reference made to this colour!

17.2 Liveries - Pre Rehabilitation.
17.2.1 GNY.

The Metrovicks were painted in accordance with the 'General Instructions for Painting Main Line Diesel Locomotives' which incorporated a number of class-specific elements e.g. light grey radiator and ventilator grille frames, light grey bogie frames, light-grey lining, together with a single set of D57xx numbers per side (under the driver's cab window) and a single crest per side at the No.2 end.

17.2.2 BR Emblem.

In strict heraldic terms, the lion in the lion-and-wheel emblem should always face towards the left; however, it appears that two versions of the crest were produced for the Metrovicks so that the crest always depicted the lion facing towards the No.1 end of the locomotive. The crests on the 2-1 side were, therefore, technically incorrect.

17.3 Liveries - Post Re-Rehabilitation.
17.3.1 GNY

Generally accepted wisdom is that all Metrovicks acquired small yellow warning panels during their time in Dukinfield for rehabilitation. However, photographic evidence seems to suggest otherwise.

Whilst BR decided that yellow warning panels should be adopted as standard on 23 July 1961, it was to be 1962, after Design Panel input regarding shape and styling, before the physical application of the panels commenced. Although the precise point in time during 1962 when panels started to be applied is unknown, it is reasonable to suspect that some Metrovicks departed Dukinfield without the panels, given that the first examples left the Works in late 1961 and early 1962.

The photograph of D5709 on page 150 shows the locomotive at Gorton Works (number readable) on 22 February 1962 with no yellow warning panels, only a matter of days before the *Engine History Card* shows this locomotive as completing its Dukinfield Works repairs. Another photograph (see below) shows D5709 active on 1 June 1962 without yellow panels, and whilst the locomotive number is not readable, the 25kV sign position is consistent.

This inevitably begs the question as to whether any other Metrovicks departed Dukinfield without yellow panels. As D5709 was the second of the class to depart Dukinfield, it is perhaps reasonable to assume that D5719, the first loco, was also ex-works without yellow panels.

It is also arguable that D5713, D5707 and D5708, the third, fourth and fifth locomotives from

D5709, Bilsborrow (between Lancaster and Preston), 1 June 1962. Barrow-Liverpool passenger. Post-Dukinfield rehabilitation, with no yellow panels. (*Arnold W. Battson [Transport Treasury]*)

Dukinfield, may also have left in all-over green. This is based on the fact that these three locomotives (and D5709/19) subsequently carried somewhat 'makeshift-looking' small yellow warning panels with larger radius curves to the top corners of the yellow panels, as compared with D5703, D5710 and D5705, the seventh, eighth and ninth departures. It will be noted in the photograph of D5713 below that the panel corner curves do not smoothly meet the vertical and horizontal boundaries and certainly illustrate a less professional application than the panels seen on D5706 also illustrated below. This might suggest a post-Dukinfield depot application (at Barrow?) rather than Works although unfortunately there is no actual evidence to substantiate this theory.

Photographic evidence covering 1962/63 illustrates the variance on the first five locomotives rehabilitated at Dukinfield but unfortunately photos for D5712, the sixth Dukinfield departure, have not been found for this critical period.

Loco	Date ex-Dukinfield	Yellow panel top corner radii	Date seen	Number readable (nr)/ number not readable (nnr)
D5719	21/12/61	Large radius	06/08/62	nr
D5709	23/02/62	Large radius	13/09/63	nnr
D5713	15/03/62	Large radius	25/08/62	nr
D5707	29/03/62	Large radius	06/08/62	nr
D5708	19/04/62	Large radius	xx/11/63	nr
D5712	18/05/62	Small radius	15/10/66	nr
D5703	23/05/62	Small radius	28/07/62	nr
D5710	08/06/62	Small radius	11/07/64	nr
D5705	27/06/62	Small radius	29/07/63	nnr

Left: D5706, Lancaster, 12 June 1964. Small radius curves to top corners of yellow panel. (Author's Collection)

Right: D5713, Morecambe, 25 August 1962. Large radius curves to top corners of yellow panel. (Author's Collection)

The large radii corners were retained by D5713/9 and probably D5709 until withdrawal. D5708 did likewise until its GFY repaint. D5707, however, was noted with small radii corners when photographed by Noel Machell on 1 July 1966.

17.3.2 GSY

All twenty Metrovicks carried green livery with small yellow panels (GSY), although, as already seen in the previous Section, the top corner radii of the panels varied, as did the height of the yellow panels (compare the two photographs of D5702 and D5706 on page 214).

D5716, Crewe Works (Paint Shop Yard), 8 November 1964. Lower height yellow warning panel. *(Alec Swain [Transport Treasury])*

D5711, Unknown location and date. *(RCTS Archive)*

17.3.3 GFY

Full yellow front ends for all main line locomotives became official policy at the BRB meeting on 9 June 1966. BR's Design Panel meeting in November 1966 agreed to adopt the increased yellow front end design for the new blue livery. With regard to the use of full yellow front ends on locomotives still in green, the Chief Engineer (T&RS) asked the General Manager Workshops on 22 February 1967 to paint green locomotives with full yellow front ends in future where their paintwork required only to be touched up.

D5707 and D5708 received the full yellow end treatment during their workshop visits in April-June 1967 and October-December 1967 respectively.

D5702 (August-October 1967), D5705 (April-August 1967) and D5706 (September-October 1967) also visited Crewe Works during this period, but all retained the small yellow panels.

D5707, 10A Carnforth, June 1968. A livery alteration which did absolutely nothing to improve the aesthetic qualities of the Metrovicks! 25kV signs appear to be going missing with only one remaining on the front and none on the bodyside. (Colour-Rail)

17.3.4 BFY

Only one locomotive, D5701, was outshopped in standard BR rail blue with a full yellow end. This was carried out at Crewe Works as part of a classified overhaul during October-November 1967. For the first time, two sets of numbers were carried on each side of the locomotive.

D5701, 10A Carnforth, 25 June 1968. *(Bill Wright)*

D5701, 10A Carnforth, August 1968. *(Colour-Rail)*

17.4 D-Prefixes.

All locomotives were originally released to traffic with sans serif D-prefixes. Locomotives known to have subsequently carried serif D-prefixes were: D5700/2/7/11/4/6-8.

D5701 carried sans-serif D-prefixes prior to repainting blue, when it received 'block'-style asymmetric numbers and lettering.

Locomotives known to have had sans-serif D-prefixes at withdrawal were: D5704/5/8-10/2/3/9. D5703/6/15 are also believed to have carried sans-serif D-prefixes right up to withdrawal.

Interestingly, D5708, one of the two locomotives to receive GFY livery, carried sans serif D-prefixes throughout, whereas D5707, the other GFY locomotive, changed from sans serif to serif at the same time as the full yellow ends were applied.

D5706, Crewe Works, 8 November 1964. 'Sans-Serif' D-prefix. Touch-up repaint. Boiler testing equipment attached to the buffer beam pipe for the venting of steam. (*A. Swain [Transport Treasury]*)

D5702, Crewe Works, 16 May 1965. Serif D-prefix. Ex-works with full repaint; note that the yellow panel does not extend as high as the panel on D5706. (*Noel A. Machell*)

Loco No.	Last sighting Sans serif	First sighting Serif	Additional Notes
D5700	xx/07/64	04/09/65	To serif during Crewe Works 01/11/64-07/02/65 visit. Serif at withdrawal.
D5701			Sans serif whilst GNY/GSY. To BFY with block-style asymmetric numbers (11/67).
D5702	04/07/63	16/05/65	To serif during Crewe Works 07/02/65-23/05/65 visit. Serif at withdrawal.
D5703	?	?	Sans serif at withdrawal (?); sans serif on 07/08/65.
D5704			Sans serif at withdrawal.
D5705			Sans serif at withdrawal.
D5706	?	?	Sans serif at withdrawal (?); sans serif on 08/11/64.
D5707	10/07/66	04/06/67	Sans serif whilst GNY/GSY. To serif during Crewe Works 09/04/67-11/06/67 visit. Serif whilst GFY up to withdrawal.
D5708			Sans serif at withdrawal.

Loco No.	Last sighting Sans serif	First sighting Serif	Additional Notes
D5709			Sans serif at withdrawal.
D5710			Sans serif at withdrawal.
D5711	10/07/66	15/01/67	To Serif during Crewe Works 14/08/66-15/01/67 visit. Serif at withdrawal.
D5712			Sans serif at withdrawal.
D5713			Sans serif at withdrawal.
D5714	xx/xx/xx	18/10/66	To Serif during Crewe Works 24/07/66-18/09/66 visit. Serif at withdrawal.
D5715	?	?	Sans serif at withdrawal (?); sans serif on 06/08/67.
D5716	01/09/64	01/11/64	To serif during Crewe Works 12/08/64-06/12/64 visit. Serif at withdrawal.
D5717	07/04/66	07/05/67	To serif during Crewe Works 05/06/66-18/09/66 visit. Serif at withdrawal.
D5718	26/06/66	07/05/67	To serif during Crewe Works 09/10/66-18/12/66 visit(?). Serif at withdrawal.
D5719			Sans serif at withdrawal.

17.5 Works Repaints.
17.5.1 Full Works Repaints.
Locomotives known to have received full works repaints at Crewe Works are:

D5701	26/11/67	To BFY	Classified repair?
D5702	23/05/65	GSY retained	Following fire damage sustained 21/01/65.
D5711	15/01/67	GSY retained	Following fire damage sustained 20/07/66.
D5714	18/09/66		Following fire damage sustained 31/05/66 at Barrow depot.

17.5.2 Touch-Up and Varnish.
Locomotives known to have received touch-up repaints at Crewe Works are:

D5700	07/02/65		
D5706	08/11/64		
D5707	11/06/67	To GFY	Classified repair?
D5708	26/11/67	To GFY	Classified repair?
D5710	28/02/65		
D5716	29/11/64		
D5717	25/04/64		Cab repaint
D5718	18/12/66		

Chapter 18
UNIQUE IDENTIFIERS

18.1 Selected Identifiers.

For the Metrovicks there were very few readily apparent physical detail differences which allowed locomotives to be quickly identified when the individual numbers were not visible or indecipherable. This was a problem for the Metrovicks both in their early GNY days, and again post-Dukinfield in their GSY guise. Window modifications to certain members of the class pre-Dukinfield, together with some limited livery changes (to GFY or BFY) post-Dukinfield allowed some scope for individual locomotive identification.

The situation today is made so much worse when trying to identify locomotives from photographs because of the fact that, apart from D5701 in blue, the Metrovicks were only numbered at one end; so any 'three-quarter' photographs taken with the secondman's cab nearest are highly likely to cause problems!

There are unfortunately numerous photographs out there where the locomotive is incorrectly identified. Use of a number of very 'minor' locomotive detail differences allow these errors to be recognised for what they are, either the incorrect recording of locomotives in the first place, or, in a small number of cases, the deliberate spurious captioning of photographs. Where the locomotive number is clearly visible, it is also sometimes possible using these unique identifiers, to expose incorrect quoted dates.

Four key identifiers are:

- Front-end 25kV warning signs (number and positioning).
- Bodyside 25kV warning sign (position).
- Red Circle coupling symbols above the buffer beam (present or not), and,
- Depot allocation 'stencils' above the buffer beam or on the cab sides (present or not, and actual depot code if applied)

18.2 25kV Electrification Warning Signs – General.

In the main, 25kV signs were fixed during works visits (although possibly not exclusively); there is certainly a distinct link between the Metrovick works dates and their change from single signs to pairs of signs on the cab fronts.

Single front-end 25kV signs started to be fitted in 1960 at Derby, then Dukinfield and possibly Horwich. It appears that all Metrovicks which received modified cab windows prior to the Dukinfield rehabilitation also received the 25kV signs. Once Crewe took over overhauls in 1963, pairs of signs were attached to each front-end.

25kV signs were also fitted onto the locomotive's bodysides adjacent to the boiler water filler access doors, one per side. As can be seen from the tables, the exact positioning of the signs varied considerably, thereby aiding locomotive identification.

18.2.1 Front-End 25kV Signs: GNY Livery.

The methodology for describing the positioning of the 25kV signs on GNY-liveried locomotives is provided in the captions for the two photographs on page 217.

As already mentioned, 25kV warning signs were fitted to the Metrovicks from mid-1960; however, it is highly likely that several locomotives did not receive them until their release from rehabilitation at Dukinfield. Single signs were located on the right-hand gangway door. Vertical positioning varied very considerably.

Details of the fitting of 25kV signs to GNY locomotives are tabulated on page 217.

Unique Identifiers • 217

D5700, 17A Derby, 30 April 1961 (*Colour-Rail*).

D5705, 17A Derby, 4 May 1961. Single 25kV signs only were applied to certain Metrovicks carrying GNY livery. In the following table the positioning of the single signs is made using the top of lower disc structures as the reference point; the vertical length of the sign is defined as 100 per cent. Thus, for D5700, the bottom of the sign is level with the top of the disc structure (i.e. 0%) and so, by definition, the top of the sign is +100% above the structure. Similarly for D5705, the bottom of the sign is -100 per cent below the top of the disc structure and the top is level (0%). Note that the first % number represents the position of the bottom of the sign;, the second % number represents the position of the top of the sign. (*Arnold W. Battson [Transport Treasury]*)

Loco No.	Notes	Date Sighted	nr/nnr	Cab End	No. of Signs	Vertical Positioning	Additional Notes
D5700		07/05/61	nr	No.1	Single	0/+100%	Mod windows pre-Dukinfield
D5701	(3)						Mod windows pre-Dukinfield
D5702							
D5703							
D5704		26/09/60	nr	No.2	Single	-40/+60%	Mod windows pre-Dukinfield
D5705		04/05/61	nr	No.1	Single	-100/0%	Mod windows pre-Dukinfield
D5706							
D5707	(4)						
D5708	(4)						
D5709	(4)	22/02/62	nr	No.2	Single	-30/+70%	During Dukinfield mods
D5710	(1)	24/09/60	nnr	No.1	Single	-120/-20%	
	(1)	09/10/60	nnr	No.2	Single		
	(3)						Mod windows pre-Dukinfield

218 • THE METROPOLITAN-VICKERS TYPE 2 CO-BO DIESEL-ELECTRIC LOCOMOTIVES

Loco No.	Notes	Date Sighted	nr/nnr	Cab End	No. of Signs	Vertical Positioning	Additional Notes
D5711		xx/xx/61	nr	No.2	Single	-10/+90%	Mod windows pre-Dukinfield
D5712							
D5713	(4)						
D5714	(2)	14/05/61	nnr	No.1	Single	-100/0%	
D5715							
D5716							
D5717	(3)						Mod windows pre-Dukinfield
D5718	(3)						Mod windows pre-Dukinfield
D5719	(4)						

nr = number readable.   nnr = number not readable.

Notes:

(1) D5710 possibly received 25kV signs *prior* to receiving modified windows (see photograph on p59 of *Modern Railways Illustrated* No.226 dated 24/09/60 – No.1 end, number not readable). Also D5710 (flickr photograph dated 09/10/60 [No.2 end, again number not readable]).

(2) Similarly, D5714 may have received 25kV signs whilst GNY and carrying the original front windows (see photograph below); number not readable.

Notes (1) and (2) above indicate that at least two Metrovicks carried 25kV signs whilst still being fitted with the old-style windows.

(3) No photographic evidence has been seen of D5701/10/7/8 with 25kV signs on GNY livery; however, these locomotives received modified windows prior to entering Dukinfield for major repairs and, therefore, like D5700/4/5/11, probably received the 25kV signs whilst in GNY livery.

(4) Like D5709, D5707/8/13/9 may have left Dukinfield following rehabilitation repairs without yellow warning panels (see Section 17.3.1) and *may*, therefore, represent an additional four locomotives which carried single 25kV signs on the cab fronts whilst still carrying GNY livery.

D5714, 18A Toton, 14 May 1961. No.1 end. Unmodified windows, 25kV sign on front end. But is this D5714? Another photo of D5714 (No.2 end) taken at Cricklewood on 11 April 1962 *without* front-end 25kV sign is also available via Rail-Online; however, the date for this one is clearly incorrect as D5714 was in Dukinfield on this date. (*Rail-Online*)

Unique Identifiers • 219

18.2.2 Front-End 25kV Signs: GSY Livery.

All locomotives in GSY, GFY and BFY liveries carried *single* signs or a *pair* of signs on the cab fronts. The methodology for describing the positioning of the 25kV signs on GSY-liveried locomotives is provided in the captions for photographs 1804, 1807 and 1808.

A number of locomotives which carried 25kV signs whilst in GNY livery had them removed whilst undergoing rehabilitation at Dukinfied, these being re-applied in a different position prior to release. Whether this applied to all locomotives is unknown at this stage, particularly given the question mark over how many Metrovick were initially released from Dukinfield carrying GNY livery (see Section 18.3.1).

The relevant information for each locomotive, derived wholly

Above left: **D5711, 17A Derby, 1961.** (*Peter Sedge*)

Above right: **D5711, Barrow-in-Furness, 11 July 1964.** Single 25kV sign re-positioned, presumably undertaken during the locomotive's time in Dukinfield. (*Keith Long*)

Left: **D5710, 12C Barrow, 11 July 1964.** Both locomotives exhibit the single front-end 25kV signs on the right-hand gangway door but note the radically different positioning of the signs. D5702/7/12/6/8 were also present on this visit to Barrow. On the basis of the position of the 25kV sign on the Metrovick adjacent to D5710, this second locomotive is believed to be either D5707 or D5712, with D5712 being the most likely contender as that one was recorded in Keith Long's notebook next to D5710. Note the absence of a windscreen wiper on the secondman's window of D5710. In the following tables the positioning of the 'Single' signs is made using the top boundary of the yellow warning panel as the reference point, with the vertical length of the sign defined as 100 per cent. Thus, for D5710, the bottom of the sign is +10 per cent of the sign's height *above* the warning panel and so, by definition, the top of the sign is +110 per cent above the yellow panel. Similarly for D5712, the bottom of the sign is -130 per cent below the yellow panel and the top -30 per cent below. (*Keith Long*)

220 • THE METROPOLITAN-VICKERS TYPE 2 CO-BO DIESEL-ELECTRIC LOCOMOTIVES

D5702, 10A Carnforth, 22 June 1968. *(Transport Topics)*

D5709 (sic), 12B Carlisle Upperby, July 1966. Both locomotives illustrate a 'Pair' of 25kV signs. Using the same reference point of the top of the yellow warning panels and logic explained in the caption for the photograph on page 219 (lower), the positioning of the signs on D5702 is -30/+70 per cent and for D5709 is -40/+60 per cent (although the right-hand sign is slightly higher than the left). All is not what it seems, however, and here we have the classic problem with the Metrovicks. The number for 'D5709' is at the far and not readable. Using the known positioning of the 25kV signs, it becomes clear that this locomotive cannot be D5709 as it never carried a pair of 25kV on the front-end and, indeed, went to the grave yard with only a single sign. The twin 17A/12E depot coding identifies this locomotive as D5715 (see Sections 18.5 and 18.6). *(Rail-Photoprints)*

from photographic evidence, is provided in Section 18.6; entries are deliberately marked 'nr' (number readable) or 'nnr' (number not readable). Dated 'nnr' reports are, where possible supported by 'nr' reports. In all records the locomotive end (No.1 or 2) is recorded.

The tables may at first sight look like an assembly of somewhat random information but actually there are some very interesting patterns to be found amongst the mass of data, as follows:

1. Seven GSY locomotives carried single 25kV signs *within* the yellow warning panels. These were the first seven Metrovicks released from Dukinfield i.e. D5703/7-9/12/3/9.
2. Eight GSY locomotives carried single 25kV signs *immediately above* the yellow warning panels (i.e. 0-100% or +10-+110). These were the eighth to the fourteenth Metrovicks released from Dukinfield i.e. D5700/1/4-6/10/4/6.
3. Five GSY locomotives carried single 25kV signs *substantially above* the yellow warning panels in various positions. These were the last six Metrovicks out-shopped from Dukinfield i.e. D5702/11/5/7/8.
4. D5704/9/13 only ever carried a single 25kV sign on each front end. The remaining seventeen subsequently acquired pairs of signs.
5. All Metrovicks categorically *known* to have been fitted with 25kV signs prior to Dukinfield (D5700/4/5/11), had their single signs moved to a higher position on despatch from Dukinfield.

The first two observations raise the interesting possibility that further locomotives departed Dukinfield without yellow warning panels than those already suggested in Section 18.3.1. The hypothesis here was that D5707-9/13/9 and maybe D5712 left Dukinfield in GNY livery, with 'makeshift' yellow panels added at a later date. However, it is maybe possible that D5703 also left Dukinfield in GNY livery, with yellow panels painted on later around the pre-existing low-level 25kV signs. After D5703, the next seven Dukinfield departures were subsequently noted with yellow panels and 25kV signs neatly positioned immediately above.

18.2.3 Front-End 25kV Signs: GFY Livery.
Pairs of signs only were carried by locomotives in GFY livery. Without the small yellow warning panel to use as the positioning reference point, it is necessary to revert to the top of the lower disc structure as the reference.

Two locomotives, D5707/8, were repainted into GFY. In both cases the position of the front end 25kV signs actually remained unchanged, with the different % positioning numbers reflecting the reference point change.

18.2.4 Front-End 25kV Signs: BFY Livery.
Pairs of signs only were carried on the BFY livery; D5701 carried single signs whilst in GSY livery and only carried the pairs of signs when in blue. Reference % points again refer to the top of the lower disc structure.

18.3 25kV Signs: Bodyside.
Single bodyside 25kV signs were placed immediately to the right of the boiler water access doors on both sides. Heights varied as per the table in Section 18.6; however, in the majority of cases, once fitted they seem to have remained in the same position throughout their lives despite works visits.

The methodology for describing the positioning of the bodyside 25kV signs is provided in the caption for the photograph below.

D5705, Worksop, 1 September 1991. The 25kV sign is visible to the right of the access door midway along the bodyside. The positioning of the signs varied vertically and in Section 18.6 the positioning of the sign is described by using the cantrail as the reference point with the vertical length of the sign defined as 100%. Thus, for D5705, the bottom of the sign is -130 per cent of the sign's height *below* the cantrail and so, by definition, the top of the sign is -30 per cent below the cantrail. (*Anthony Sayer*)

18.4 Red-Circle Multiple-Working Symbols.

British Railways locomotives deployed different multiple-working coupling arrangements and to distinguish between the various types, a symbol was applied above the buffer beam to allow quick recognition of the suitability of coupling between different locomotives types. In the case of the Metrovicks the code was Red Circle, reflecting electro-magnetic control; the photograph on page 223 illustrates the positioning and size of the symbol.

No photographic evidence has been found showing locomotives carrying the red circle symbol prior to entering Dukinfield. By no means all of the Metrovicks carried the Red Circles; observations of locomotives seen carrying the symbol are listed in Section 18.6.

18.5 Depot Identification.

Locomotives variously carried painted '17A' (Derby), '14A' (Cricklewood), '12E'/'12C' (Barrow) and '12B' (Carlisle Upperby) markings above their buffer beam (usually below the left hand gangway doors), and subsequently 'NWL' or 'NW' (North Western Lines) above the buffer beams or on the cab sides to notify their operational allocation; in at least one case two markings were carried simultaneously!

The tables in Section 18.6 give full details of depot codes carried post-Dukinfield. Pre-Dukinfield, D5700-7/9-11/3-5/8 are known to have carried the '17A' code (all below the left-hand gangway door).

Loco No.	Date	Cab	nr/nnr	Depot Code	Date	Cab	nr/nnr	Depot Code
D5700	09/05/59	No.2	nr	17A	30/04/61	No.1	nr	17A
D5701	17/07/59	No.1	nr	17A				
D5702	xx/xx/59	No.2	nnr	17A				
D5703	16/08/59	No.2	nr	17A				
D5704	09/05/59	No.1	nr	17A	26/09/60	No.2	nr	17A
D5705	30/04/60	No.2	nr	17A	xx/09/60	No.2	nr	17A
D5706	26/09/60	No.2	nnr	17A				
D5707	09/05/59	No.1	nr	17A				
D5708	17/05/59	No.2	nr	17A				
D5709	13/06/59	No.2	nnr	17A	22/02/62	No.2	nr	17A
D5710	19/04/59	No.2	nnr	17A				
D5711	30/04/60	No.2	nr	17A				
D5712								
D5713	xx/xx/59	No.2	nr	17A				
D5714	30/04/60	No.2	nr	17A				
D5715	30/04/60	No.2	nr	17A				
D5716								
D5717	08/07/60	No.2	nr	14A?				
D5718	30/04/60	No.1	nr	17A	xx/05/60	No.2	nr	14A?
D5719								

Unique Identifiers • 223

D5715, 12B Carlisle Upperby, July 1966. Red Circle coupling code markings. Note the 17A and 12E markings on the buffer beam below the gangway doors. *(Rail-Photoprints)*

18.6 Summary of Identifying Characteristics (Post-Dukinfield).

A post-Dukinfield loco-by-loco summary covering 25kV signs, Red Circle symbols and depot codes is provided in the tables below.

All locos GSY livery unless otherwise stated in "Comments" column.
Front-end 25kV sign reference points relate to yellow panel (top boundary) unless otherwise stated in "Comments".

Abbreviations:-
nr/nnr	Loco. number readable/number not readable.
Cab end viewed	No.1 (radiator end), No.2 (non-radiator end).
Front-end 25kV signs	As per descriptions in Sections 18.2.2, 18.2.3 and 18.2.4.
Red Circle MW Code	Yes/No.
Allocation Code	12B Carlisle Upperby, 12C/12E Barrow, 17A Derby, NW/NWL (NorthWestern Lines).
	Depot code position: blhgd/brhgd - below left or right hand gangway door; cs - cab side.
Side Viewed	1-2 (No.1 end left and No.2 end right).
Bodyside 25kV signs	As per description in Section 18.3.

D5700

Photo Date	nr/nnr	Cab End Viewed	25kV Signs	Red circle MW Code	Allocation Code	Side Viewed	25kV Sign	Comments
xx/08/63	nr	No.1	Single: 0/+100%	Y	12E (blhgd)	1-2	-170/-70%	Signs higher post-Dukinfield.
06/06/64	nnr	No.2	Single: 0/+100%	Y	12E (blhgd)	1-2	-170/-70%	
xx/07/64	nr	No.1	Single: 0/+100%	Y	12E (blhgd)	1-2	-170/-70%	
								Crewe Works: 01/11/64-07/02/65.
xx/xx/xx	nnr	No.1	Pair: -60/+40%	N	Nil	2-1	-180/80%	Crewe Works (Paint Shop Yard).
07/08/65	nnr	No.1	Pair: -60/+40%	N	Nil			
04/09/65	nr	No.2	Pair: -60/+40%	N	Nil			
29/01/67	nr	No.2	Pair: -60/+40%	N	Nil	1-2	-170/-70%	Stored.
30/08/67	nr	No.2	Pair: -60/+40%	N	NWL (cs)			Stored.

D5701

Photo Date	nr/nnr	Cab End Viewed	25kV Signs	Red circle MW Code	Allocation Code	Side Viewed	25kV Sign	Comments
xx/xx/63	nr	No.1	Single: 0/+100%	Y	12E (blhgd)			
01/06/63	nr	No.2	Single: 0/+100%	Y	12E (blhgd)	1-2	-140/-40%	
xx/07/65	nr	No.1	Single: 0/+100%	Y	12E (blhgd)			
xx/09/65	nr	No.2	Single: 0/+100%	Y	12E (blhgd)	2-1	-140/-40%	See Note (1).
25/05/66	nr	No.1	Single: 0/+100%	Y	12E (blhgd)	2-1	-140/-40%	
08/07/66	nr	No.1	Single: 0/+100%	Y	12E (blhgd)	1-2	-140/-40%	
19/03/67	nr	No.2	Single: 0/+100%	Y	12E (blhgd)	2-1	-140/-40%	See Note (1).
02/07/67	nr	No.1	Single: 0/+100%	Y	12E (blhgd)	2-1	-140/-40%	See Note (1).
								Crewe Works: 01/10/67-26/11/67.

Unique Identifiers • 225

Photo Date	nr/nnr	Cab Front-End Characteristics			Bodyside		Comments
		Cab End Viewed	25kV Signs	Red circle MW Code	Allocation Code	Side Viewed	25kV Sign	
21/04/68	nr	No.2	Pair: +25/+125%	N	Nil	2-1	-130/-30%	Crewe Works Arr/Dep Sidings.
06/06/68	nnr	No.1		N	Nil			<u>BFY</u> livery. See Note (2).
25/06/68	nr	No.1	Pair: +25/+125%	N	Nil	2-1	-140/-40%	<u>BFY</u> livery. See Note (2).
xx/08/68	nr	No.1	Pair: +25/+125%	N	Nil			<u>BFY</u> livery. See Note (2).

Note (1) 1967 12E allocation marking metamorphosed to 12C (partially painted out E to give angular C)
Note (2) BFY livery - 25kV sign <u>disc</u> reference point.

D5702

Photo Date	nr/nnr	Cab Front-End Characteristics			Bodyside		Comments
		Cab End Viewed	25kV Signs	Red circle MW Code	Allocation Code	Side Viewed	25kV Sign	
04/07/63	nr	No.2	Single: +40/+140%	Y	12E (blhgd)	2-1	-100/0%	
10/06/64	nnr	No.2	Single: +30/+130%					
08/08/64	nnr	No.2	Single: +30/+130%					
								Crewe Works: 07/02/65-23/05/65.
16/05/65	nr	No.2	Pair: -40/+60%	N	Nil	2-1	-100/0%	Crewe Works Paint Shop Yard (ex-works).
27/03/66	nr	No.2	Pair: -30/+70%	N	Nil	2-1	-100/0%	
03/04/66	nnr	No.1	Pair: -40/+60%	N	Nil	2-1	-100/0%	Crewe Works Arr/Dep Sidings.
12/08/66	nnr	No.1	Pair: -40/+60%	N	Nil	2-1	-100/0%	
20/08/67	nr	No.2	Pair: -30/+70%	N	Nil	2-1	-100/0%	
15/06/68	nr	No.1	Pair: -30/+70%	N	Nil	2-1	-100/0%	
22/06/68	nr	No.2	Pair: -30/+70%	N	Nil	2-1	-100/0%	
03/08/68	nnr	No.2	Pair: -30/+70%	N	Nil	1-2	-100/0%	
xx/05/69	nr	No.2	Pair: -30/+70%	N	Nil			Withdrawn.

Note (1) Minor height variation between left and right signs when fitted with pairs of signs on front end.

D5703

Photo Date	nr/nnr	Cab Front-End Characteristics			Bodyside		Comments
		Cab End Viewed	25kV Signs	Red circle MW Code	Allocation Code	Side Viewed	25kV Sign	
28/07/62	nr	No.2	Single: -110/-10%	N	12E (blhgd)	2-1	-150/-50%	
xx/xx/xx	nr	No.2	Single: -110/-10%	N	12E (blhgd)	2-1	-150/-50%	
								Crewe Works: 03/01/65-20/06/65.

D5704

Photo Date	nr/nnr	Cab End Viewed	25kV Signs	Red circle MW Code	Allocation Code	Side Viewed	25kV Sign	Comments
xx/06/65	nr	No.1	Pair: -50/+50%	N	12E (blhgd)	1-2	-150/-50%	Crewe Works Paint Shop Yard.
07/08/65	nr	No.2	Pair: -50/+50%	N	12E (blhgd)	1-2	-150/-50%	
25/09/67	nnr	No.1	Pair: -50/+50%					Stored (on transfer).

D5704

Photo Date	nr/nnr	Cab End Viewed	25kV Signs	Red circle MW Code	Allocation Code	Side Viewed	25kV Sign	Comments
12/06/63	nr	No.1	Single: +10/+110%					Signs higher post-Dukinfield.
22/06/63	nnr	No.1	Single: +10/+110%	Y	12E (blhgd)			
25/09/66	nnr	No.1	Single: +10/+110%	Y?	Nil	2-1	-100/0%	Stored. Crewe Works Stripping Shop.
xx/xx/67	nr	No.1	Single:			1-2	-110/-10%	Stored (on transfer).
xx/xx/68	nr	No.2	Single: +10/+110%	?	NWL (cs)			Withdrawn.

Note (1) As D5704 became progressively filthy over the years it became increasingly difficult to ascertain whether it carried the Red Circle and Depot codes.

D5705

Photo Date	nr/nnr	Cab End Viewed	25kV Signs	Red circle MW Code	Allocation Code	Side Viewed	25kV Sign	Comments
01/07/62	nr	No.2	Single:			2-1	-130/-30%	
17/07/62	nnr	No.2	Single: +10/+110%	Y	12E (blhgd)	1-2	-140/-40%	Signs higher post-Dukinfield.
29/07/63	nnr	No.1	Single: +10/+110%	Y	12E (blhgd)			
29/08/64	nr	No.2	Single: +10/+110%	Y		2-1	-130/-30%	
09/06/65	nr	No.2	Single: +10/+110%	Y	12E (blhgd)	1-2	-140/-40%	
								Crewe Works: 25/07/65-14/11/65.
29/01/67	nr	No.1	Pair: -40/+60%	Y				See Note (1).
05/03/67	nr	No.2	Pair: -40/+60%	Y	12C (blhgd)	2-1	-130/-30%	See Note (1).
15/10/67	nr	No.2	Pair: -40/+60%	Y	12C (blhgd)	1-2	-140/-40%	See Note (1).
03/09/72	nr	No.2	Pair: -40/+60%	Y	12C (blhgd)/ NWL (cs)	2-1	-130/-30%	Numbered S15705. See Note (1).

Note (1) Minor height variation between left and right signs when fitted with pairs of signs on front end.

D5706

Photo Date	nr/nnr	Cab End Viewed	25kV Signs	Red circle MW Code	Allocation Code	Side Viewed	25kV Sign	Comments
		Cab Front-End Characteristics				**Bodyside**		
12/06/64	nnr	No.1	Single: 0/+100%	Y	12E (blhgd)	2-1		
08/11/64	nr	No.2	Pair: -100/0%	Y	12E (blhgd)	2-1	-140/-40%	Crewe Works: 12/08/64-08/11/64. Crewe Works.
15/07/66	nnr	No.2	Pair: -100/0%	Y	12C (blhgd)			
26/03/68	nnr	No.1	Pair: -100/0%	Y	Nil	2-1	-140/-40%	Crewe Works: 10/09/67-01/10/67.

D5707

Photo Date	nr/nnr	Cab End Viewed	25kV Signs	Red circle MW Code	Allocation Code	Side Viewed	25kV Sign	Comments
		Cab Front-End Characteristics				**Bodyside**		
06/08/62	nr	No.1	Single: -120/-20%	N	12E (blhgd)	1-2	-150/-50%	
06/08/62	nnr	No.2	Single: -140/-40%	N	12E (blhgd)	1-2	-150/-50%	
09/02/63	nnr	No.1	Single: -120/-20%	N	12E (blhgd)	2-1	-150/-50%	
30/08/64	nr	No.1	Single: -120/-20%	N	12E (blhgd)			
30/08/65	nnr	No.2	Single: -140/-40%	N		1-2	-150/-50%	
02/04/66	nr	No.1	Pair: -70/+30%	N		1-2	-150/-50%	Crewe Works: ??? See Notes (1 & 2).
15/06/66	nr	No.1	Pair: -70/+30%	N	12C (blhgd)	1-2	-150/-50%	See Note (2).
01/07/66	nr	No.2	Pair: -70/+30%	N	12C (blhgd)	2-1	-150/-50%	See Note (2).
02/08/66	nnr	No.2	Pair: -70/+30%	N	12C (blhgd)	1-2	-150/-50%	See Note (2).
12/08/66	nnr	No.2	Pair: -70/+30%	N	12C (blhgd)	1-2	-150/-50%	See Note (2).
30/09/66	nnr	No.2	Pair: -70/+30%					See Note (2).
xx/03/67	nr	No.2		N	12C (blhgd)	2-1	-150/-50%	
04/06/67	nr	No.2	Pair: +40/+140%	N	12C (blhgd)	2-1	-150/-50%	Crewe Works: 09/04/67-11/06/67. GFY livery. See Note (3). Crewe Works.
01/06/68	nr	No.2	Pair: +40/+140%	N	12C (blhgd)			GFY livery. See Notes (3 & 4).
22/06/68	nr	No.1 & 2	Pair: +40/+140%	N	12C (blhgd)	1-2	-150/-50%	GFY livery. See Notes (3 & 4).
xx/05/69	nr	No.1	Pair: +40/+140%	N				GFY livery. See Note (3). Withdrawn.

Note (1) Change from single to pair of 25kV signs - may be a depot alteration or unknown/unrecorded Works visit.
Note (2) Patch on yellow panel (-120/-20%) where single sign had been removed, which may substantiate a depot alteration.
Note (3) GFY livery - 25kV sign <u>disc</u> reference point; actual positioning same as 1966/67.
Note (4) Right-hand sign at No.2 end 'lost'.

D5708

Photo Date	nr/nnr	Cab End Viewed	25kV Signs	Red circle MW Code	Allocation Code	Side Viewed	25kV Sign	Comments
21/09/63	nnr	No.2	Single: -140/-40%	N				
xx/11/63	nr	No.1	Single: -120/-20%	N	12E (blhgd)	1-2	-160/60%	
17/09/66	nr	No.1	Single: -120/-20%	N	12C (blhgd)	2-1	-160/-60%	Crewe Works: ???
23/03/67	nnr	No.2	Pair: -90/+10%	N	12C (blhgd)	1-2	-160/60%	See Note (1). Crewe Works: 01/10/67-26/11/67.
03/05/69	nr	No.2	Pair: +30/+130%	N	12C (blhgd)/ NW (cs)	2-1	-160/-60%	GFY livery. See Note (2). Withdrawn.

Note (1) Change from single to pair of 25kV signs - may be a depot alteration or unknown/unrecorded Works visit.
Note (2) GFY livery - 25kV sign <u>disc</u> reference point; actual positioning same as 1967.

D5709

Photo Date	nr/nnr	Cab End Viewed	25kV Signs	Red circle MW Code	Allocation Code	Side Viewed	25kV Sign	Comments
22/02/62	nr	No.2	Single: -25/+75%	N	17A (blhgd)	2-1	-150/-50%	GNY livery. See Note (1). Gorton.
01/06/62	nnr	No.2	Single: -25/+75%	N	17A (blhgd)	2-1	-140/-40%	GNY livery. See Note (1).
xx/xx/xx	nr	No.2	Single: -125/-25%			2-1	-140/-40%	See Notes (2 & 3).
13/09/63	nnr	No.2	Single: -125/-25%					
xx/09/64	nnr	No.2	Single: -125/-25%	N		1-2	-150/-50%	See Note (3)
07/04/65	nnr	No.2	Single: -125/-25%	N		1-2	-150/-50%	
xx/xx/67	nr	No.2	Single:					Stored (on transfer).

Note (1) GNY livery - 25kV sign <u>disc</u> reference point.
Note (2) Single sign same level as 22/02/62 when seen at Gorton Works in GNY livery immediately post-Dukinfield rehabilitation.
Note (3) Damage repairs to driver's side corner of No.2 cab obliterated part of yellow panel.

D5710

Photo Date	nr/nnr	Cab End Viewed	25kV Signs	Red circle MW Code	Allocation Code	Side Viewed	25kV Sign	Comments
03/09/62	nnr	No.1	Single: +10/+110%	Y	12E (blhgd)			Signs higher post-Dukinfield.
05/05/63	nr	No.2	Single: +10/+110%	Y		2-1	-130/-30%	
11/07/64	nr	No.2	Single: +10/+110%	Y				Crewe Works: 20/12/64-28/02/65.

Unique Identifiers • 229

Photo Date	nr/nnr	Cab End Viewed	25kV Signs	Red circle MW Code	Allocation Code	Side Viewed	25kV Sign	Comments
		Cab Front-End Characteristics				**Bodyside**		
07/02/65	nnr	No.2	Pair: -60/+40%	N?	Nil	2-1	-180/-80%	Crewe Works Paint Shop Yard.
22/08/65	nnr	No.2	Pair: -60/+40%					
30/08/65	nr	No.2	Pair: -60/+40%	Y	Nil	2-1	Nil	
								Crewe Works: 26/09/65-14/11/65.
25/06/66	nr	No.2	Pair: -60/+40%	Y	Nil	2-1	Nil	Stored. Crewe Works Arr/Dep Sidings.
03/10/66	nr	No.2	Pair: -60/+40%	Y	Nil	2-1	Nil	Stored. Crewe Works Arr/Dep Sidings.
xx/xx/67	nr	No.2	Pair: -60/+40%			2-1	Nil	Stored (on transfer).

D5711

Photo Date	nr/nnr	Cab End Viewed	25kV Signs	Red circle MW Code	Allocation Code	Side Viewed	25kV Sign	Comments
		Cab Front-End Characteristics				**Bodyside**		
11/07/64	nr	Nos.1 & 2	Single: +50/+150%	Y	12E (blhgd)	2-1	-130/-30%	Signs higher post-Dukinfield.
08/08/64	nnr	No.2	Single: +50/+150%	Y	12E (blhgd)			
10/07/66	nr	No.2	Single:	Y	12C (blhgd)	1-2	-130/-30%	
								Crewe Works: 31/07/66-15/01/67.
15/01/67	nr	No.1	Pair: -40/+60%	N	Nil	1-2	-200/-100%	Crewe Works (ex-Works).
05/03/67	nnr	No.2	Pair: -50/+50%	N	Nil	1-2	-200/-100%	
24/05/68	nr	No.1	Pair: -40/+60%	N	Nil	1-2	-200/-100%	
28/07/68	nr	No.1	Pair: -40/+60%	N	Nil	1-2	-200/-100%	

D5712

Photo Date	nr/nnr	Cab End Viewed	25kV Signs	Red circle MW Code	Allocation Code	Side Viewed	25kV Sign	Comments
		Cab Front-End Characteristics				**Bodyside**		
06/05/63	nnr	No.2	Single: +20/+120	Y	12E (blhgd)			
								Horwich Works: 03/08/63-20/08/63.
23/04/66	nr	No.2	Single: -125/-25%	N		1-2	-150/50%	
08/10/66	nr	No.1	Single: -125/-25%	N	12C (blhgd)	1-2	-150/50%	
15/10/66	nr	No.2	Single: -130/-30%	N	12C (blhgd)	2-1	-140/-40%	
								Crewe Works: ???
01/04/67	nr	No.1	Pair: -50/+50%		12C (blhgd)	2-1	-140/-40%	See Notes (1 & 2).
15/04/67	nr	No.1	Pair: -50/+50%	N	12C (blhgd)	2-1	-150/-50%	See Note (2).
16/09/67	nr	No.1	Pair: -50/+50%	N	12C (blhgd)	1-2	-150/-50%	See Note (2).

230 • THE METROPOLITAN-VICKERS TYPE 2 CO-BO DIESEL-ELECTRIC LOCOMOTIVES

Photo Date	nr/ nnr	Cab End Viewed	25kV Signs	Red circle MW Code	Allocation Code	Side Viewed	25kV Sign	Comments
12/05/68	nr	No.2	Ex-Single: -125%/25% plus, Pair: -50/+50%	N	12C (blhgd)	2-1	-150/-50%	
26/05/68	nr	No.1	Ex-Single: -125%/25% plus, Pair: -50/+50%	N	12C (blhgd)	1-2	-150/-50%	
03/05/69	nr	No.1	Ex-Single: -125%/25% plus, Pair: -50/+50%	N	???/NW (cs)	1-2	-150/-50%	Withdrawn.

Note (1)   Change from single to pair of 25kV signs - may be a depot alteration or unknown/unrecorded Works visit.
Note (2)   Patch on yellow panel (-125/-25%) where single sign had been removed, which may substantiate a depot alteration.
Note (3)   Minor height variation between left and right signs when fitted with pairs of signs on front end.

D5713

Photo Date	nr/ nnr	Cab End Viewed	25kV Signs	Red circle MW Code	Allocation Code	Side Viewed	25kV Sign	Comments
25/08/62	nr	No.1	Single: -110/-10%	N	12E (blhgd)	1-2	-180/-80%	
03/10/64	nnr	No.2	Single: -240/-140%	N	12E (blhgd)	1-2	-180/-80%	
01/08/65	nr	No.2	Single: -240/-140%	N		2-1	-160/-60%	
xx/xx/xx	nr	No.2	Single: -240/-140%	N	12C (blhgd)	2-1	-160/-60%	Stored. Crewe Works Arr/Dep Sidings.
xx/xx/67	nr	No.2	Single:	N		2-1	-160/-60%	Stored (on transfer).
08/10/67	nr	No.2	Single: -240/-140%	N	NWL (brhgd)			

D5714

Photo Date	nr/ nnr	Cab End Viewed	25kV Signs	Red circle MW Code	Allocation Code	Side Viewed	25kV Sign	Comments
xx/xx/xx	nr	No.2	Single: +10/+110%	Y	12E (blhgd)	2-1	-120/-20%	
05/06/64	nr	No.2	Single: +10/+110%	Y	12E (blhgd)			
								Crewe Works: 10/10/64-20/12/64, 07/01/65-24/01/65, 17/10/65-14/11/65, 24/07/66-18/09/66.
18/10/66	nr	No.1	Pair: -75/+25%	Y	Nil	1-2	-150/-50%	
23/12/67	nr	No.2	Pair: -75/+25%	Y	Nil	2-1	-120/-20%	
13/07/68	nr	No.2	Pair: -75/+25%	Y	Nil	2-1	-120/-20%	
29/07/68	nr	No.1	Pair: -75/+25%	Y	Nil	1-2	-150/-50%	

D5715

| Photo Date | nr/nnr | Cab Front-End Characteristics |||| Bodyside || Comments |
		Cab End Viewed	25kV Signs	Red circle MW Code	Allocation Code	Side Viewed	25kV Sign	
27/07/63	nnr	No.2	Single: +20/+120%	Y	12E (blhgd)	2-1	-130/-30%	
15/08/64	nnr	No.1	Single: +40/+140%	Y	17A/12E(blhgd)	2-1	-120/-20%	
xx/xx/65	nnr	No.1	Single: +40/+140%	Y	17A/12E(blhgd)	2-1	-120/-20%	Crewe Works: 09/05/65-12/09/65, 16/01/66-29/05/66.
xx/07/66	nnr	No.2	Pair: -30/+70%	Y	17A/12E(blhgd)	1-2	-120/-20%	
12/02/67	nr	No.2	Pair: -30/+70%	Y	17A/12E(blhgd)	2-1	-130/-30%	
xx/xx/67	nr	No.2	Pair: -30/+70%	Y	NWL (cs)	2-1	-120/-20%	17A/12E painted out.
06/04/67	nr	No.1	Pair: -30/+70%	Y	NWL (cs)	1-2	-120/-20%	17A/12E painted out.

Note (1) Minor height variation between left and right signs when fitted with pairs of signs on front end.

D5716

| Photo Date | nr/nnr | Cab Front-End Characteristics |||| Bodyside || Comments |
		Cab End Viewed	25kV Signs	Red circle MW Code	Allocation Code	Side Viewed	25kV Sign	
xx/04/63	nnr	No.2	Single: +10/+110%	Y	12E (blhgd)			
06/05/63	nnr	No.2	Single: +10/+110%	Y				
xx/xx/64	nr	No.1	Single: +10/+110%	Y		2-1	-120/-20%	
01/09/64	nr	No.1	Single: +10/+110%					Crewe Works. Crewe Works: 12/08/64-29/11/64.
01/11/64	nr	No.1	Pair: -75/+25%	N	Nil			Crewe Works Paint Shop Yard (ex-Works).
08/11/64	nr	No.1	Pair: -75/+25%	N	Nil	1-2	-125/-25%	Crewe Works Paint Shop Yard (ex-Works).
06/12/64	nr	No.2	Pair: -75/+25%	N		2-1	-125/-25%	
xx/05/65	nr	No.1	Pair: -75/+25%	N		1-2	-125/-25%	Crewe Works (incorrect date?). Crewe Works: 31/10/65-13/02/66.
08/10/67	nr	No.2	Pair: -75/+25%	N	NWL (brhgd+cs)	2-1	-120/-20%	
07/04/68	nr	No.2	Pair: -75/+25%	N	NWL (brhgd+cs)	2-1	-120/-20%	

D5717

Photo Date	nr/nnr	Cab End Viewed	25kV Signs	Red circle MW Code	Allocation Code	Side Viewed	25kV Sign	Comments
		Cab Front-End Characteristics				**Bodyside**		
xx/xx/xx	nr	No.1	Single: +80/+180%	Y	12E (blhgd)	1-2	-100/0%	
xx/xx/xx	nr	No.1	Single: +80/+180%	Y	Nil	1-2	-100/0%	Crewe Works.
06/07/63	nnr	No.1	Single: +80/+180%	Y	12E (blhgd)			
								Crewe Works: 27/01/64-02/05/64.
25/04/64	nr	No.1	Single: +80/+180%	Y	Nil	1-2	-100/0%	Crewe Works.
xx/06/64	nr	No.2	Single: +80/+180%	Y	Nil	2-1	-100/0%	
22/08/64	nnr	No.1	Single: +80/+180%	Y	Nil			
29/08/64	nr	No.2	Single: +80/+180%	Y	Nil	2-1	-100/0%	
								Crewe Works: 06/06/65.
07/04/66	nr	No.2	Pair: -30/+70%	Y				
								Crewe Works: 05/06/66-02/10/66.
18/09/66	nnr	No.2	Pair: -30/+70%	Y				Crewe Works.
07/05/67	nr	No.2	Pair: -30/+70%	Y	12B (blhgd)	2-1	-100/0%	
20/08/67	nr	No.2	Pair: -30/+70%	Y	12B (blhgd)	2-1	-100/0%	
26/05/68	nr	Nos.1 & 2	Pair: -30/+70%	Y	12B (blhgd)	2-1	-100/0%	
02/04/69	nr	No.1	Pair: -30/+70%	Y				
03/05/69	nr	No.2	Pair: -30/+70%	Y		2-1	-100/0%	Withdrawn.

D5718

Photo Date	nr/nnr	Cab End Viewed	25kV Signs	Red circle MW Code	Allocation Code	Side Viewed	25kV Sign	Comments
		Cab Front-End Characteristics				**Bodyside**		
06/09/63	nr	No.2	Single: +40/+140%	Y	12E (blhgd)	1-2	-110/-10%	
								Crewe Works: 06/04/64.
xx/09/65	nnr	No.1	Single: +10/+110%	N		2-1	-110/-10%	
26/06/66	nr	No.1	Single: +10/+110%	N	12C (Blhgd)			
								Crewe Works: 09/10/66-18/12/66.
xx/xx/66	nr	No.2	Pair: -60/+40%	N	12C (Blhgd)			
07/05/67	nr	No.2	Pair: -60/+40%	N	12? (blhgd)	2-1	-100/0%	
22/04/68	nr	No.1	Pair: -60/+40%	N	NWL (brhgd)	2-1	-100/0%	

D5719

Photo Date	nr/nnr	Cab Front-End Characteristics				Bodyside		Comments
		Cab End Viewed	25kV Signs	Red circle MW Code	Allocation Code	Side Viewed	25kV Sign	
06/08/62	nr	No.2	Single: -125/-25%	N	12E (blhgd)	2-1	-160/-60%	
08/09/63	nr	No.1	Single: -125/-25%	N	12E (blhgd)	1-2	-140/-40%	
14/06/64	nr	No.2	Single: -125/-25%	N	12E (blhgd)	1-2	-140/-40%	Crewe Works
								Crewe Works: 07/03/64-04/09/64.
14/08/66	nr	No.2	Ex-Single: -125%/25% plus, Pair: -100/0%	N		2-1	-160/-60%	
15/04/67	nr	No.1	Ex-Single: -125%/25% plus, Pair: -100/0%	N	12E (blhgd)	1-2	-140/-40%	
15/07/67	nr	No.2	Ex-Single: -125%/25% plus, Pair: -100/0%	N	NWL (cs)			12E painted out.
xx/xx/69	nr	No.2	Ex-Single: -125%/25% plus, Pair: -100/0%	N	NWL (cs)	1-2	-140/-40%	Withdrawn.

Chapter 19
STORAGE – 1965-68

19.1 Official Storage Data (versus Published Information).

Storage details from the Engine History Cards in comparison with published sources (*Locomotive Directory* (Strickland) (December 1983) and *Modern Locomotives Illustrated* No.226) are listed below:

	EHC	Locomotive Directory	MLI 226
D5700	S(u): 06/06/66 (no reinstatement date)		
D5701			
D5702			
D5703	S(u): 06/06/66 (no reinstatement date)	OOU: 05/67 until Wdn.	
D5704	S(u): 30/01/65 (no reinstatement date)	OOU: 06/65 until Wdn.	S(u): 04/66, R/I: 12/66
D5705			
D5706			
D5707			
D5708			
D5709	S(u): 03/09/65 (no reinstatement date) N.B. Might be 03/04/65; poor hand writing.	OOU: 11/65 to 01/67 (poss. until Wdn.)	S(u): 11/65, R/I: 12/66
D5710	S(u): 18/10/65 (no reinstatement date)	OOU: c04/66 until Wdn.	S(u): 04/66, R/I: 12/66
D5711			
D5712			
D5713	S(u): 30/11/64 (no reinstatement date)	OOU: 06/65 to 12/66	S(u): 01/66, R/I: 12/66 (poss. until Wdn.)
D5714	S(u): 28/09/65-18/10/65		
D5715			S(u): 07/66, R/I: 02/68
D5716			
D5717		OOU: 02/64 until after 02/67	S(u): 02/64, R/I: 12/66
D5718			
D5719		OOU: c04/64 to 12/66	S(u): 04/64, R/I: 12/66.

Notes:
(1) OOU: Out of use, S(u): stored (unserviceable).
(2) From the above comparison it is clear that there is minimal commonality between the official information and previously published material.

(3) Magazine reports:
- 'Two Metro-Vick Type diesels, Nos. D5704/13 are reported by a correspondent to have been withdrawn.' (*Modern Railways*, August 1965)
- 'Seven of these unfortunate diesels were stored unserviceable in July (*1966*), mostly at Carlisle Upperby and Crewe Works.' (*Railway Observer*, September 1966) i.e. D5700/3/4/9/10/3, plus one more (possibly D5711 or D5717 - see Section 19.2).

19.2 Individual Locomotive Storage Histories.

Whilst previously published information covering the periods in store of the Metrovick fleet is quite clearly wholly inaccurate, it is also clear that the official information is also less than perfect. Storage periods, prior to ultimate withdrawal, based on a combination of EHC data, Fire Reports and sighting information, can be pinned down with greater accuracy. The results obtained from this approach are listed below:

	Storage Periods
D5700	02/66-12/67
D5701	09/68
D5702	Worked up to withdrawal (09/68).
D5703	06/66-12/67
D5704	11/64-1267
D5705	Worked up to withdrawal (09/68).
D5706	09/68
D5707	07/68-09/68
D5708	Worked up to withdrawal (09/68).
D5709	06/65-12/67
D5710	09/65-12/67
D5711	09/68
D5712	09/68
D5713	11/64-12/67
D5714	09/65-11/65, then worked up to withdrawal (09/68).
D5715	12/67-05/68
D5716	09/68
D5717	09/68
D5718	02/68-05/68
D5719	Worked up to withdrawal (09/68).

Notes:
The following five Metrovicks also spent periods of 4 months or more (per visit) at Crewe Works:

D5705	07/65-11/65, 04/67-11/67
D5711	07/66-01/67
D5715	05/65-09/65, 01/66-05/66
D5717	01/64-05/64, 06/66-10/66
D5719	03/64-09/64

Chapter 20
STORAGE LOCATIONS 1965-68

20.1 Barrow.

D5713 and D5704, 12C Barrow MPD, 1 August 1965. Note damage to the solebar and undergear; batteries removed from the box between the bogies.
(R. Lush [Modern Traction Photo Group])

Storage Locations 1965-68 • 237

20.2 Crewe Works.

D5704, Crewe Works (Stripping Shop), 25 September 1966. Boiler and vacuum brake pipes removed, windscreen wipers missing and battery box empty. (*Author's Collection*)

238 • THE METROPOLITAN-VICKERS TYPE 2 CO-BO DIESEL-ELECTRIC LOCOMOTIVES

D5710, Crewe Works (Arrival Sidings), Undated. (*Transport Topics*)

D5713, Crewe Works (Arrival Sidings), Undated. (*Transport Topics*)

Storage Locations 1965-68 • 239

Various reports in *Modern Railways* during 1967 commented on developments:

'By the end of December at least five Metro-Vick Co-Bo diesels, Nos. D5704/9/10/5/7 were stored at Crewe and were believed to be awaiting a decision on their future.' (February 1967 edition)

'The five Metro-Vick Type 2 Co-Bos at Crewe Works, Nos. D5704/9/10/3/5, were stripped of engines and fittings and were dispersed in various parts of the works at the end of January.' (March 1967)

'Two Metro-Vick Co-Bos have undergone heavy repairs and modifications and one is now being tested thoroughly before work is started on a further four locomotives of the class stored in the works.' (April 1967)

'D5703/4 (sic)/5/7 were still in Crewe at the beginning of May in the course of being re-engined.' (July 1967)

The LCGB *Bulletin* (April 1967) anticipated that 'The MV Co-Bos, which have lain around the works (*Crewe*) for many moons now, are to be towed away to Upperby in the near future, to be 'stored unserviceable'. D5704/9/10/3 moved late February/early-March 1967 and are depicted in the photographs on pages 239 to 241.

Stanier 5MT 45135, D5713, D5710, D5704 and D5709, Warrington Dallam (en route from Crewe Works to 12B Carlisle Upperby), Undated. Believed to be late-February/early-March 1967. All seen at Crewe Works on 19/02/67; not present on 05/03/67. Batteries removed from all four locomotives. *(Dave Lennon)*

240 • THE METROPOLITAN-VICKERS TYPE 2 CO-BO DIESEL-ELECTRIC LOCOMOTIVES

D5713, D5710, D5704 and D5709, Warrington Dallam, Undated. Note the side-swipe accident damage along the solebar of D5713 (see also photographs on pages 236 and 238). *(Dave Lennon)*

D5710, D5704 and D5709, Warrington Dallam, Undated. *(Dave Lennon)*

Storage Locations 1965-68 • 241

D5704 and D5709, Warrington Dallam, Undated. *(Dave Lennon)*

D5709 Warrington Dallam, Undated. Note the 'puncture' damage to the No.2 end cab, driver's side, which may have precipitated its visit to Crewe Works in 1965 after which the locomotive never worked again. *(Dave Lennon)*

242 • THE METROPOLITAN-VICKERS TYPE 2 CO-BO DIESEL-ELECTRIC LOCOMOTIVES

D311 and D5703, Greenholme (en route from Crewe Works to 12B Carlisle Upperby), 25 September 1967.
(*Ernie's Railway Archive*)

20.3 Carlisle Upperby (12B) (1967-9).

D5700, 12B Carlisle Upperby, Undated. Batteries, windscreen wipers and part of roof section removed.
(*Author's Collection*)

Storage Locations 1965-68 • 243

D5700, 12B Carlisle Upperby, 30 August 1967. *(Dave Lennon)*

D5713, 12B Carlisle Upperby, 8 October 1967. Still exhibiting side-swipe damage. *(Rail-Online)*

Visit reports:
21/10/67 (Sunday)
12B Carlisle Upperby: D5713 . . . D5709 . . . D5710, D5703, D5700, D5704 (in order noted).

06/01/68
Ex-12B Carlisle Upperby:
D5703/9/10/3

20.4 Carlisle Kingmoor (12A – Steam & Diesel Depots) (1967-9).

The February 1969 edition of the *Railway Observer* reported:

'Since the closure of Kingmoor and Upperby M.P.D.'s on 1st January 1968, diesel locomotives are stabled at various points within the locality. The steam shed at Kingmoor, despite the loss of connections with the main and goods lines at Etterby last February, still contains stored and condemned locomotives, access being gained through the ground frames on the up through siding adjacent to the shed.'

D5704, Ex-12A Carlisle Kingmoor (Steam), Undated. Note the NWL lettering below D5704's cabside number. The identity of the second locomotive, assuming it is one of the original six withdrawals, and, on the basis of the positioning of the pair of 25kV signs and the (removed) single sign, is D5703. Pantograph windscreen wiper partially broken giving the impression of a double-length wiper! *('70023venus2009')*

D5719, 12A Carlisle Kingmoor (Steam), 4 January 1969.
North end of the old steam depot, with the Metrovick keeping company with an equally redundant Clayton Class 17 (at least as far as the Carlisle area was concerned). The Clayton is believed to be D8533. *(John Grey Turner)*

Carlisle Kingmoor withdrawn locomotive sightings reports are provided below:

02/01/68 (*Traction Annual 2010/11*).
Diesel (12A): D5704/15

'The new Kingmoor diesel depot on the opposite side of the WCML had six diesel locos present . . . D5704 which had recently been withdrawn . . . and stored D5715 which was eventually withdrawn on 4/5/68.'

06/01/68 (SMA)
Steam (Ex-12A): D5704 (+D5715)

Diesel (12A): No withdrawn Metrovicks listed (+D5702/5)

27/01/68 (RO 04/68)

'On 27th January . . . Dumped at Kingmoor were . . . D5703/9/10/3. The diesels were minus engines and for scrap. In the adjacent workshop were D5704/15.'

Question: Definition of 'adjacent workshop'; Diesel Depot, or, former Steam Depot repair shop?
N.B. One day later, D5704 was seen on the Steam depot, and, D5715 on the Diesel Depot.

28/01/68 (SMA)
Steam (Ex-12A): D5703/4/9/10/3 (*with D5715 and D5716-8 on the Diesel Depot*)

10/02/68 (RL 03/68)
Steam (Ex-12A): D5700/3/9/10/3
Diesel (12A): D5704 (+D5711/2/5/9)

25/02/68 (RL 04/68)
Steam (Ex-12A): D5700/3/9/10/3
Diesel (12A): No withdrawn Metrovicks listed (+D5706-8)

17/03/68 (SMA)
Steam (Ex-12A): D5700/3/4/9/10/3

Storage Locations 1965-68 • 245

11/04/68 (AW)
Steam (Ex-12A): D5700/3/9/10/3
(all minus engines)
Diesel (12A): D5704
(+D5706/12/4/9)

13/04/68 (AR)
Steam (Ex-12A): D5700/3/9/10/3
(all minus engines)
Diesel (12A): D5704
(+D5706/8/12/4/9)

15/04/68 (RL 05/68)
Steam (Ex-12A): D5700/3/9/10/3
Diesel (12A): No withdrawn
Metrovicks listed (+D5706/12/9)
N.B. D5704 not listed on either the
Diesel or Steam depots.

18/04/68 (RL 05/68)
Steam (Ex-12A): D5700/3/4/9/10/3
Diesel (12A): No withdrawn
Metrovicks listed (+D5711/2/9)

11/05/68 (SMA)
Steam (Ex-12A):
D5700/3/4/9/10/3/8
Diesel (12A): D5715

06/06/68 (*Steam World* No.139)
Steam (Ex-12A):
D5700/3/4/9/10/3/8

15/06/68 (RO/SMA)

'Carlisle. The diesel depot
contained the following on
15th June: . . . D5705 . . . Nearby
were D5715, withdrawn, and
D5717 whilst stored in the
old steam shed at Kingmoor
were . . . D5700/3/4/9/10/3/8.'

Steam (Ex-12A):
D5700/3/4/9/10/3/8
Diesel (12A): D5715 (+D5705/17)

21/06/68 (SMA)
Steam (Ex-12A):
D5700/3/4/9/10/3
Diesel (12A): No withdrawn
Metrovicks listed (+D5705)

20/07/68 (*Traction Annual 2010/11*)
Diesel (12A): No withdrawn
Metrovicks listed (+D5707/8)
Carlisle (Unspecified,
presumably Steam (Ex-12A):
D5700/3/4/9/10/3/8 (Withdrawn/
stored)

27/07/68 (SMA)
Steam (Ex-12A):
D5700/3/4/9/10/3/8
Diesel (12A): No withdrawn
Metrovicks listed
(+D5701/5/7/8/17/9)

29/07/68 (SMA)
Diesel (12A): No withdrawn
Metrovicks listed (+D5701/8/16/9)

10/08/68 (RL 09/68)
Steam (Ex-12A): D5700/4/9/10/3
Diesel (12A): D5703/18
(+D5708/11/2/9)

25/08/68 (SMA)
Steam (Ex-12A): D5700/4/9/10/3
Diesel (12A): D5715/8 (+D5712/9)
N.B. D5703 not listed.

06/09/68 (SMA, RO)
'Carlisle. Observations on 6th
September produced the following.
'Locomotives at Etterby Rd.: . . .
D5712 . . . (*Diesel Depot*)
'In Kingmoor shed: . . .
D5701/6/9/10/1/3/5-8.'
(*Steam shed*)
N.B. D5709/10/3/5/8 early
withdrawals; D5700/3/4 already
dispatched for scrap..

08/09/68 (SMA)
Steam (Ex-12A):
D5701/6/9/10/1/3/5-8
Diesel (12A): D5712

30/09/68* (*Traction Annual 2010/11*)
Kingmoor (Unspecified):
D5701/2/6-8/11/4-9 (Withdrawn/
stored)
N.B. D5705/12 not listed.

*List states 'Monday June 30,
1968' - incorrect date given that (i) the
early Metrovick withdrawals would
have been present, and, (ii) June 30
1968 was a Sunday not a Monday.
However, 30/09/68 was a Monday
and this date fits with all of the
Metrovicks having been withdrawn.

09/10/68 (SP)
Diesel (12A): D5712.
N.B. Diesel or Steam not specified,
presumably Diesel.

24/10/68 (AW)
Kingmoor Steam (Ex-12A):
D5701/2/6-8/11/2/4-7/9
N.B. D5718 not listed.

07/12/68 (RL 01/69)
Kingmoor (*assumed Steam [ex-12A]*):
D5701/2/6-8/11/2/4/7/9
Diesel (12A): D5716

08/12/68 (RO 02/69)
Diesel (12A): D5716
'Kingmoor maintenance depot
situated opposite the steam
shed . . . on 8th December . . . for
disposal was . . . D5716 (D10).'

31/12/68 (BWTE No.15)
'Locos stored on the sight
of the former Kingmoor
mpd on 31st December,

1969 (sic 1968), were as follows: D5701/2/6/7/11/2/4/6/7/8/9 (sic D5701/2/6-8/11/2/4/6/7/9).'

03/01/69 (AW)
Steam (Ex-12A): D5716/9 (outside north end of shed)

04/01/69 (JGT)
Steam (Ex-12A): D5701/2/6-8/11/2/4/6/7/9

11/01/69 (SMA)
Steam (Ex-12A): D5701/2/6-8/11/2/4/6/7/9 (in order recorded: D5707/19/16...06/02/12/08/17/14/01...11)

Undated (RM 05/69)
'At Carlisle Kingmoor depot...5701/2/6/7/8/11/2/4/6/7/9 remain in store.'

20.5 Carlisle Kingmoor Yard (1969).
The eleven Metrovicks latterly stored at 12A Carlisle Kingmoor (Steam) shed were moved to Carlisle Yard in February 1969

Kingmoor Yard sighting reports and photographic evidence are listed on pages 247 and 248.

Map of the Middle Section of Carlisle Kingmoor Yard (1963). The two large fans of sidings at the top centre of the map are the Up Sorting Sidings, and the pair at the bottom centre are the Down Sorting Sidings. The most easterly lines constitute the West Coast Main Line (WCML) and the more widely spaced fan of sidings at the bottom right of the map between the WCML and the Up Sorting Sidings are the Up Departure Sidings. During 1969/70 withdrawn locomotives were stored in the fan of six dead-end sidings immediately to the north of the Down Sorting sidings, with the longest of the six utilised for storing the Metrovicks during 1969 (marked in yellow).
(© Crown Copyright and Land Information Group Ltd 2018/ Old-Maps.co.uk)

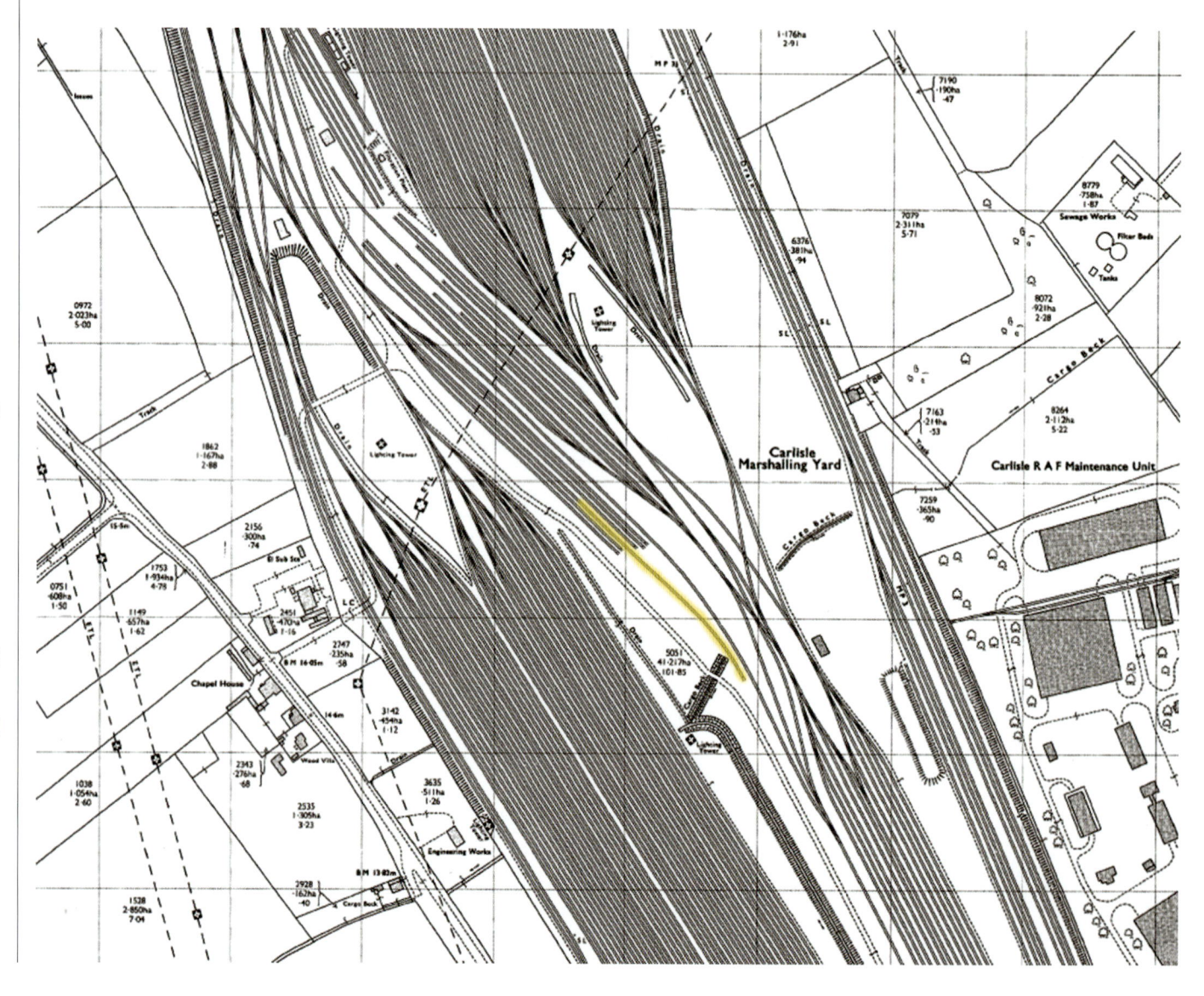

02/04/69 (AW)
D5701/2/6-8/11/2/4/6/7/9

In order recorded/photographed:

S										N
D5708, 2-1	D5716, 1-2	D5712, 2-1	D5717, 1-2	D5706,	D5719,	D5702,	D5714,	D5707, 2-1	D5711, 2-1	D5701

03/05/69 (Rail-Online)
In order:

S				N
D5708, 2-1	D5716, 1-2	D5712, 2-1	D5717, 1-2	....

Major shunt round.

xx/05/69 (RCTS Archive)
In order:

S				N
D5719, ?	D5702, 1-2	D5707, 2-1	D5711, 2-1	....

12/05/69 (SP)
D5701/2/6-8/11/2/4/6/7/9

26/05/69 (RO 07/69)
D5701/2/6-8/11/2/4/6/7/9

06/07/69 (SMA)
D5701/2/6-8/11/2/4/6/7/9

05/08/69 (AW)
D5701/2/6-8/11/2/4/6/7/9

21/08/69 (SB)
In order:

S												N
D5719, 1-2	D5702, 1-2	D5707, 2-1	D5711, 2-1	D5714, 1-2	D5701, 2-1	D5708, 2-1	D5716, 1-2 -75%/+25% 25kV sign	D5712,	D5717,	D5706		

N.B.
1. After D5708, the order of D5716/12/17/06 (S to N) is assumed to be the same as per the early-April sighting.
2. Whilst the numbers of D5716/12/17/06 are unreadable, the locomotive to the north of D5708 has -75%/+25% 25kV sign positioning supporting the assumption that this locomotive is D5716.

23/08/69 (TS)
D5701/2/6-8/11/2/4/6/7/9 (in order recorded: D5719/02/07/11/14/01/08/12/16/17/06)

24/08/69 (SMA)
D5701/2/6-8/11/2/4/6/7/9 (in order recorded: D5707/11/14/01/08/16/12/17/06 . . . D5719/02)

04/09/69 (APS)
D5701/2/6-8/11/2/4/6/7/9

Major shunt round prior to despatch to scrap yards.

19/09/69 (SMA)
D5712

20/09/69 (RO 11/69)
D5712

22/10/69 (AW)
D5712

Additional Notes:
1. Locomotive orientations in Carlisle Kingmoor Yard (South to North):
    1-2: D5702/6/12/4/6/7/9
    2-1: D5701/7/8/11
    N.B. Orientation of D5706 based on picture of Metrovicks in transit to Cashmore, Great Bridge (see picture on page 258).
    Orientation of D5716 based on Rail-Online picture dated 3 May 1969.
2. May 1969 shunt-around:
   The following comment in *The Railway Magazine* (July 1969) may explain the reason for the shunt around of locomotives in May 1969: ' . . . A.E.I. have recently removed radiator fan motors from withdrawn Metro-Vick/Crossley locomotives for the C.I.E. in Ireland.'
3. The late-August/early-September 1969 shunt-round ensured that the Metrovicks departed for scrap more-or-less in numerical order (i.e. D5701/2/6 (15/09/69), then D5707/8/11 (16/09/69), then D5716/7 (17/09/69) and finally D5714/9 (18/09/69).
   This was a repeat of the first six Metrovicks which were sent for scrap to Scotland in numerical order in 1968 (i.e. D5700/3/4 (28/08/68) and D5709/10/3 (11/09/68). And it was repearted again when the final twelve Claytons left Carlisle for Scotland. Why? Scheduled by someone with a tidy mind, perhaps!

Storage Locations 1965-68 • 249

D5708, Carlisle Kingmoor Yard, 3 May, 1969. *(Rail-Online)*

D5712, Carlisle Kingmoor Yard, 3 May, 1969. *(Rail-Online)*

250 • THE METROPOLITAN-VICKERS TYPE 2 CO-BO DIESEL-ELECTRIC LOCOMOTIVES

D5717, Carlisle Kingmoor Yard, 3 May, 1969. *(Rail-Online)*

D5702 (with D5719), Carlisle Kingmoor Yard, May 1969.
(RCTS Archives [MJB])

Storage Locations 1965-68 • 251

D5707 (with D5702), Carlisle Kingmoor Yard, May 1969. *(RCTS Archives [MJB])*

D5719, D5702, D5707, D5711, D5714, D5701, D5708, D5716, D5712..., Carlisle Kingmoor Yard, 21 August 1969. *(Stewart Blencowe)*

252 • THE METROPOLITAN-VICKERS TYPE 2 CO-BO DIESEL-ELECTRIC LOCOMOTIVES

D5701 (with D5714 and D5708), Carlisle Kingmoor Yard, 21 August 1969.
(Stewart Blencowe)

D5719 (with D5702), Carlisle Kingmoor Yard, Undated.
(Photographer unknown)

Chapter 21
WITHDRAWAL

21.1 Withdrawal Rationale: National Traction Plans.

As already described in Section 11, the updated National Traction Plan of November 1967 signed the death-knell of the Metrovick re-engining proposal and also of the class itself. Type 2 locomotive requirements summarised in the Plan are tabulated below:

Region	Stock at 31.7.67	Year Ending				
		1967	1968	1969	1970	1971
London Midland	385	407	426	412	402	392
Total	1002	972	947	918	891	864
Metrovicks		20	10	-	-	-

Thus:

'Due to reduced requirements the proposed re-engining of the 20 Met/Vic. locomotives has now been abandoned. Six locomotives are unserviceable and the remainder have only short life expectancy. A submission is being prepared for their condemnation.'

This submission initially took the form of a memorandum to the BRB Works & Equipment Committee (W&EC) and the Supply Committee dated 18 January 1968, and is fully reproduced below;

Diesel Train Locomotives: Condemnation Type 2 1,200 hp Met-Vic/Crossley.

Introduction.
1. The existing stock of Type 2 diesel train locomotives includes 20 diesel-electric locomotives (Nos. D5700-5719) of a type built by Metropolitan Vickers Ltd. in 1968/59. All are allocated to the London Midland Region.
2. The power equipment of this type of locomotive incorporates a 1,200 hp Crossley two-stroke engine which has been costly to maintain and has given repeated trouble with fractured crank cases and cylinder heads as well as excessive wear of the cylinders.
3. The engine manufacturers endeavoured to overcome the problems but as the difficulties continued to be experienced, the Board by Minute No.66/14(b) of 27.1.66, authorised a scheme to re-engine all 20 locomotives with the English Electric 8CSVT engine at a total estimated outlay of £386,000.
4. The necessity during 1966 to cut back Capital expenditure held up the implementation of the re-engining scheme. The project was removed from the 1967 Investment Programme and has since remained deferred.
5. Six of these locomotives are at present stored unserviceable and all current modifications have been cancelled.

Proposal.

6. A recent re-appraisal of the locomotive requirements under the National Traction Plan has shown the practicability of advancing the target date for the complete elimination of steam traction from mid-1969 to August 1968. The consequent opportunity to rationalise and reconstruct locomotive working diagrams will reduce overall locomotive requirements and enable this locomotive class to be eliminated by the end of 1969.

7. It is proposed that the re-engining project be abandoned, the 6 unserviceable locomotives condemned forthwith, and the remaining 14 locomotives of this class withdrawn individually when expensive repair becomes necessary.

8. The deferment of the re-engineering project was currently notified to the contractors concerned. No commitments have, therefore, been entered into in this connection. The approval of this proposal will also necessitate rescinding the authority recorded in Supply Committee Minute 409 A(vi) (10.2.66) to place orders with the English Electric Company and BR (Workshops).

9. The residual value of the 20 locomotives, less cost of recovery, is estimated at £20,000. The remaining net book value of the locomotives, estimated at £1,020,000, will be written off to Capital Deficit Account, or as part of the capital reconstruction at 31st December, 1968.

The six unserviceable locomotives will be displaced from Capital Account at the end of 1967 and the remainder as they are withdrawn from service when a heavy repair is necessary.

The value of stores held for these locomotives is £180,000 which will become redundant when the locomotives are displaced and written off to Stores Obsolescence Account.

Recommendation.

10. It is recommended that:
    a) the re-engineering project authorised by Board Minute No. 66/14(b) (27.1.66) at an estimated outlay of £386,000 be cancelled,
    b) the six locomotives stored unserviceable be displaced forthwith without replacement,
    c) the remaining 14 locomotives of this class be displaced without replacement when an expensive repair becomes necessary,
    d) Supply Committee Minute 409A(vi) (10.2.66) be rescinded.

'Signed Chief Engineer, Chief Operating Officer, Supplies Manager, and Chief Accountant.'

The W&EC agreed at a meeting held on 23 January 1968 (recorded in Minute No.3059 [5]) to recommend the contents of the Memorandum to the Board for approval. The W&EC also suggested that the stock of Metrovick spares might be disposed of to the CIE and/or other Administrations.

A Memorandum dated 9 February 1968, summarising the earlier Memorandum dated 18 January, was sent to the British Railways Board, as follows:

Type 2 1200 hp Met.Vic/Crossley Locomotives.

'The Board by Minute 66/14(b) of 27th January, 1966 authorised the re-engining of all the 20 locomotives of this type at a total estimated cost of £386,000.

'The project was deferred on account of capital investment cuts, and a recent reappraisal of locomotives under the National Traction Plan makes it possible for the re-engining project to be abandoned.

'The attached submission recommends that re-engining should not be carried out, the six unserviceable locomotives being condemned forthwith and the remaining 14 withdrawn as and when expensive repair becomes necessary. The action proposed is recommended for the approval by the Board. The possibility of disposing of the stock of spares to other Administrations operating this type of locomotive will be explored.

'Signed: Chairman (Works & Equipment Committee), Chairman (Supplies Committee).'

Minute 68/48 2[A]) of the BRB Meeting held on 22 February 1968 recorded the W&EC recommendations as 'cleared in correspondence'. It will be noted in Section 21.3 below that D5700/3/4/9/10/3 were actually withdrawn during w/e 30/12/67, well in advance of the various memoranda and Committees mentioned above. Clearly decisions had already been taken either verbally or 'in correspondence' to secure the withdrawal of the first six locomotives by the year-end of 1967.

The final twelve locomotives of the fleet were officially removed from traffic en masse during the first week of September 1968, one month after the cessation of steam operations on BR. The fact that all twelve went together suggests business simplicity rather than operational pragmatism and waiting until excessive repair costs of individual locomotives prevented continued activity.

D5701/6/11/6/7 were noted stored in 12A Carlisle Kingmoor (Steam) shed on 6 September 1968, presumably having been taken out of traffic awaiting exams and/or repairs. D5712 was similarly out of use at 12A Carlisle Kingmoor (Diesel) on the same date. In addition, D5707 was variously noted out of use at Carlisle Kingmoor, Carnforth and Reddish during the period July to September 1968. As a consequence, it is believed that D5702/5/8/14/9 worked right up to their withdrawal deadline before being switched-off for the last time, still in operational condition.

21.2 Withdrawal Dates: Numerical Listing.
See Section 5.

21.3 Withdrawal Dates: Chronological Listing.

D5700/3/4/9/10/3	Period 13/67 (1w/e 30/12/67)	Ex-12B
D5715/8	Period 05/68 (1w/e 04/05/68)	Ex-12A
D5701/2/5-8/11/2/4/6/7/9	Period 09/68 (1w/e 07/09/68)	Ex-D10

Chapter 22
DISPOSAL

22.1 Introduction.
Information surrounding the disposal of the Metrovicks is distinctly poor. There is some official information regarding transfers from depots to scrapyards, but sightings at both Shettleston and Great Bridge were few and far between, to the extent that seven Metrovicks can be considered as 'Disposal Not Proven'.

This situation probably explains the contradictory cut-up dates for many of the locomotives provided in books, part-works and magazines over the years. Unfortunately, there appear to be no photographs of any Metrovicks in scrapyards, either extant or in the throes of final disposal.

22.2 J. MacWilliam, Shettleston.
22.2.1 Official BR Documentation (Source: Derby Industrial Museum).

Internal Memo:
From: CM&EE Derby.
To: General Manager, Movements Office, Crewe; Divisional Manager, Preston.
Date: 22 Jul 1968.

> Sale of Condemned Locomotives.
> I give below details of condemned locomotives which have been sold by the Supplies Manager, and shall be glad if you will arrange delivery and inspection/preparation as indicated in my letter of the 29th June, 1967.
> Loco.No.: D5700/3/4/9/10/3
> Location: Carlisle Kingmoor
> Firm to which sold: J. MacWilliam & Sons Ltd, Sandyhills Yard, Shettleston, Glasgow E2.
> Delivery instructions: As soon as possible to firm's sidings at Shettleston, Glasgow.
> Sale Order No.: 17/230/521T/46
> Sale Order Date: 17/7/68

Internal Memo:
From: Divisional Manager, Preston 25.
To: General Manager, Derby 49.
Date: 11.9.68.

> Sale of Condemned Locomotives.
> Week Ending: 7.9.68.
> The undermentioned condemned locomotives were despatched to Private Buyers during the week:
> Locomotive No.: D5700/3/4
> From: Carlisle
> Firm to which sold: J. MacWilliam, Shettleston
> Date of Despatch: 28.8.68

Internal Memo:
From: Divisional Manager, Preston 25.
To: General Manager, Derby 49.
Date: 19.9.68.

> Sale of Condemned Locomotives.
> Week Ending: 14.9.68.
> The undermentioned condemned locomotives were despatched to Private Buyers during the week:
> Locomotive No.: D5709/10/3
> From: Carlisle
> Firm to which sold: J. MacWilliam, Shettleston
> Date of Despatch: 11.9.68

Internal Memo:
From CM&EE Derby.
To General Manager, Movements Office, Crewe; Divisional Manager, Stoke; Divisional Manager, Preston.
Date: -9 Aug 1968.

> Sale of Condemned Locomotives.
> I give below details of condemned locomotives which have been sold by the Supplies Manager,

and shall be glad if you will arrange delivery and inspection/preparation as indicated in my letter of the 29th June, 1967.
Loco.No.: D5715
Location: Crewe
Loco.No.: D5718
Location: Carlisle Kingmoor

Firm to which sold: J. MacWilliam & Sons Ltd, Sandyhills Yard, Shettleston, Glasgow.

Delivery instructions: As soon as possible to firm's sidings at Shettleston, Glasgow.
Sale Order No.: 17/230/521T/50.
Sale Order Date: 7/8/68.

Internal Memo (N.B. Poor quality document):

Advice of Despatch from Mr Yates Stoke 5264:
D5715 Crewe DD. Crewe to Carlisle on 15/8/68.
Then by spcl train (Special Notice 2438G........[?])

22.2.2 Sighting Reports.
31/08/68	RO, November 1968	D5700/4 intact, plus cabs of D5703
06/10/68	RO, August 1969	D5700/4/9/10/3, plus D5718 being cut-up.

22.2.3 Book publications – Comparative disposal details.
Four sources are provided for comparison:
Locomotive Directory, D.C. Strickland (LocDir).
Modern Locomotives Illustrated No.226, C.J. Marsden (MLI226).
Allocation History of BR Diesels and Electrics (Part 5) (AHBRDE5).
Diesels & Electric Locomotives for Scrap, A. Butlin (D&ELfS).

	Arr/Cut dates Loco Dir	Date cut-up MLI 226	Date cut-up AHBRDE5	Arr/Cut dates D&ELfS	Notes
D5700	08/68-09/68*	09/68	11/68	07/68-11/68	Despatched Carlisle 28/08/68; intact 06/10/68.
D5703	08/68-07/68(sic)*	06/68 (sic)	08/68	07/68 (sic)	Despatched Carlisle 28/08/68.
D5704	08/68-09/68	08/68	09/68	08/68	Despatched Carlisle 28/08/68; intact 06/10/68.
D5709	09/68-10/68*	10/68	10/68	09/68	Despatched Carlisle 11/09/68; intact 06/10/68.
D5710	09/68-10/68*	09/68	10/68	09/68	Despatched Carlisle 11/09/68; intact 06/10/68.
D5713	09/68-10/68	10/68	11/68	09/68-11/68	Despatched Carlisle 11/09/68; intact 06/10/68.
D5715	10/68-xx/xx	09/68 (sic)	No date	11/68	Still at Carlisle 24/10/68
D5718	10/68-10/68	09/68	10/68	09/68	Noted being cut 06/10/68.

* The *Locomotive Directory* information was subject to numerous supplementary changes as follows:
D5700. Cut-up date changed to 11/68 (Supplement 7).
D5703. Cut-up date changed to 'soon after 08/68' (Supplement 3/4)
D5709/10. Cut-up dates changed to 'Date Not Known Which: . . . D5709 cut 12/68 or 10/68; D5710 ditto . . . ' (Supplement 7).
D5715/8. Arrival date changed to 09/68 (Supplement 7).

Three Class 28s en route to J.Cashmore, Great Bridge hauled by a Class 47, Undated (presumably 15 September 1969). These locomotives are believed to be D5701/2/6 based on the *Railway Observer* report. Blue-liveried D5701 is the middle locomotive of the convoy; the positioning of the front-end 25kV warning flashes would suggest that the nearest locomotive is D5706, so, in order of travel, D5702, D5701, D5706. This is further corroborated by a report in edition No.1 of the *Northern Counties Transport Society* magazine, as follows: 'On Monday 15th September, 1969, D5706, D5701 and D5702 were seen being hauled by (*Brush Type 4*) 1795 through Blackburn.' (Stephen Fisher)

22.2.4 Disposal Not Proven.
D5715 should be considered as 'Disposal Not Proven'.

N.B. This is not to say that this locomotive was not cut at Shettleston, rather that there is no confirmed evidence to absolutely confirm disposal at this yard.

A. Whitaker (*Traction*, April 2004) states that 'D5715 was moved to Shettleston in November 1968 . . .' which fits with its last known Carlisle sighting of 24/10/68 and absence on 07/12/68.

22.3 J. Cashmore, Great Bridge.
22.3.1 Transfers.
The November 1969 edition of the *Railway Observer* carried the following report:

'The Metrovick diesels recently congregated at Carlisle have been sold to J.Cashmore, Great Bridge. They were booked to leave Carlisle in convoys during week ended 20th September (*1969*), as follows: 5701/2/6 on 15th, 5707/8/11 on 16th, 5716/7 on 17th, 5714/9 on 18th.'

The convoys were routed via the Settle & Carlisle to Hellifield, and then via Blackburn to rejoin the West Coast Main Line at Preston

R. Harris (AHBRDE5) states that D5712 was ' . . . hauled to J.Cashmore, Great Bridge, W. Midlands on 17/11/69'. Why this locomotive was delayed by two months compared with the other ten Metrovicks purchased by J. Cashmore is unknown.

22.3.2 Sighting Reports.
xx/11/69   RW, February 1970   'Among those in the yard for cutting up . . . were 5708/11/12/14/19.'

N.B. The comment 'Among those in the yard' might be interpreted to mean that other unidentified locomotives were in the yard awaiting scrapping, including other Metrovicks.

A. Whitaker (*Traction*, April 2004) quotes D5712 and D5716 as being the last locos to be cut up.

22.3.3 Book publications - Comparative disposal details.
The same four publications are used for comparison as in Section 22.2.3 above.

	Arr/Cut dates Loco Dir	Date cut-up MLI 226	Date cut-up AHBRDE5	Arr/Cut Dates D&ELfS
D5701	09/69-10/69	09/69	10/69	09/69
D5702	09/69-11/69	09/69	11/69	09/69-11/69
D5706	09/69-11/69	09/69	11/69	09/69-11/69
D5707	09/69-10/69	09/69	10/69	09/69
D5708	09/69-11/69	09/69	11/69	09/69-11/69
D5711	09/69-11/69	09/69	11/69	09/69-11/69
D5712	09/69-12/69	12/69	By 20/12/69	11/69
D5714	09/69-10/69	09/69	10/69	09/69
D5716	09/69-12/69	09/69	By 20/12/69	09/69-12/69
D5717	09/69-11/69	09/69	11/69	09/69-11/69
D5719	09/69-10/69	09/69	10/69	09/69

22.3.4 Disposal not proven.
D5701/2/6/7/16/7 should be considered as 'Disposal Not Proven'.
N.B. This is not to say that these locomotives were not cut-up at Great Bridge, rather that there is no confirmed evidence to absolutely confirm disposal at this yard.

Chapter 23
D5705 POST WITHDRAWAL

23.1 D5705/S15705

D5705 moved from Carlisle to the Derby Research Centre during the latter part of 1968, apparently under its own power. The Research Centre was looking to secure its own dedicated motive power, rather than having to rely on Etches Park, where the Research Train duties were accorded a low priority.

The irony of D5705 returning to Derby apparently did not go unnoticed amongst the engineering staff who recalled the antics of the Metrovicks ten years earlier!

S15705, Derby Works, circa August 1972. Possibly 26 August 1972 on the occasion of the annual Works Open Day. (Photographer unknown)

However, it will be recalled that this locomotive was the example fitted with a re-designed Crossley crankcase and is understood to have performed more successfully during its second stint at Derby.

It has been reported, unofficially, as being re-numbered S15705 in February 1969 and, following preparation work, embarked on its new duties hauling test trains in the Derby area specifically involving investigation of wheel/rail interaction under varying conditions of adhesion and the development of plasma torch technology aimed at clearing dirt and grease from rail surfaces to improve friction between wheel and rail.

As the Metrovick only operated relatively infrequently and because the stabling facilities were somewhat rudimentary, the locomotive inevitably suffered from exposure, especially during the winter months. Leaking joints and coolant loss caused frequent failures. Whilst the Metrovick's electrical equipment was of far better quality and reliability than its Crossley engine, the control, auxiliary and traction equipment all suffered from the effects of the damp conditions caused by its intermittent use and outdoor stabling.

The general condition of S15705 deteriorated over time and, after suffering a traction motor flashover, it ran for an extended period with one traction motor isolated. Ultimately, an increasing list of defects finally brought about its demise. Not fit for further service without considerable expenditure, S15705 was withdrawn from Derby Research Unit duties in 1974.

The Metrovick was nominated for unpowered mobile train heating duties and as such was booked to be hauled away from the Derby Research Centre in September 1974.

23.2 TDB968006.

S15705 was booked to be hauled from Derby to Gloucester on 18 September 1974. By 27 September, it was noted at Swansea. *Railway Observer* (February 1975) records that 'S15705 was moved from Swansea (High Street) carriage sidings to Danygraig early in December (*1974*), but had left the latter by the 23rd.'

During January 1975, the locomotive was again renumbered, this time to TDB968006. In this guise, the Metrovick was ostensibly allocated to carriage pre-heating duties. The locomotive showed no external signs of modification for these duties and it is questionable as to how much pre-heating work it actually undertook.

TDB968006 spent much of 1975 at the Danygraig Wagon Works/Repair Shops before being transferred to Bristol Bath Road on 10/11 February 1976. The Metrovick was variously reported as destined for Laira and Penzance for further carriage heating duties, but the Metrovick took up residence at Bath Road depot for four years. During its time at Bristol, the locomotive suffered fire damage; based on photographic evidence this occurred sometime between 5 June 1976 and 23 October 1977. Various sources quote TDB968006 as being withdrawn in September 1977.

TDB968006 was eventually acquired for preservation in April 1980 and moved to Swindon in June 1980.

TDB968006, Swansea East Dock, 1975.
(*John Grey Turner*)

D5705 Post Withdrawal • 261

TDB968006, Bristol Bath Road, 5 June 1976.
(*Graham Smith [Rail-Photoprints]*)

TDB968006, Bristol Bath Road, 10 November 1977. Same position seventeen months later showing evidence of the fire-damage sustained whilst stored at Bristol. Worksplate now removed. (*G.H. Taylor [Transport Treasury]*)

23.3 Preservation and back to D5705.

TDB968006, Swindon, 26 September 1981. (Anthony Sayer)

TDB968006 was acquired for preservation April 1980 and was transferred to Swindon for storage in June. On 7 April 1986, it moved to Matlock (Peak Rail) and on to Bury (East Lancashire Railway) on 10 January 1997. During its time in preservation, D5705 has been displayed at a number of BR Open Days including Coalville, Worksop, Leicester and Crewe Works.

D5705 Post Withdrawal • 263

D5705, Worksop (BR Open Day), 1 September 1991. *(Anthony Sayer)*

Chapter 24
CONCLUSIONS

The 'Achilles heel' of the Metrovicks was undoubtedly the Crossley engine and despite several attempts to recover the situation, by progressively strengthening the crankcase, etc., the potentially successful version ultimately deployed in D5705 in November 1967 came too late. The analytical work undertaken as part of the build-up to the November 1967 National Traction Plan had already triggered the decision to withdraw the Metrovicks, against the backdrop of deteriorating traffic volumes, and the consequent reduced requirement for Type 2 motive power. The Sulzer-engined BR and BRCW Type 2s along with the Brush Type 2 (progressively being equipped by English Electric engines at this time), at over 850-strong collectively, were more than sufficient to cope with anticipated future needs. The smaller classes including the twenty Metrovicks, the ten 'Baby Deltics', together with fifty-eight N.B.L. diesel-electric Type 2s all ultimately became supernumerary. There was simply no need to continue any further unnecessary and costly re-engineering development work.

Some of the 'quirkier' aspects of the Metrovick design will in all probability also have influenced their early demise, including the strange cab door positioning, the highly unusual Co-Bo wheel arrangement and associated ride characteristics, the seemingly 'inefficient' general equipment layout, and the antiquated driver controls to name but a few. Despite all this, the Metropolitan-Vickers electrical equipment was highly robust and very reliable.

It can be argued that the Pilot Scheme rationale actually worked with respect to the Metrovicks in a very broad sense, despite the fact that the pilot fleet of 174 locomotives were never properly trialled before the mass ordering of 'production' fleets of diesel locomotives. With R.C. Bond's engineering experience and by keeping aware of developments of the Metrovick fleets in Ireland (and possibly Australia), he was able to steer away from the Crossley-engined machines and concentrate on Sulzer and English Electric products whilst at the same time adhering to the decisions of his lords and masters to accelerate the procurement of diesel traction.

Inevitably there remain some factual and photographic gaps in the Metrovick history; I have provided below my wish-list of 'top-ten' items which I would personally like to see developed:

- Photographs of Metrovicks undergoing rehabilitation at Dukinfield.
- Photographs of D5703/7-9/12/3/9 <u>immediately</u> post-Dukinfield (1961-62) to check/confirm whether they carried GNY livery immediately post-rehabilitation.
- Photographs of D5709 during the 1963-68 period (with number visible).
- Official documentation regarding nominated Metrovicks for re-engining.
- Crewe Works visit report for 26/02/67 to fine-tune the date when D5704/9/10/3 were transferred from Crewe Works to Carlisle Upperby.
- Date of D5705's move Derby Research Centre.
- Photographs of Metrovicks at 12A Carlisle Kingmoor (Steam) depot.
- Photographs of Metrovicks being dragged away from Carlisle to Shettleston or Great Bridge for scrap.
- Dates for the transfers of D5715/8 to J. MacWilliam, Shettleston.
- Photographs of Metrovicks in J. MacWilliam's, Shettleston and J. Cashmore's, Great Bridge scrapyards.

Any contributions to the editorial office, please. Thank you.

Conclusions • 265

D5711, Disley, circa 1960. *(A.H. Bryant (Rail-Photoprints))*

D57xx, Drigg (Workington-Liverpool), Undated. *(Transport Treasury)*

266 • THE METROPOLITAN-VICKERS TYPE 2 CO-BO DIESEL-ELECTRIC LOCOMOTIVES

D5702, Grange-over-Sands, 3 August 1968. *(Michael Atkinson)*

Conclusions • 267

D5709, Broughton (Barrow-Euston), 7 April 1964. *(Paul Claxton)*

D5702, Broughton (Euston-Barrow), 26 March 1964. *(Paul Claxton)*

268 • THE METROPOLITAN-VICKERS TYPE 2 CO-BO DIESEL-ELECTRIC LOCOMOTIVES

D5707, 12A Carlisle Kingmoor, 26 March 1967. A Metrovick sandwich with a 'Britannia' 7MT Pacific to the right and a 9F 2-10-0 to the left. (Rail-Photoprints)

'Britannia' Pacific 70013 "Oliver Cromwell" alongside an unidentified Metrovick, 12B Carlisle Upperby, 9 December 1967. The identity of the Metrovick is probably D5703; see also photograph on page 243. (Michael Atkinson)

Conclusions • 269

D5716, Bolton-le-Sands, April 1963. (Colour-Rail)

D5715, Carlisle Citadel station, Undated. (Colour-Rail)

BIBLIOGRAPHY

Books:
Bond, R.C., *A Lifetime with Locomotives,* Goose & Son Publishers, 1975.
Brock, P., *Calling Carlisle Control,* Ian Allan Publishing, 1990.
Clough, D.N., *Diesel Pioneers,* Ian Allan Publishing, 2005.
Cooper, B.K., *BR Motive Power since 1948,* Ian Allan Publishing, 1985.
Haresnape, B., *British Rail Fleet Survey: 1. Early Prototype and Pilot Scheme Diesel-Electrics,* Ian Allan Publishing, 1981.
Harris, R., *The Allocation History of BR Diesels & Electrics: Parts 4, 5 & 6 (Third & Final Edition),* 2004/05/06 respectively. (AHBRDE4/5/6A respectively)
Marsden, C.J., *The Complete UK Modern Traction Locomotive Directory,* TheRailwayCentre.com, 2011.
Rogers, H.C.B., (Colonel), *Transition from Steam,* Ian Allan Publishing, 1980.
Strickland, D.C., *Locomotive Directory - Every Single One There Has Ever Been,* D&EG, 1983, plus Supplements No.1-7 (1983-87). (LocDir)
Tufnell, R.M., *The Diesel Impact on British Rail,* Mechanical Engineering Publications, 1979.
***British Railways Illustrated**,* Summer Special No.5, Irwell Press, 1997, specifically:pp30-9, 'Diesel Dawn - Out and Out Disaster'.'
Traction Annual *2010/11,* Warner Group Publications, specifically:pp24-37, 'Locating MacLocos', P.Robinson.

Magazines:
The Locomotive, December 1958, pp231-235,' Metropolitan-Vickers 1200hp diesel-electric locomotives'.
Trains Illustrated/Modern Railways/Railway World (Ian Allan) (TI/MR/RW), specifically:
TI, February 1958, pp86-89, 'The A.B.C. of the diesel engine - Part One', R. Tourret.
   TI, January 1959, pp12-13, 'Type "2"'1,200 hp diesel-electric Co-Bo units for BR'
TI, April 1959, p175, '"Condor", BR's fastest freight'.
TI, January 1960, pp45-49, '"Condor" – British Railways' fastest freight train'.
Traction, specifically:
   September 1995, pp4-8, 'Derby & the R.T.C. Part 2', S. Allsopp.
   July 1996, pp4-5, 'Co-Bo's In Decline, A. Ian Appleby.
   December 1998, pp38-41, 'Classic Classes - The Co-Bos', J. Hypher.
   January 1999, pp46-49, 'Classic Classes - The Irish Metro-Vicks', P. Jones.
   December 2003, pp32-33, 'Oranges and Lemons', B. Nicholls.
   April 2004, pp39-41, 'The Slow Death of the Metrovick Co-Bos', A. Whitaker.
   March 2006, pp10-13, 'The Co-Bos - a Re-Appraisal', D.N. Clough.
   November/December 2018, pp20-3, 'Metrovick's Stockton-on-Tees Factory', G. Pickering.
Modern Locomotives Illustrated, No.226, 'Class 23 – "Baby Deltic" & Class 28 – "Co-Bo" Fleets', August-September 2017. (MLI226)

British Railways Illustrated, specifically:
    May 2010, pp340-345, 'Diesel Dawn - The Met-Vics', A.C. Baker.
    December 2010, pp154-155, 'A Reader Writes (inc. letters from A. Whitaker and P. White)'.
    March 2012, pp270-275, 'Metrovicks at the Edge - Barrow's Unsung Co-Bos', T. Hartle (Lakeside Railway Soc.).
Motive Power Monthly, specifically:
    October 1986, pp16-20, 'Profile of the Class 28 Co-Bo'.
    September 1991, pp30-35,' Class by Class - The 28's', A. Whitaker.
Rail, specifically:
    January 22-February 4 2014, pp64-67, 'Class 28s: Duds or Victims?', D.N. Clough.
Railways Illustrated, specifically:
    November 2018, pp78-83, 'The Enigmatic Metrovicks', no author specified but presumably D.N. Clough (very similar to *Traction* March 2006 article).
Heritage Railway, specifically:
    February 14-March 13, 2013, 'Metrovick Finale', M. Burns.
Cumbrian Railways, specifically:
    Vol.7, No.11, pp180-183, 'Bank Engine Days', P.C. Johnstone.
    Vol.9, No.4, pp88-92, 'Metro-Vick Memories', P.C. Johnstone.
    Vol.9, No.4, pp93-94, 'The Metro-Vick - an Historical View', M. Peascod.
Railway Observer (RCTS). (RO)
Journal (SLS).
Bulletin (LCGB).
Railway Locomotives (BLS). (RL)
Buckley Wells Transport Enthusiasts (BWTE), subsequently:
Northern Counties Transport Society (NCTS).
Link (Engine Shed Society [ESS])

Archive Sources:
Barrow Archive and Local Studies Centre.
Derby Industrial Museum.
National Archive, Kew.
BTC and BRB Committee Meeting Minutes and Supporting Papers.
BR National Traction Plans (February 1965, November 1967, December 1968). (NTP)
BR Fires on Diesel Train Locomotives Reports 1961-68, Locomotive Performance & Efficiency Development Unit, Derby. (FDTL)
BR Engine History Cards. (EHC)
National Railway Museum, York.

Official BR Documents:
Main Line Diesel Locomotive Layout Diagrams (various editions).
Main Line Diesel Locomotive Diagram Book, June 1969.
BTC report: Two 1200hp Crossley/Met.Vick. D.E. Locos. Hauling Special Container Train Hendon-Gushetfaulds October 1958, C.M. & E.E. Department, Derby, August 1959.

Websites:
Welcome to Co-Bo World!
Flickr, specifically Rob Mason's site (Metrovick engineering drawing re. Sulzer re-engining proposal).

272 • THE METROPOLITAN-VICKERS TYPE 2 CO-BO DIESEL-ELECTRIC LOCOMOTIVES

Photographic Sources:
RCTS Archives, Colour-Rail, Rail-Photoprints, Rail-Online, Transport Topics, Transport Treasury, Rail Image Collections, Rail Pictorial: The Paul Claxton Collection, Online Transport Photography.

Michael Atkinsin, Stewart Blencowe, David Dippie, Ernie's Railway Archives, Stephen Fisher, Bill Hamilton, Mark Hoofe, Mike Jackson, Andrew Lance, Dave Lennon, Keith Long, R.Lush, Noel A. Machell, Stuart Martin, Mick Mobley, Peter Sedge, Clinton P.R. Shaw, N.Skinner, John Grey Turner, Mark Walker collection, George Woods, Bill Wright, together with 'Regional Bus Photos', '70023venus2009' and the Modern Traction Photo Group.

Sighting Sources:
Geoff Arnold, Stewart Blencowe, Tom Bowman, Chris Capewell, Chris Coates, Dennis Dey, Peter Dix, Vic Forster, Bill Hamilton, Richard Lillie, Steve Perkins Archive, Alan Robinson, Peter Robinson, Roy Schofield, Alex Scott, Tony Skinner, Richard G.Strange, M.Stokes, John Grey Turner, Alan Whitaker.

Shed Master Archives

D5719, Penrith, 15 July 1967. M6 motorway under construction beneath the railway bridge. (*C. Davies [Rail-Photoprints]*)